The Pleasure Boatmen
of
Eastbourne

TED HIDE

S.B. Publications

Front Cover: *Albert 'Tuppy' Sayers - Old Eastbourne Pleasure Boatman b1860. d1946.*

Title Page: *Pleasure boat 'Children's Friend' owned and operated by the Prodger family of Royal Parade c1920.*

First published in 2007

ISBN 978-1-85770-333-7

Designed and Typeset by EH Graphics (01273) 515527

Contents

The Pleasure Boatmen of Eastbourne.

The following is a record especially for those present day Eastbourne families whose ancestors were part of the Pleasure Boating and Fishing Community that once thrived, and finally declined through a hard, rugged life style over some two hundred years, serving Eastbourne in its rise to become a premier seaside resort.

Throughout this chronological record of events and happenings where possible, dates, names of Boatmen and boat names are given. As to names, the same Christian names were given through generations in a lot of seafaring families and it has been difficult to differentiate between father, son, cousins etc.

My family was involved in the Boating business from the early days and I have drawn on their material to give some examples. Material I have obtained from other Boating families I also give examples of. Unfortunately research has failed to trace the whereabouts of the all important 'Books of Boat and Boatman Licences Issued' and 'Foreshore Plans of Boat Stand Sites' that were held within the Eastbourne Council and the old Eastbourne Borough Police Force's care. These particular documents were not passed on to the East Sussex Records Office, Lewes or to the Sussex Police Archives. Hopefully they are not lost forever and will surface one day.

A thorough study of the old Watch Committee and other old Committees' minutes have produced a fairly accurate record of numbers of licences issued over the years and is duly reproduced. It can be assumed that Boat Stand sites were numbered lowest first - No1 starting from between the Wish Tower and Bandstand then through to the Pier, Marine Parade and to the end of Royal Parade. Over the years re-numbering and moving of Boat Stands did take place and Boatmen did 'jockey' for the best sites - there being more than one Boat Stand between the groynes.

Also recorded are some other events which took place on the seafront parades giving a picture of life at a seaside resort, especially during the 19th and 20th centuries.

I am grateful to the following for the help and support given to me. My thanks to Brian Allchorn, Pearl Tyler (nee Prodger), the late Fred 'Mucky' Erridge, the late Jack Hurd, the late Frank Smith, the Langford sisters - Thelma and Pam, Mike Strong, Ken and Jim Simpson, Gary Brookshaw, Lionel Jones, Dave Simkin, the late Olive Wilkins (née Simpson), the late Phil Webb, George Boniface and many others. Finally to the staff at Eastbourne Library and East Sussex Records Office, Lewes, my thanks.

I would also like to acknowledge the following, without whom I could not have compiled the information:- The Argus, Beckett Publications, the British Museum, the British Library, Eastbourne Local History Society, Eastbourne Town Council minutes, Eastbourne Central Library, East Sussex Records Office, Coastwise Craft, T.C. Lethbridge, Arthur Beckett, Sussex County Magazine, 'Eastbourne Fishermen and Boatmen' by Tom Reed and Liz Howe for the design and typography of this book. Many thanks to my son, Richard who has greatly assisted with the collation and editing of my work.

Chapter One

1770 ~ 1889

C.1770 Eastbourne was made up of four hamlets - Meads, Bourne (Old Town area), Southbourne (Town Hall area) and Sea Houses. The 'Sea Houses' were so called from the 14th century and as the name suggests, were situated on the seashore roughly from where the Pier entrance is today and reached east along Marine Parade. This was the first site of a developing seaside resort at Eastbourne. Just to the west of the Sea Houses stood the 'Round House'. Formerly a horizontal mill worked in those days by miller Richard Simpson and converted c.1760 into two lodgings for visitors. Sea bathing had begun to become popular, with bathing taking place at the 'Sea Houses' as far back as 1754.

Pleasure Boating at Eastbourne could be said to have started back in 1780, with the visit of the children of King George III. Prince Edward stayed in the 'Round House'. Edward's brother Prince Octavius, and two sisters the Princesses Elizabeth and Sophia stayed in a house at the Sea Houses which were later pulled down and

Plan of Eastbourne. C.1800 showing Sea Houses.

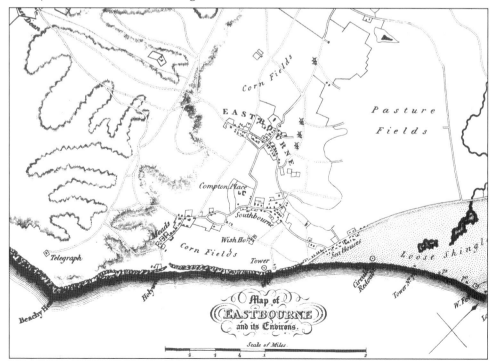

Sea Houses. 1785.

the Albion Hotel built on the site. This Royal patronage no doubt popularised Eastbourne. The local Fishermen soon adapted their boats to take visitors for trips and fishing expeditions, traditionally launching off the beach and adding to their income during the summer months with the winter being spent commercial fishing. The terms used for Fishermen following these occupations were 'Longshoremen'. Another term for a Boatman is 'Waterman' and 'Pleasuring' the term used for Pleasure Boating.

Boatmen were graded into 1st and 2nd class.

1st class Boatmen were competent in handling Sailboats with passengers, handling skiffs (row boats) with passengers and being able swimmers.

2nd class Boatmen were only competent in handling skiffs with passengers and being able swimmers.

Later with the arrival of the Pleasure Motor Boat, the grade of Motor Boat Steersman/Driver was introduced.

In those early days, trips took place from the 'Stade' where the 'Sea Houses' stood. 'Stade' was a local Sussex word signifying *"a place on shore where vessels may run ashore for the discharge of cargo and landing of fish"*. This was the original Fishing Station and living area for the Fishing and Boating community of Eastbourne. They later moved eastwards between Marine Parade and the Great Redoubt, then in 1884 to east of the Great Redoubt.

In John Heatherley's 1819 guide to 'East-Bourne', the Boatmen of Eastbourne were quoted thus: -

"The sands at the Sea Houses are very fine and dry. Parties can enjoy boat trips in good boats, well fitted out and crewed by men who have a thorough knowledge of the tides and are well versed in nautical skills, they are likewise much respected for their civility".

Another source of income was the hiring of Bathing Machines for sea bathing, then in its infancy.

With the Marine Parade being constructed c.1820, Pleasure Boating took place from there. Later with the development of the Grand Parade 1845-70, this opened up the seafront for more Boat Stands and Bathing Machines as the town grew under the stewardship of William Cavendish, 7th Duke of Devonshire and Mr Davies Gilbert. Eastbourne's renown as a coastal resort is mainly due though to the 7th

Duke for the fine way he developed his land from Grand Parade to Holywell and Meads, earning Eastbourne the title 'Empress of Watering Places'.

In 1884 with the forced removal of the Fishermen from their ancient Fishing Station between Marine Parade and the Great Redoubt, the Royal Parade was built affording more Boat Stands and employment for the Boating Fraternity. With the Fishing Station moved east of the Great Redoubt, Mr Gilbert developed the land side into a residential area where the Boating and Fishing community moved.

Marine Parade. C.1860. Pleasure Boats & Bathing Machines.

Pleasure, Sail and Row Boats continued through till after the turn of the 19th century, when Motorboats slowly took over from sail. Pleasure Boating being in decline before this, partly due to the introduction of the Paddle Steamers operating off the Pier head in the 1890's with cruises along the coast.

Between the 1st and 2nd World Wars, there was somewhat of a revival, but towards the end of the 1930s fewer boats were operating. After the 2nd World War fewer boats still until the 1960s saw just two Boating families, Allchorn and Sayers, plying the big Motorboats from Grand Parade. Rowing boats were represented by Ned Sayers before giving way completely to the Council operated 'floats and pedalos'. One family still operated in the 1990s, this being Allchorn Bros. having taken over Sayers business in 1965, finally selling the business in 1995. The Pleasure Boats 'William Allchorn' and 'Southern Queen' still ply for hire off the beach giving trips to the Lighthouse, Beachy Head and Channel cruises under the Allchorn name.

The company now operating Allchorn's has acquired more vessels for Pleasuring and operates some trips from the Sovereign Harbour.

Some Pleasure Boating families of long ago; Swain, Knight, Simpson, Hurd, Paul, Penfold, Prodger, Breach, Erridge, Allchorn, Tutt, Tyrell, Huggett, Mockett, Sayers, Wood, Matthews, Boniface, Hide, Novis, Grooms, Elms, Hardy, Hunt, Godden, Reed, Chester and many more names, can still be found among the inhabitants of Eastbourne to this day.

In those days gone by amongst the Fishing and Boating community there would have been a strong Sussex dialect spoken, alas long gone. The following poem gives an example: -

This poem is by Winnie Botting, herself descended from a Saxon chief called Botta.

Owd Sussex.

Who dare speak agen our Sussex,
Owd Sussex as stan 's by de sea?
Wid her medders an' Weald an' Downland,
Owd Sussex 's like heaven to me,
Ye may boast of yer castles an' cities,
Yer palaces gay over the sea,
But I' ll never leave dear owd Sussex,
Owd Sussex as stan's by de sea.

There be sea, an' there's uplan's an' lowlan's,
Owd Sussex pervides all these three,
There be villages, towns an' there's hamlets,
In owd Sussex as stan's by de sea.

Though folkses may prate about Lunnon,
The Riviery an' the Frenchies' Paree,
I doant think they can beat dear owd Sussex,
Owd Sussex as stan's by de sea.

They say as we be Sussex sheep, like,
An' we wunt be druv! What care we?
I wouldn't be druv-no I wouldn't-
From Sussex-de sheer by de sea.

c.1800 - 1889.

During the summer months of the 1850's there was a demand for Pleasure Boating by the ever-increasing number of visitors coming to the town, due to the opening of the railway line to Eastbourne in 1849.

Cliff Cottage where Jenny Lind 'The Swedish Nightingale' stayed can be seen between the Wish Tower and Mount Pleasant House where Tennyson stayed.

The low cliff between the 'Field House' (where the Queens Hotel now stands) and the Wish Tower, was developed and the Grand Parade Seawall built from 1848. The Grand Parade buildings included the Burlington and Cavendish Hotels being completed by 1866. Eastbourne became a thriving seaside resort, catering for the well to do as well as the day-tripper arriving by train. During this period the Boatmen voluntarily cleared the foreshore of rocks giving an ease of launching and landing.

The Grand Parade had displaced two noted residencies on that stretch of seashore, namely 'Cliff Cottage' where the world famous opera singer, Jenny Lind, known as the Swedish Nightingale, stayed from time to time, giving the Boatmen on the beach a free listen to her voice. Robert Cooper in his book 'Eastbourne Reminiscences' tells of her sweet voice and how people used to gather

Grand Parade before Cavendish Hotel & Pier built. C.1863.

near Cliff Cottage in the hope of hearing her sing without having to go to the Opera. The other residence was 'Mount Pleasant', a fine house where the poet Tennyson stayed.

Early beach scene. C.1865. Pier under construction. Victorian day-trippers.

Bathing Machines, introduced from the early days when sea bathing became popular, shared the beach with the Boatmen for many years and in many cases the Bathing Machines were owned and operated by the Boatmen themselves. This situation continued up to 1920 when the machines were taken over by the Corporation and turned into static bathing huts. Early Bye-Laws were made in 1875 and sites for the machines were the Wish Tower (gentlemen), Grand Parade (ladies), Marine Parade (ladies) and later the Great Redoubt (Gentlemen). No mixed bathing in those days. *Charges: single bathe 9d, for a series 6d each.*

Another Bye-Law prohibited persons bathing without a Bathing Machine after 8.00am on any part of the shore between the Wish Tower and Great Redoubt.

It is said Bathing Machines had been introduced to Eastbourne by a Doctor Thomas Gibbs c.1800. Doctor Gibbs was a man of high regard with a practice in Old

The new sea wall. Grand Parade. C.1865.

Grand Parade after Cavendish Hotel & Pier built. C.1870.

Town. He is said to have been the first to appreciate the value of sea bathing and to have had made a Bathing Machine for the use of his son. When it was wheeled down from the Old Town it was followed by a crowd of people who said the Doctor had built a box to drown his son in. Doctor Gibbs also had his own house built on the Marine Parade.

From the Vestry Minutes of June 9th 1793, an entry shows *"it was decided on application of Doctor Thomas Gibbs, surgeon, apothecary and man midwife, that he should undertake the care of the poor of the parish for the sum of £20 per annum, Small pox excepted".*

A notable Boatman of the period 1866 was Fisherman George 'Dot' Hide, who started 'Pleasuring' at the age of 12 years in 1826. Now being 52 years of age and not in good health and being unable to carry on his living of fishing, he was given the grand gift of a Pleasure Boat and gold sovereigns from the 'Shipwrecked Fishermen and Mariners Society' and Mr Herbert F. Eaton, an Eton schoolboy. The presentation was fully reported in the local papers at the time.

28th July 1866

'Presentation of a Boat to George Hide, an old Eastbourne Fisherman'.

On Tuesday a very interesting ceremony took place here, it being the occasion of the presentation of a very nice Pleasure Boat to an old Eastbourne Fisherman, named George Hide. The pleasing ceremony came off at the Railway Station, where the boat had arrived by train from the builders, Messrs, Forrest, of London.

Mr Henry E. Eaton said; 'I am much pleased to be able to present this boat to you from the Shipwrecked Fishermen and Mariners' Society, and from my brother Herbert Eaton and to take this opportunity of thanking you for your kind attention to him last year whilst in Eastbourne'.

Miss Fanny Eaton then presented George Hide with a purse of 20 sovereigns, remarking that all vessels going to sea required ballast. (Cheers and laughter)

George Hide said, 'I beg to return my sincere thanks to you and to Mr Herbert

Eaton for this present and for your coming to Eastbourne to give it to me. I wish you every happiness. I hope that Mr Hall will express my thanks to the Shipwrecked Fishermen and Mariners' Society and tell them that, crippled as I am, I will in case of need, still endeavour to render assistance to vessels in distress which my knowledge of the coast can afford.'

Mr. Tenderly said, 'George Hide, as your oldest friend in Eastbourne, it falls to my lot to say a few words on behalf of the Shipwrecked Fishermen and Mariners' Society, and of my young friend Mr Herbert F. Eaton, who should have stood in my place, but is not unwilling but unavoidably absent at Eton College. You have done well in thanking that excellent Society, of which Mr Hall is the agent, for the part they have taken in this matter, for certainly on the strength of their support this deserving award has now been accorded to you, and their approbation with a donation of 10 pounds, is of the more value as being a special gift and coming from a Society which embraces within its blessings the whole surface of the globe, for where-ever there is a sea coast or the possibility of a wreck, the benefits granted to seamen are inestimable, for wherever a British seaman is thrown ashore, destitute and helpless, he is there clothed and restored, free of expense, to his own home. You are not at all to consider this gift in any way as charity, but as testimonial of your

George 'Dot' Hide with sons John on right and Ben to his left with Henry E and Herbert F Eaton on board Pleasure Boat 'Guardsman' 1866.

being ever ready to risk your life to assist others who are in danger and also as an encouragement to everyone to follow your good example, and it will, at the same time, prove to you and to all who hear me that a British public is always grateful and ready to reward those who, at their own personal risk, volunteer to save others, and although it is many years since your last act of devotion was performed, you now find that it is never too late for acknowledgement of service. I will now as briefly as possible, state why this testimonial of public sympathy has been awarded to you. It pleased Almighty God to give you great courage, with very personal strength, and a most kind and good English heart in the right place, and this has been the more particularly shown in the first case which I shall bring before you. It is quite true that there was no great personal risk to yourself or your companions on that occasion, but you were all boys, and it was the good feeling evinced to a foreigner in distress, which proved what I before stated that your heart was in the right place. The ages of yourself and three companions were as follows: - Frederick Hide 17 (now dead), George Hide 15, Richard Hide scarcely 13 and James Hutchins 15 (now dead). The above happened as far back as the year 1828, when a large

Backboard of the 'Guardsman' Pleasure Boat.

French lugger, laden with fish from the North of England, came in for water, when the captain, not being aware of the shallowness of the coast, and being detained on shore, the tide had fallen and the wind risen, producing a heavy swell and the vessel was beating heavily on the shore; the colours were hoisted for assistance, which the captain was unable to afford from the smallness of his boat. Sadly the Fishermen of Eastbourne were unwilling to render aid, so yourself and your three young companions volunteered and took the captain off with his water, the anchor was got up, and the vessel went safely to sea. - The second case was in 1833. The 'Isabella', West Indiaman, of London was wrecked. Two trips were made in the lifeboat and twenty-nine lives saved, for this you received a medal from Mr Fuller M.P. The third case was in 1840, when the 'Joseph', of Sunderland, was driven on shore and no communication could be obtained by rocket or otherwise, when you volunteered and saved the lives of 10 persons by swimming off three times, and the last time you were brought on shore insensible, and were laid up ill for a considerable time. A medal and certificate was presented from Lloyd's of London. The fourth case was in 1845 when the 'Twee Cornelissen', a Dutch East Indiaman was wrecked and the captain and part of the crew saved by yourself and companions in the lifeboat. To the above may be added the boats 'Rob Roy', 'Bee', 'English Rose', and others of minor importance. And now, George Hide, I am sure that all here will join in wishing you success, and that your 'Guardsman' (the name of the new boat) will ever prove to you as a loyal and true a friend as the British Guards have ever proved to their country.

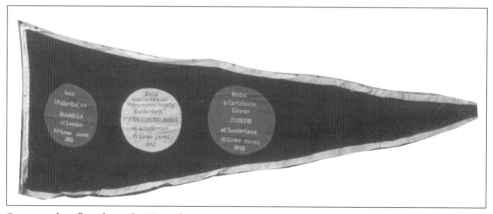

Pennant that flew from the 'Guardsman'.

After three hearty cheers, George Hide then took possession of the boat, a procession being formed. Two seamen of the Coastguard leading with the colours of the Shipwrecked Fishermen and Mariners' Society, and George Hide following the boat to the beach. It was christened by Miss Fanny Eaton who named it 'Guardsman' after which this young lady took a trip in it on the water.

The back-board of the boat 'Guardsman' was inscribed and reads:

Presented June 1866 by the Shipwrecked Mariners' Society and friends of Herbert F EATON to GEO HIDE For heroic exertions in saving life and property from the perils of the sea.

The backboard measures some 5 feet across, so it can be assumed the boat was some 18-20 feet in length. A large pennant 8 feet long flew from the 'Guardsman' when she was plying for hire. The pennant is embroidered with the details of George Hide's three most famous rescues.

The presentation date was originally to be June 1866 as on the backboard. Obviously something happened because Herbert F. Eaton's brother Henry E. actually made the presentation in July 1866. It is interesting to see that the boat builders Messrs. Forrest of Limehouse, London built the 'Guardsman'. They also built the second Eastbourne Lifeboat 'Mary Stirling' in 1863, which replaced the first Eastbourne lifeboat, the 'Samaritan'.

Shown is the c.1866 photo of the two Eton College boys Henry E. and Herbert F. Eaton on board the Pleasure Boat "Guardsman" with George Hide and two of his sons John and Benjamin.

On 30th November 1876, the Pleasure Boat 'Guardsman' was involved in the saving of life off Eastbourne, when the fishing boat 'Emma' sank.

"It was shortly after 4 o'clock on Thursday afternoon that considerable excitement was occasioned on the beach by a report that a boat had gone down. It appears that Thomas Mitchell, an old Fisherman between sixty and seventy (he was a member of the crew of the 'Samaritan' in the first lifeboat rescue, in 1833), had put out in his boat 'The Emma' in company with another old man named 'Story' Adams, on a hook and line fishing expedition. Two or three other boats also went out, but the wind being high and the water very choppy, they returned to shore early in the afternoon. The 'Emma' continued fishing for some time, and their boat was watched with some anxiety on shore as the afternoon advanced and the shades of evening drew on. At length the boat, which had only her mizzen up, was seen to be coming ashore, but when a quarter of a mile out, she was suddenly lost sight of, and the painful news ran like wildfire along the beach that she had gone down. With commendable promptitude two boats put out to the rescue, one belonging to Arthur Matthews (landlord of the Beach Hotel) and the other to George Hide Snr. The boat with Boatmen John Hide, Charles Hide, James Collins, Jesse Huggett, Peter Waymark, George Gausden (boat builder) and John 'Kruger' Prodger aboard, succeeded in riding through the waves and the poor fellows Mitchell and Adams, were picked up just in time to save the former from being drowned, for he was quite exhausted and must have sunk had the assistance not been forthcoming at the moment it was. The cause of the accident a heavy wave had struck the boat filling

her with water caused her to sink and the occupants were immersed in the sea. Fortunately they each had sufficient presence of mind to seize an oar, and upon this slender support they managed to keep afloat till they were rescued as above stated. The gallant conduct of the crew who saved the men is worthy of all praise, and in this the occupants of the Arthur Matthews boat may well share, for they pulled away right bravely till their frail craft had shipped so much water that further persistence would have been sheer madness. After reaching shore Adams was able with assistance to walk home, but Mitchell was too prostrate to be able to stand on his feet. The sunken boat was washed ashore in the evening, as were also a number of fish which had been taken in her."

September 1866.

A Local Regatta was held for the Boatmen and Fishermen of Eastbourne off the Grand Parade. Sail boats were the order of the day, with the skill of boat handling to the fore. There were also rowing, swimming and other events. (The very first Eastbourne Regatta had been held on 26th August 1859. George F Chambers wrote in 'Eastbourne Memories' 1910 - quote *"The 26th August 1859 saw the first Regatta at Eastbourne. Along the Seafront opposite 24 Grand Parade to the Wish Tower was all cliff - no houses except 2 old cottages and swarms of people lined the cliff."*)

The report on the 1866 Regatta reads as follows: -

"Without exception it has been one of the best-managed gatherings that has been our lot to chronicle for some past. The officials proved themselves of undertaking and carrying out successfully a 'Full-rigged Regatta'. The sports were not open to the coast, but confined to the town and besides a cup and medal, nearly £30 were given away in prizes. The affair was organized by and under the management of the Eastbourne Swimming and Rowing Club. The gentlemen of the Committee took up their position in a boat moored some distance out, while others stationed themselves in the middle of the course on a platform erected in front of the Grand Parade. The Regatta took some 3 hours to complete and here are the results: -

Fishing Boats - lugger rigged, not exceeding 22 ft.
Prizes. £3.0s.0d. £2.0s.0d. £1.0s.0d.
1st 'Saucy Lass' - E Matthews.
2nd 'Monarch' - J Hoad.
3rd 'Forester' - C Wood.
4th 'Rebecca' - J Huggett.
5th 'Five Sisters' - W Hide.
There was not much wind on but quite enough to make the boats sail smoothly. Saucy Lass took the lead, maintained it throughout and won easily.

Waterman's pair-oared skiffs, not exceeding 19 ft.
Prizes. £1.10s.0d. £1.10s.0d. £0.10s.0d.
1st 'Arrow' - C Wood.
2nd 'Rose' - A Sayers.
3rd 'Swift' - J Collins.
4th 'Violet' - W Jackson.
5th 'Reindeer' - D Breach.

Very close till the home run when Arrow shot out like an arrow ought to do, and won easily.

Swimming race - Half a mile.
Prizes. A silver medal, £1.0s.0d. £0.10s.0d.
1st Mr Wrangham.(visitor)
2nd Jesse Huggett.
3rd Mr Lawrence.

Messrs. R Swain, W Wood, J Brown and Mr Savage also started. This was a well-contested race between Mr Wrangham, Mr Huggett and Mr Lawrence, the men kept up well together nearly all the way, Wrangham finally came in first by a boat's length, a dead heat between Huggett and Lawrence, who divided the 2nd and 3rd prizes. (This was Jesse Huggett who became Coxswain of the Eastbourne lifeboat in 1884.)

Amateur single sculls, not exceeding 19 ft.
Prizes. A Cup, £1.0s.0d. £0.10s.0d.
1st 'Swift' - J Sayers.
2nd 'Rose' - S Prodger.
3rd 'Reindeer' - C Haine.
4th 'Violet' - J Squire.
5th 'Arrow' - H Gardner.

Rose was first to get round the buoys and came away at a rattling pace. Swift kept close attendance, and upon nearing the goal challenged the Rose, and won easily by three lengths. Prodger pulled a good oar but could not hold out, in fact when challenged he almost broke down. The Reindeer was well up; bad fourth the Arrow went as heavy as a tub, and gave up. (C.Haine was Charles the son of John, founder of Haine the Undertaker business in South Street).

Sailing boats, not exceeding 20 ft.
Prizes. £3.0s.0d. £2.0s.0d. £1.0s.0d.
1st 'Five Brothers' - W Hide.
2nd 'Forester' - C Wood.
3rd 'Conqueror' - R Swain.
4th 'Royal Turk' - J Collins.
5th 'Favourite' - E Hobby.
6th 'William Augustus' - A Cooper.

Another good race. The first three came in almost 'neck and neck'.

(J Collins was Jacob Collins, Fisherman of Meads (Holywell) coming in 4th in the sailing boat 'Royal Turk'. She was built at Meads. Meads was known locally as 'Turkey' - there was a great rivalry between the Fishermen of Meads and the Fishermen of Eastbourne according to Fred 'Mucky' Erridge. Jacob lived to a ripe age of 90 plus years. He lived in Coppards Cottages - now 81- 87 Meads Street. Jacob was good on the oars, winning the next race.)

Watermen's single sculls, not exceeding 19 ft.
Prizes. £2.2s.0d £1.0s.0d. £0.10s.0d.
1st 'Swift' - J Collins.
2nd 'Violet' - W Jackson.

3rd 'Rose' - A. Sayers.
4th 'Arrow' - C Wood.

Arrow went off with a vengeance and threatened to carry all before her, Wood however, was soon passed and when half way round the course upon looking round, seemed amazed at the gap his opponents left behind him. He proved a regular 'old screw' and gave up. Collins in the 'Swift' proved himself a thorough master of his business and won at a 'canter'. There were two lengths between 2nd and 3rd."

Apart from the usual Regatta competitions, the following took place: -

A Duck Hunt - but it was thought by many that the birds had not a fair chance as might have been given - the result in one or two cases being an easy capture. On the other hand the feathery victims led much astray those who at one time thought themselves sure of a prize.

(Not sure what they did to the duck! perhaps clipped it's wings?)

The Regatta closed with what is termed a 'pole dance'. A leg of mutton was attached to a spar affixed to a boat, the spar over-hanging the water by about 18 feet. The one who managed to walk out the whole length of the pole before falling into the water gained the prize. There were many competitors and many futile attempts, but eventually the mutton was awarded to Boatman Richard Swain who had got nearest to the meat. This contest caused great merriment. On shore a few lads raced for rolls and treacle. Not less than 5,000 persons attended the Regatta.

August 1867.

The following year the Open Regatta at Eastbourne saw the sailing races postponed due to lack of wind, and the 'Tub Race' cancelled due to lack of entrants - each entrant had to find his own tub and shovel!

James 'Navarino' Hide b.1798. d.1883. Copy of original portrait.

April 1868.

Boatmen James 'Navarino' Hide and his son Philip were summoned before the court for using abusive language. They were charged with being drunk and abusing a Mr. W E Ellis. Mr Ellis was the owner of a yacht and on the day in question had been out for a sail, taking a gentleman with him. On his return, Mr Ellis was met by the defendants who began to abuse him and collected a crowd around him. They were under the impression that Mr Ellis was 'injuring their avocation' (pinching their customers for sea trips). This was not the first time they had annoyed Mr Ellis. Since the summons had been served, the defendants had seen Mr Ellis and begged him not proceed with the charge against them and expressed their regret for what had occurred. The defendants had agreed to pay the cost of the summons. A written apology was produced, also a request by Mr Ellis that the case be dropped. Mr Ellis did not appear in court and the Bench remarked on this. Dismissing the case the Bench remarked that Mr Ellis must understand that they cannot listen to his complaints if he suffers this case to be dismissed.

In 1927 Mark Hookham, Builder, a native of Eastbourne, recalled 'Navarino' and his son Phillip working a couple of Row Boats (1880s) from the east end of Marine Parade Nos.29-30.

Whilst at his Boat Stand on the beach at Marine Parade 'Navarino' was instrumental in saving the life of a boy in October 1872.

"A small two oared rowing boat was hired late in the afternoon, to a youth who was staying at the Burlington Hotel. No enquiry was made as to whether this boy could row or understood the management of a boat. The wind was blowing hard from the north off the shore, consequently the boat went rapidly out to sea. When more than a mile out and opposite the Anchor Hotel (Albermarle), a gentleman upon the beach observed something like a handkerchief waved as a signal from the boat. He called the attention of 'Navarino' to this signal who saw at once it was a signal of distress and he and the gentleman put off in his boat, the 'Cleopatra'. Having overtaken the lad's boat drifting rapidly out to sea and about two miles off Langney Point, they found the youth quite prostrated from sickness, exhaustion and fright. Had the signal not been observed by the gentleman at the time it was, he must, as it was growing late and dark, have been carried out to sea, and both he and the boat in all probability, lost. The gentleman and 'Old Navarino', who was upwards of 70 years of age, after a hard pull, head to wind, with the drifting boat in tow, brought both boy and boat safely to shore. 'Old Navarino's' reward was the thanks of the boy, and not of the Boatman, whose boat he had saved".

This is not the first instance of 'Navarino' having helped to save life. He was for years one of the crew of the Eastbourne Lifeboat indeed serving on the first Lifeboat the 'Samaritan'.

James 'Navarino' Hide (1798-1883) acquired his nickname from the year 1827. Having been convicted of smuggling in 1824 and sentenced to 5 years servitude in the Royal Navy, he saw action at the Battle of Navarino October 1827, when a combined British, French and Russian fleet defeated the Turkish fleet. A native of Eastbourne, he married Susan Allchorn a member of the old Eastbourne Boating family. They lived for many years at No.37, Marine Parade, a cottage in the twitten between Seaside and Marine Parade, still there to this day.

Arthur Beckett the Sussex historian wrote an article on 'Navarino' and the Hide family in the Sussex County Magazine No.10, Volume 11, October 1928.

August 1869.

Eastbourne's Athletic Sports day was held - the very first being in 1861 and every year the event became more successful. At the meeting held at the Cricket ground (situated in the Ashford Road area where there used to be a row of cottages named Cricketfield Cottages long since demolished to make way for a multi storey car park), the attendance was 2,000, mainly upper classes.

Interestingly they had a Boatmen's running race over 100 yards.
The prizes were £1.0s.0d. £0.10s.0d. £0.7s.6d.
1st Tom Swain.
2nd Peter Waymark.
3rd Henry Hide.

The same month in 1869 gives an insight to life on Eastbourne's seafront when a disgruntled visitor wrote to the local paper complaining of the noises on the Parades.

"One afternoon last week I was exposed to a mob of 'amusements' rivalling Derby day, wandering Ethiopians not so black as painted, callisthenic monkeys performing musketry drill. A sort of musical wheelbarrow or perambulating grinder, attended by a dog not seeming to like the performance. A gang of acrobats with big drums accompanying, and the most irrepressible nuisance of them all, a would be Irishman, who's perpetual jig, flourish and palaver drove me mad. Then the dreary weary duet, then the forlorn soloist, then hearing in the distance a squeak! which announced the only true national branch of drama! 'Punch and Judy'. Altogether a broken Babel of discord".

Grand Parade. C.1870. With 'harp busker' on the beach.

This visitor certainly wanted peace and quiet. Today we still get Punch and Judy shows, and have our Bandstand. (As recently as 1996 saw the prosecution of a musician (busker) playing his synthesiser on the Wish Tower slopes.)

Bye-Laws were brought in to curb the excesses of entertainers! See the interesting photograph c.1870 of a (busker) musician playing his Harp on the beach!

What about the current Airborne Weekends for noise?

Itinerant preachers were also the order of the day in that same year. Two preachers on the beach preaching their gospel complained that they were assaulted at the instigation of a gentleman on the parade who incited the Boatmen by giving them money to assault them. They maintained a rope was placed around one of their necks, nearly strangling them. They both refused to press charges. Over the years the Parades have been a site for various religious meetings, but not so much these days.

Going back to the visitors, Eastbourne was very busy during the summer months. A visitors list was printed in the local paper - visitors being important to the economy of the town. With the invasion of 'well to do' visitors it caused bad blood between the young gentlemen and the young working classes of Eastbourne. Imagine the young gentlemen - 'jolly dogs' as they were called, promenading along the Parades. In 1869 a young Boatman Charles 'Bones' Hide got involved in a fracas with the 'jolly dogs' resulting in him being assaulted. This caused a general 'riot' to take place from the seafront through to Terminus Road between the 'jolly dogs' and the Boatmen and Artisans of the town, resulting in a Court case and a 'jolly dog' being fined.

The Bread and Soup Charity for Relief of the Poor.

Whilst we are told of the elegance of Eastbourne, the Empress of Watering Places, how the town was expanding and to the forefront of health resorts and praises sung of the development of the town by the Duke of Devonshire, one could not escape from the poverty and hunger that abounded in 1870.

A collection by the Bread and Soup Charity Committee raised £59. This money was used to purchase and distribute 3,500 qts. of soup and 3,800 lbs. of bread to 1,700 families and 50 young men. With the balance of cash left 1 cwt of coal was distributed to each of 80 families. They had just come through the winter months!

Life was terrible if you were one of Eastbourne's poor and going back to 1845 the distress in Eastbourne was something appalling. Carts were made with long shafts and cross heads for unemployed men to pull up to the Downs and bring down the furze firewood to sell to get bread for their families. It would take 8-10 men to pull these carts. Another example of poverty was of over 50 men at times assembled by the Lamb Inn, all unemployed. No work and no food for the family other than potatoes and salt.

September 1869.

The Regatta of September 1869 gives another example of competition amongst the Boatmen of the time.

One oared scull race. 200 yds. Open to boats of any size worked by one scull.
Prizes. £1.0s0d. £0.10s.0d. £0.5s.0d. Entrance free.
1st 'Young Gruff' - Samuel Huggett.
2nd 'Wang Wang' - Charles Hide.
3rd 'Slap Bang' - Frederick Hide.

Only the above contested, and after an amusing and exciting race. It was Young Gruff who took the lead and kept it.

One oared race. 150 yds. Not less than 5 boats to enter. Fee 2s.6d.
Prizes. £1.10s0d. £0s.15s.0d. £0.5s.0d.
1st Charles Hide.
2nd Joseph Mockett.
3rd Charles Mitchell.

This race created much amusement by the alternate working of the oar and various foulings, just before the finish Hide and Mockett pulled hard for the first prize.

Single sculls. Not exceeding 18 feet.
Prizes. £3.0s.0d. £1.10s.0d. £0.10s.0d.
1st 'Fly' - John Collins.

2nd 'Ellen Rose' - Charles Hide.
3rd 'Champion' - John Pearce.
4th 'Newport' - Arthur Matthews.

The Fly won easily.

August 1871.

With the opening of the Eastbourne Pier (1870), a Regatta was held in August 1871, organised by the first Pier Master, Mr John Vine. Crowds could watch from the Parades and now also from the Pier.

Sailing match. Boatmen.
1st prize Mackerel net. 2nd prize Shrimp net.
1st 'Florence' - William Mitchell.
2nd 'Marion' - John Hide.
3rd 'Emma' - Tom Mitchell.

Paired-oared skiffs. Boatmen.
1st prize Anchor & Chain. 2nd prize 1 lb tobacco.
1st 'Lily' - John Hide & John Jones.
2nd 'Peep-o-day' - Will Mitchell & Harry Allchorn.
3rd 'Snow-drop' - Samuel Hide & Cassy Reed.
4th 'Topsy' - Charles Hide & Richard Graves.

'Biddy' Stonham of Hastings performs at Eastbourne. C.1930. His tub can be seen in the Hastings Fishermen's Museum.

There were a variety of other competitions finishing with the: -

Tub Race for a silver watch (a tub and spade required for this race)
1st 'Livonia' - Thomas Bennett.
2nd 'Sappho' - Charles Hide.
3rd 'Cambria' - Frederick Hide.
4th 'Dart' - Thomas Knight.
5th 'Dauntless' - James Hide.

As shown the 'Tubs' had interesting names - a tub being a beer barrel sawn in half. One famous 'Tub' man was 'Biddy' Stonham of Hastings. He used to perform with his tub at the Eastbourne Regattas before and after the 2nd World War. His 'Tub' can be seen in the Hastings Fishermen's Museum.

September 1871.

At the end of the summer season, we again have a visitor giving a view of Eastbourne town and the busy bustling Parades. After praise, we do come in for some subtle criticism.

The visitor says, *"One source of annoyance to his dyspeptic nerves is, the main armies of two town bands, and the lighter troops skirmishing on their flanks. Next comes the, two rival town criers, whose several jurisdictions have not been accurately defined. Each having a long list of announcements, chiefly relating to articles lost by ladies on the beach, and every announcement introduced by a loud clanging overture on a large bell. Another grievance stated, is, the cry of fish in general, and of 'Fresh-biled prawns' in particular, pervades the streets all day and the night is made hideous with the cry of 'fine live hysters (oysters)' creatures as big as saucers and requiring the full power of a strong man to open them, and more than the power of a strong man to digest them.*

The choicest noises, the obtrusive hawkers, and the most insolent beggars, the jugglers and buffoons, reserve their favours for the people on the Grand Parades, and the beach before it.

The hawkers, I believe, live by findings upon the beach, articles which have not been lost. It cannot be supposed that a lady would purchase the wares of a dirty, tipsy costermonger, and when she is accosted by him when she sits upon the beach, she naturally puts her sunshade between herself and the brute, who is concealed from her view and he has the chance to pick up unobserved any article she may have beside her. Soon afterwards clang goes the bell of the crier offering a reward for the recovery of a ladies morocco bag, lost on the beach opposite. These hawkers have no licences and need hounding".

June 1874.

The Hard Hearted Local Board - Mr Charles Dowdall wrote a letter saying he had for 15 years made his living by selling sea shells on the beach and that being blind he could earn a living no other way. He asked the Board in consideration of his affliction to allow him to erect a stall as an exception to the rule. - Refused.

Messrs. Erridge for £3 were allowed to place chairs on the Parade till the end of October 1874, providing the charge for their use did not exceed 1d. Five years later in June 1879, Messrs. Erridge were charged £20 to place chairs on the Parade during the summer season.

Pleasure Boat Bye-Laws and other Bye-Laws covering the seafront were certainly needed in those early days. It was back in 1868 when George Chambers, a member of the Local Board published in his 'Guide to Eastbourne' - *"of Pleasure Boats, many for hire on the beach, but control of them has not yet been assumed by the Local Board, that is a reform which has yet to take place - there is consequently no stated tariff in force, 2/- an hour is the usual charge for a rowing boat".*

The Bye-Laws were a long time coming, but come they did in 1875 along with the appointment of the first Parade Inspector, Mr Francis Gilbert. Bye-Laws with regard to Pleasure Boats were made under the provisions of the Public Health Acts, 1875. The term 'Waterman' was used on the licences issued to 'Boatmen' under those first Bye-Laws.

An early example of the Parade Inspector and the Bye-Laws in operation was in 1876 when the Street, Lawns and Trees Committee who then controlled the Parade and Boatmen, dealt with the behaviour of Boatmen Jesse and Samuel Tutt who had taken a larger number of passengers in their boats than they were licenced for. The

Committee recommended the Parade Inspector be instructed to take proceedings against all parties committing a similar offence in the future. No action against the Tutts, only a warning. It was also mooted by the Committee to consider the placing of enamel plates on Pleasure Boats displaying owners' names.

Shortly after the above episode there came the worst Boating incident ever to happen in Eastbourne, with the drowning of 12 persons occurring on Sunday morning 11th June 1876.

The sad tale is as follows:

"The mackerel boat 'Nancy's Pride' belonging to Samuel 'Pork' Huggett was lying on the beach near the old Lifeboat House, between Marine Parade and the Great Redoubt, this being the Fishing Station. 'Nancy's Pride' was 22 feet long and 7 feet across the beam. 'Pork' Huggett along with his father, also named Samuel, touted for passengers to take a trip that morning - a thing they should not have done, the boat not being a Pleasure Boat and as such was not licensed to carry passengers. 'Nancy's Pride' strangely, did not contravene the Bye-Laws because she was not a Pleasure Boat. In any event Huggett had 12 passengers aboard that morning, 11 young men and a boy of 3 years.

At about 10.30am 'Nancy's Pride' put off with its passengers and with just 'Pork' Huggett Jnr. on board. Once clear of the beach he set her foresail and mizzen sail, and (unfortunately) being the only seaman on board, made both sails fast. The wind being on the right quarter took them out to sea. When she was about a mile off shore she was seen suddenly to capsize. Fishermen and Boatmen on the beach quickly launched their boats and proceeded to the spot where she had gone down. A boat belonging to George Hide succeeded in saving the only survivor, a young man named Richard Deen, Benjamin Hide being the rescuer. The bodies of the 12 drowned persons were all later recovered and taken to the 'Victoria Tavern' (Hotel) in Tower Place (now part of Latimer Road) for identification.

It was on Monday 19th June, at the Victoria Tavern, that the inquest was held and the following facts came out about the tragedy. Huggett was at the tiller and the wind had been slight, coming from the north or north east, then came a sudden puff of wind and the boat dipped and took in about a bucket of water. Huggett told some passengers to move over to the lee side, but they all panicked and went to the lee side causing the boat to capsize tipping all into the sea. The survivor Deen said he got an oar and within minutes all others had disappeared. He recalled 'Pork' Huggett as being the first to go down. He put his hands over his head and went straight down. Ben Hide gave evidence of saving Deen and recovering the bodies of two of the deceased. The 'Nancy's Pride' he considered a safe boat. She was 5 years old having been built by local boat builder, Gausden. Ben Hide considered 13 persons would not have overcrowded the boat but it should have had two Boatmen aboard for management. It was known Huggett fixed the sails. Had they been loose it might not have capsized, as Ben Hide had been off with passengers in a similar circumstance. People on board did get into dangerous positions and only laughed when told".

After hearing all the evidence a verdict of accidental death was brought in. A fund was raised in the town to help the relatives of the deceased and in July £70 was paid to each dependant and 7s 6d, each to the Boatmen who recovered the bodies.

August 1876.

 As a result of the above tragedy, the Local Board met at the Vestry-Rooms and stated there had been contact with the body appertaining to Pleasure Boat Bye-Laws. It had been decided that all Pleasure Sailboats must have two competent Boatmen in attendance when at sea and the Parade Inspector to have full power to stop unlicenced boats taking passengers to sea. A notice board was to be placed on the Parades warning persons not to use unlicenced boats.

January 1877.

New Years Day 1877 opened with a violent storm along the coast and Eastbourne was hit badly with the land end of the Pier being washed away. The Pier Master, Mr Sawdie and two employees Henry Barber and Caesar Mitchell had to make a very late escape from the collapsing Pier by jumping for it, Barber breaking a leg. From the original Splash Point opposite the Queens Hotel, hundreds of people watched the destruction of the Pier.

The Local Board met on the evening of New Years Day to discuss the damage to the Parades and there was much aggravation between members of the Board with regard to the Lower Parade. The problem had been caused, alleged Mr Tomes the Board's Surveyor, by not carrying out his recommendation to pave the Parades.

Rueben Climpson said, "The problem arose from the removal of the shingle beach from the foreshore and this could not be allowed to continue. The Duke of Devonshire could take the beach shingle (building materials) for his own purpose but no-one else had a right to".

Climpson went on to say the shingle was used on the Duke's estate no doubt, but not all for the Duke's purpose.

William Francis thought if one party were allowed to take beach, everybody ought to have the same privilege. George Chambers took it there was no remedy to the matter. The foreshore had been conveyed to the Board with reservations, one of which was that his Grace might delegate his powers of removal of shingle to any one he pleased. The meeting was concluded without any firm action.

Who was going to tell his Grace to leave the shingle alone? By the action of removing the shingle, the sea wall (promenade) had been breached and by rights they should have billed the Duke!

Grand Parade. C.1890. Row Boats placed on promenade due to neap tide.

July 1877.

The gales of January had washed away most of the beach shingle along the Grand Parade and in July there were complaints from the visitors about the state of the beach - one writing and threatening to go elsewhere for his sea bathing. The Boatmen had to pull up their boats on to the Lower Promenade, there being very little shingle left when the tide came in, thereby obstructing the Promenade and causing complaints. One belligerent Boatman named Wood crossed swords with the Parade Inspector Francis Gilbert over this problem and ended up in Court.

Edwin Wood, a Licenced Boatman, was summoned under the Bye-Laws of the Eastbourne Local Board for refusing to comply with the orders of Mr Gilbert and for using abusive language to him when ordered to remove his boats. Wood pleaded guilty to both charges.

 Gilbert told the court that Mr Tomes, Board Surveyor, instructed him to get all boats removed from the Parade. He spoke to the Boatmen and all with exception of Wood complied. Wood said he would not remove his boats for any person and began to abuse him, using the most indecent language. Wood not only contravened these Bye-Laws, but also had failed to display a plated copy of the Bye-Laws in a conspicuous place on his boats. Wood denied this and went on to say he had been a Boatman for over 50 years and had never experienced such 'awful times' as the present. This was owing to the beach being so rocky due to the loss of shingle and the boats were liable to receive damage. The Bye-Laws stated two boats could be placed abreast on the parade. Mr Tomes replied stating the Bye-Law regarding boats on the parade only applied in bad weather or neap tides. On the day in question the sea was dead calm.

Boatmen on Grand Parade. C.1870. John Hide on extreme right, others unknown.

These were the first charges brought under the Bye-Laws and the Bench said they would be lenient on this occasion. Wood was fined a total of 15s 0d plus costs, 7 days imprisonment in default.

As regards the Bye-Laws covering the Pleasure Boats, plated copies of the Bye-Laws had to be displayed on the boats in 1877.

May 1878.

Whit Monday was a fine day at Eastbourne and thousands of visitors poured into the town during the forenoon. The Parades had been completed to Holywell and even the haughty neighbours Brighton, expressed themselves delighted with Eastbourne's beautiful seafront. The one drawback to the town however was the dusty streets, which were blown about in clouds. It was unfortunate the Board had not provided against this as it was most irritating.

The tide was out in the morning and thousands of people dotted the sands. Later in the day the tide was in and looked lovely but the day was not so good for the Boatmen, the wind being up and 'ruffling' the sea that it would unsettle many a head.

Mr H.P. Hughes' smart little American yacht raced a Mr Hannay's yacht 'Annie' over a 3-mile course in the morning. Mr Hughes craft won with Alleyn 'Old Rig' Sayers being her sailing master.

This for the Boatmen of Eastbourne was another source of income, crewing private

yachts for well to do residents and visitors. The previous year in September 1877 the Boatmen received invitations from Mr. Hughes to attend the Boatman's Annual Dinner at the Anchor Hotel. A report from the local paper shows it to have been a grand affair. Mr Hughes was an old and respected visitor to the town for over 28 years and a benevolent friend of the Fishermen and Boatmen of Eastbourne. He must have been quite well off as nearly one hundred accepted his kind invitation.

July 1878.

An enterprising Eastbourne Boatman, Thomas Sayers, took a lady and gentleman to Littlington by water. The trip proved a very pleasant one and its practicability proved it likely that Mr

John Hide b.1837. d.1918. & Boatmen's Dinner invitation 1877.

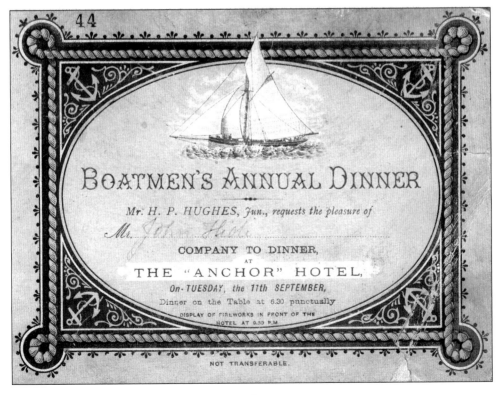

Russell's beautiful Pleasure Tea Gardens would receive many visitors that summer by way of the sea.

Sailing by Beachy Head, through the river mouth and windings of the River Cuckmere, must have been very exciting and of soothing character and the Littlington Gardens offered every land pleasure on arrival there. The sailing and boating skills of Tom Sayers were second to none when considering the tide, wind and handling the boat under restricting conditions. Indeed the Boatmen of Eastbourne can be said to have possessed superior skills over a deep sea going Seaman.

There was a distinction between a Boatman and a Seaman. A Boatman was brought up from childhood and skill in boat work came with years of practice. The Seaman's calling was different and he was usually trained to it when a grown man hating boat work and dreading the broken water amid which much of the Boatman's life was spent.

July 1878.

Eastbourne Court July 20th and Boatman Samuel Tutt was summoned for not wearing his Boatman's numbered licence badge. Tutt held licence No.72 for his boat 'Eagle' but had not been wearing it on his hat when plying for hire. Tutt denied this saying he was not plying for hire and that was why he was not wearing it. Parade Inspector Gilbert gave evidence that Tutt was plying. The Bye-Laws stated the licence badge should be worn on a hat. It was a numbered badge with the words 'Licenced Boatman' surrounding. The non-wearing of the badge had been mentioned to Tutt before and he had been abusive. Tutt was found guilty and fined £1.0s.0d with 16s.0d. costs.

Samuel Tutt with his brother Jesse, as seen back in 1876 was a source of aggravation to the Parade Inspector!

Marine Parade. C.1890.

October 1878.

Rough weather again at the end of October and damage again to the foreshore of Marine Parade. A gale had reaped terrible havoc, sweeping away thousands of tons of shingle, leaving bare, undermining and destroying the foundations of what were once dwelling houses for the Coast Guard Officers.

View east from Marine Parade showing original Fishing Station before the building of Royal Parade. C.1879.

The Lifeboat House was nearly washed away, the Lifeboat being kept out for safety. The Coastguard and Rocket Apparatus House was swept to its foundations and the footing of the signal mast almost washed away. Boats had been dragged into the roadway for safety with fishing gear etc. also removed. The Rowing Club Boat House was washed to its foundations. The sea overflowed a wall of shingle to the east of Marine Parade and poured in torrents down through Mann's Row (now St. Aubyn's Road) into Seaside tearing up the road.

'Pug up' was the cry down Mann's Row as the sea was imminent in its approach. An age old custom of 'pugging up' doors of the terraced cottages in Mann's Row to keep the sea out was related by the late Fred 'Mucky' Erridge (nicknamed by his fellow Fishermen and Boatmen because of his smart and clean turnout on all occasions - Fred died at the age of 93 in 1990.)

The flooding over the foreshore between Marine Parade and the Great Redoubt (now strangely called Redoubt Fortress) into Seaside had happened on other occasions and as a result the Local Board finally brought in the Eastbourne Improvement Act 1879. This resulted in the Fishermen being thrown off their ancient site between Marine Parade and the Great Redoubt and moved eastward to the present site east of the Great Redoubt.

A new Sea Wall was built and the keystone of the new parade (Royal Parade) laid by the first Mayor of Eastbourne, Mr G A Wallis on 4th January 1884. Under the supervision of Mr

Royal Parade completed 1884.

Tomes, Board Surveyor, the Sea Wall was finally completed on 11th February 1884.

The building of the Sea Wall and Royal Parade only partly stopped the flooding of Seaside as it flooded well into the 20th century and the loss of the shingle beach increased especially by the Marine Parade. We are told in a report from 1896 of the great loss there and up at Holywell, where some ten years previously there were great swathes of shingle now all gone. Indeed the shingle washed onto Marine Parade in a storm (1896) was carted away for building material and not replaced on the beach. The loss of shingle from the foreshore is a never-ending problem. The year 2000 saw some £20 million spent on groyne protection and shingle replacement, but 2 years later vast quantities of shingle had still been swept away.

September 1880.

On the Grand Parade and a narrow escape from drowning with Boatman Edward Walter Allchorn's prompt action.

It was on Wednesday 1st, when a young gentleman named Anson St.Clair-Ford, aged 15 years the son of Capt. and Mrs. St.Clair-Ford, got into a boat on the Parade intending to row himself up and down near the shore for a while. He had not been long in the boat when he was overcome with faintness and sank against the side of the boat his head and neck at once becoming immersed in the sea. Boatman Edward Allchorn saw the peculiar position the boy was in and at once got into the nearest boat and rowed out and rescued the lad. A few seconds more and life would have been extinct. Allchorn rowed quickly to shore bearing what he thought was a lifeless body.

Doctor MacQueen was soon in attendance and assisted by Boatmen William Allchorn Snr. Charles Knight, John Mockett, Samuel Wood, Reuben Wood, Alleyn Sayers and William Allchorn Jnr. every effort was made to restore life. After some time there was a partial recovery. The boy was taken to the Victoria Baths (then at the sea end of Victoria Place, now Terminus Road) and most carefully watched by Dr. MacQueen and Boatmen Charles 'Bones' Hide, Richard Hurd and some kind

Victoria Baths where the Boatmen took young Anson St.Clair to recover from drowning.

ladies. It was not until between 8 and 9 o'clock that evening that the parents arrived. They had anxiously been awaiting their son's return unaware of the accident. The boy was removed home and made a full recovery. Capt. and Mrs. St. Clair-Ford tendered their sincere thanks to the Boatmen, to Mrs Fuller of the Victoria Baths, to Dr. MacQueen for his promptness and skill and to Police Sergeant Bourne for his great forethought displayed. The Boatmen were all personally thanked and liberally rewarded. A rowboat was built for Edward Allchorn and called after the boy he saved - 'Anson St. Clair'.

The year 1880 also saw the foreshore between Victoria Place and the Pier solely given over to Pleasure Boats - no more Bathing Machines. Previously there had been machines all along the foreshore of the Grand Parade with the exception of Pleasure Boat Stands opposite Howard Square, Cavendish Hotel and Victoria Place Steps. In 1881 the Local Board resolved that the same number of stands for Bathing Machines be allowed to Messrs Hide & Paul, Luck, Hounsom and Bennett, as last year (1880). It appears these people had a monopoly west of the Pier.

Royal Parade. C.1886 showing Erridge Bathing Machine station.

When the Royal Parade was built in 1884 the Erridge family solely ran their Bathing Machines there until they were taken over by the Council in 1920. Stabling for their horses was situated in the mews to the rear of what is now the Royal Naval Old Comrades Club, in Beach Road. A very old Eastbourne Fishing and Pleasure Boating family, the Erridges also had the franchise to supply chairs on the parades at that period.

Royal Parade. C.1900. Erridge Bathing Machine Office with Police attendance.

The building of the Royal Parade opened up sites for Pleasure Boat Stands giving more of Eastbourne's Fishing and Boating fraternity an opportunity to earn a living

With their fishing knowledge, the Boatmen also earned a living by taking visitors for rod and line fishing to places off shore where they made a good fix using prominent landmarks of the town of Eastbourne and beyond. This ancient knowledge of fishing ways was ever changing as Eastbourne grew.

Here are a couple of examples of a fix on the 'Inner Southern Shaw' west and east marking fishing grounds - 'Paradise over Trinity Mansion Hotel' and 'Millers House over Langney Coastguard Station'. Of course there are many more.

In 1881 two gentlemen visitors sang the praises of Boatmen Charles Wood and Thomas Hide and their knowledge of the tide in the boat 'Venus', when they caught 130 lb of various fish over a two-hour period. Time was of essence because of the tide.

June 1881.

When the Grand Parade was first opened, the local Boatmen took it upon themselves to clear the foreshore of all large boulders and rocks to facilitate ease of launching and landing as well as a safety measure. In June, a letter was sent from the Pleasure Boat owners to the Local Board with a complaint to the effect that they had cleared the foreshore of rocks and boulders and asked for special treatment against those boat owners (newcomers) who did nothing and were now vying with them for the Boat Stands - the Local Board had granted some licences to outsiders.

Another letter and memorial was sent in June by the local Boatmen requesting the Board to appoint Stands for boats on the foreshore. This could indicate that the traditional Boat Stand sites occupied by the Boatmen were in danger of being taken over by outsiders. Jealously guarding these Stands over the years the local Boatmen felt they had established a right to these sites. Anyway, it appears the protest worked as from what records that are available for that period all show local Boatmen on the Boat Stand sites.

John Hide's and Dennis Breach's Boat Stands C.1880. - Note the bathing costumes drying.

January 1883.

An article in the local paper appeared to the effect that Eastbourne could be in danger of losing their Pleasure Boatmen since the Fishermen had been kicked off their old Fishing Station and moved east of the Redoubt. The reply stated not to have any fears. They would return and there would be an abundance of Boatmen when the season started.

November 1883.

The Local Board, which ran the Town lasted until November 1883 when it was superceded by a Mayor and Corporation - in other words, by a Town Council under the 'Municipal Corporation Act. 1882'. It was on the innaugeral Mayor's Sunday Parade, 25th November, 1883, that the famous lifesaving incident took place when the sailing barque 'New Brunswick' was in distress off Beachy Head and the crew and residents of Eastbourne pulled the lifeboat 'William and Mary' over Beachy Head and launched her off Birling Gap into tempestous seas to rescue the crew of 11 souls.

March 1884.

The new Council agreed with a letter from Boatman William Allchorn, for Pleasure Boat Stands and Bathing Machine sites to be marked out on the Borough Surveyor's Plans. By April this had been done and so for the first time Boat Stands were marked out to individual Boatmen on the foreshore plan. The prime sites were the beach opposite Howard Square, Cavendish Hotel and opposite Victoria Place steps (top of Terminus Road), where the day-trippers arriving by train would have made their way.

September 1884.

The Eastbourne Regatta held off Grand Parade on 5th September shows the under 22 feet, lugger rigged sailing boat race result as follows: -

A handicap of one and half minutes per foot allowed for differences in length.

1st 'Sea Gull' - 19ft. 6ins. - A Sayers.
2nd 'Duke of Norfolk' - 19ft. 6ins - S Olive.
3rd 'Albion' - 17ft. - H J Tyrell.
4th 'Commodore' - 19ft. 6ins - D Breach.
5th 'Little Wonder' - 17ft. - A Matthews.
6th 'Estella' - 21ft. - D Breach Snr.
7th 'Venus' - 18ft. 6ins - J Hide.
8th 'Queen' - 19ft. 6ins - T Sayers.

There was a Ladies single sculls race won by Miss Eliza Sayers a member of the Fishing and Boating family.

A second regatta, the 'Royal Parade Regatta', was held on 30th September 1884.

It was the first Regatta to be held there and was for Watermen/Boatmen only - The Royal Parade being completed at that period opening up the beach as previously stated, for Pleasure Boating.

Watermen's sculls for Licenced Watermen of Eastbourne.

1st Jack Erridge.
2nd Will Jackson.
3rd James Merritt.

Three others started namely: John Colstick, William Bollard Hide and Edwin 'Lord' Matthews.

Matthews' boat capsized at the start, he couldn't swim and was rescued clinging to his boat (Edwin Matthews was 2nd Cox'n of the 1883 lifeboat). Jackson and Hide shared the lead between them and indeed Hide was leading when he caught a heavy sea and capsized - he swam ashore. After this, the sea being so choppy, it was decided to hold the rest of the Regatta on the Monday.

On the Monday in the Amateur paired sculls, Jesse & Arthur Bollard Hide (Sussex County cricketers) came second to John Vine & Mark Hookham.

The One oared race - open only to Royal Parade Licenced Watermen of Eastbourne.
1st C Hide.
2nd J Erridge.
3rd W Erridge.

This race caused considerable amusement. Eight entries went to the post. William Erridge got round the buoys first but Jack Erridge and Charles Hide were close on his track. The floundering appearance that the boats presented owing to the fact that the men had to row one side then another, afforded an immense amount of fun. Ultimately Charles "Bones" Hide (Coxswain of the 1883 lifeboat) came in an easy winner, Jack Erridge 2nd and William Erridge 3rd.

Pair oared race. To be rowed by the crew of the 1883 Lifeboat.
Prize given by Mr.A Hounsom of the Britannia Music Hall of Varieties.
1st William Erridge & William Stanbridge.
2nd Will Jackson & Albert Sayers.
3rd George Erridge & John Colstick.

A closely contested race. Although late members of the old Lifeboat crew of the famous 1883 rescue, they were still, along with their coxswain Charles (Bones) Hide, highly thought of by the residents of Eastbourne and always will be for their bravery in the 'New Brunswick' rescue.

The final race was a 'Hurdle Race' open to the Royal Parade Watermen. It was a swimming race where they had to clamber over and dive under about a dozen long planks placed along the course as 'obstacles'.

Hurdle Race Results.
1st J Erridge, 2nd A Erridge, 3rd J Merritt, 4th H J Tyrell, 5th W Erridge, 6th A Sayers, 7th W Jackson, 8th C(Bones)Hide, 9th F Hide.

This Regatta gives us some of the names of the Watermen/Boatmen who operated on the Royal Parade in 1884.

September also saw the sinking of the Eastbourne pleasure yacht 'Skylark' during what was described as a semi-hurricane along the coast. She was anchored 200 yards off Royal Parade, in ballast. Attempts were made to launch boats to get to her but it was too rough. Prior to this event, a fishing lugger skippered by Joseph

1886 — £ s d

Month	£	s	d
March	0	3	6
April	0	8	10½
	1	2	·
	0	11	9
	1	1	6
May	2	5	"
	1	3	6
	1	7	6
	0	12	"
June	0	19	6
	1	10	10
	2	10	"
	1	16	9
July	2	0	6
	0	18	6
	2	12	"
	1	1	6
August	1	0	"
	2	11	
	1	19	"
	4	3	"
September	5	15	6
	5	14	4½
	2	17	3
	1	18	6
	0	11	"
October	2	0	"
	0	10	6
	1	5	"
	0	5	"
	2	6	
	52	14	10
Bathing	7	0	0

1885 — £ s d

Month	£	s	d
March	1	6	
April	2	6	
	14	"	
	12	6	
	1	4	"
May	1	18	6
	1	12	3
	16	"	
	15		
June	2	12	"
	3	1	"
	1	18	3
	1	4	7
July	2	1	9
	3	12	6
	2	11	3
	2	9	"
	2	7	"
August	3	19	9
	2	15	6
	5	12	6
	2	6	"
September	1	19	6
	0	13	"
	1	18	"
	3	1	6
October	1	3	10½
	0	10	6
	0	17	"
	0	12	6
	0	16	6
	57	11	3½
Bathing	2	0	0

John Hide's Boating and Bathing Machine accounts 1885 and 1886.

Mockett, who also owned the 'Skylark' was at sea just off shore and the on-lookers experienced great worry. But under the experienced pilotage of Mockett she beached on the foreshore in splendid style. The heavy seas driven by the wind swept over the 'Skylark' and she sank. The following day when the weather had abated she was dragged ashore and found to be much damaged.

1878	£ s d			1879	£ s d		
				April	"	13	9
March	"	2	"		1	3	"
April	"	3	"		1	16	"
	2	10	2		1	3	"
May	1	6	"	May	0	13	"
	"	11	"		"	15	6
	"	"	9		1	18	6
	"	5	4		1	0	"
	"	1	9	June	"	10	6
June	1	3	6		1	12	6
	"	19	6		"	19	"
	2	13	6		1	8	6
	3	1	"	July	0	7	8
July	1	10	"		0	9	6
	1	17	6		2	1	0
	4	3	"	Fexing	"	13	0
	2	18	2		2	1	6
August	4	17	6	August	1	1	6
	0	17	6		2	17	6
	3	5	6		2	14	0
	"	19	"		1	5	6
September	5	0	"		1	4	0
	4	7	9	September	5	19	0
	0	18	9		1	12	6
	2	1	"		2	17	0
October	"	10	"		1	19	6
	"	11	6	October	"	11	9
	46	14	8		"	5	0
					"	4	6
					41	17	3

Hooking	2	5	6

John Hide's Boating and 'Hooking' accounts 1878 and 1879.

The month of September gave an interesting insight by a visitor describing the Inspector of Bathing on the beach as "say 40 years of age, strong well knit frame indicative of great strength, easy gate like a man-o-war's man, merry twinkling blue eyes and that unmistakable appearance in manner of the true Sussex Fisherman and Boatman, his name - 'Bungay on the Rock' French, others on the beach having equally curious nick-names".

1885/6.

A total of £57.11s.3¹/₂d was taken by John Hide's Pleasure Boats and £2 by his Bathing Machines for the 1885 season. 1886 shows a decrease in Pleasuring but increase in Bathing Machine takings. Earlier years' takings are also shown including returns from 'hooking' - in effect taking out fishing parties.

1887.

1887 saw Pleasure Boating at one of its busiest times and of the southern resorts, Eastbourne came out tops. The Boatmen were noted for their civility and readiness to oblige. They were fine hardy muscular fellows, which cannot be said of Boatmen at other watering places. Their well kept sailing and rowing boats bright with varnish and very clean bore out the statement by the Eastbourne Boatmen that theirs were the best-kept boats along the coast. The Boatmen of Eastbourne generally had more than one or two boats. They usually invested in several and did expect a good income during the season. For long winter months those sail boats not used for fishing lay upon the beach at the Fishing Station. Each February work began to prepare them for the coming season starting March/April through to October weather permitting. Of the boats, the principal owners usually renewed them about every 4-5 years. In this way the boats were kept to a very high standard.

In the summer of 1887, about 17 Sailing Boats worked off the Parades catering for excursions and fishing parties. Most were lugger rigged, but the largest being the 'Skylark' was dandy rigged. Owned by Joseph Mockett, she was 15 tons and carried 83 passengers. Making daily trips along the coast, her captain during this period was Charles 'Bones' Hide.

Other sailing boats recorded were: -

'Albion' owned by Harry Tyrell - 14 passengers.
'Admiral' owned by Harry Tyrell - 10 passengers.
'Industry' owned by Joseph Mockett - 4 tons -14 passengers.
'Seagull' owned by Alleyn Sayers - 4 tons - 16 passengers - 19ft 6ins long.
'Royal Albert' owned by Edwin Matthews - 20 passengers.
'Wanderer' owned by Edwin Matthews - 16 passengers.
'Golden City' owned by William Allchorn - 15 passengers - 18ft long.
'Petrel' owned by Richard Wood - 12 passengers - 17ft long.
'Nell' owned by John Francis - 10 passengers - 17ft 6ins long.
'Queen' owned by Tom Sayers - 15 passengers - 20ft long.
'Lizzie' owned by Richard Hide Jnr. - 15 passengers - 20ft long.
'I.C.U.' owned by Richard Hide Jnr. - 12 passengers - 18ft long.
'Hildegarde' owned by William(Old)Bollard Hide - 10 passengers - 17ft long.
'Commodore' owned by Dennis Breach - 20 passengers - 20ft long.
'Estella' owned by Dennis Breach - 15 passengers - 17ft long.
'Venus' owned by John Hide - 15 passengers - 20ft long.

All the foregoing sailing boats also took out fishing parties with the exception of the 'Skylark'.

Of the Rowing Boats in 1887 there were a total of 137 working off the beach with a strange variety of names. i.e. Wild Rose, English Rose, Tulip, Hyacinth, Lily, Orange Blossom, Violet, Nellie, Coral, Kate, Caroline, Annie, Ellen, Gracie, Emily,

Ocean Wave, Spray, Jack, Petrel, Nell, Diana, Iolanthe, Venus, Shamrock, Prince of Wales, Prince George, Princess Maud, Ann, Rob Roy, Noubliez Pas, Anson St Clair, Peep of Day, Young Osman and Mizpah, to name but a few.

Some recorded Rowing Boat owners and the numbers of boats owned: -

William Allchorn = 11. Dennis Breach = 8. Ellis = 4. John Francis = 3. Fred Fibbins = 5. George 'Pincher ' Hide & Allchorn = 15. John Hide Snr. = 8. William (Old) Bollard Hide = 5. William Jackson = 6. Edwin Matthews = 6. McCormack = 2. Joseph Mockett = 7. Alleyn Sayers = 10. Tom Sayers = 3. Henry Tutt = 2. Samuel Tutt = 7. Henry Tyrell = 7. Charles Wood = 5. Edward Wood = 3. Reuben Wood = 7. Richard Wood = 5. Albert Wood = 2.

From the account records of John Hide in the 1880s, there is a list of boats owned by him as follows: -

Sailing boat 'Albatross' 20ft long. To carry 14 passengers.
Rowing boat 'Little Fanny' long. To carry 7 passengers.
Rowing boat 'Bonny John' 17ft long. To carry 6 passengers.
Rowing boat 'Snowdrop' 17ft long. To carry 5 passengers.
Rowing boat 'Mo Mina' 17ft long. To carry 5 passengers.

Rowing boat 'Flying Scud' 16ft long. To carry 2 passengers.
Rowing boat 'Primrose' 16ft long. To carry 2 passengers.
Rowing boat 'True Blue' 16ft long. To carry 2 passengers.
Rowing boat 'Butterfly' 17ft long. To carry 4 passengers.
Rowing boat 'Little Ted' 17ft long. To carry 4 passengers.
Rowing boat 'Little Amy' 17ft long. To carry 4 passengers.

There were family connections to some of the names. Was 'True Blue' his political colours?

Bathing Machines in 1887 numbered some 200, working from Marine Parade to the Wish Tower, Grand Parade. The Erridge family at Marine/Royal Parade had 17 for ladies and children and 12 machines for gentlemen. Between the Pier and Wish Tower, ladies' and children's machines were run by the families Knight, Bennett, Head, Brown, Luck, 'Pincher' Hide & Paul and John Hide, then to Hounsom who had only gentlemen. Hounsom looked after some of the other proprietors'

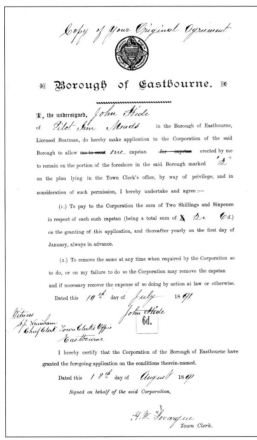

John Hide's Capstan Licence for Pleasure Boat Stand No.2 1891.

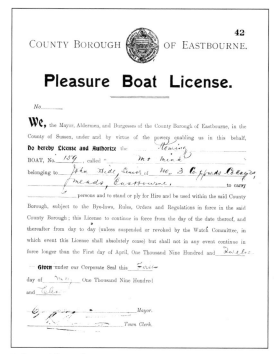

42
COUNTY BOROUGH OF EASTBOURNE.

Pleasure Boat License.

No_____

We, the Mayor, Aldermen, and Burgesses of the County Borough of Eastbourne, in the County of Sussex, under and by virtue of the powers enabling us in this behalf,

Do hereby License and Authorize the _____ *Rowing*

BOAT, No. *159*, called " *mo mira* "

belonging to *John Hide, Senior, of No. 3 Cliffords Bridges Meads, Eastbourne,* _____ to carry

_____ persons and to stand or ply for Hire and be used within the said County Borough, subject to the Bye-laws, Rules, Orders and Regulations in force in the said County Borough; this License to continue in force from the day of the date thereof, and thereafter from day to day (unless suspended or revoked by the Watch Committee, in which event this License shall immediately cease) but shall not in any event continue in force longer than the First day of April, One Thousand Nine Hundred and *Twelve*

Given under our Corporate Seal this _____ day of _____ One Thousand Nine Hundred and _____

_____ Mayor.
_____ Town Clerk.

John Hide's Pleasure Boat Licence 1911.

machines as well as his own, a total of 116. To attend to these machines he had 15 employees and worked 8 horses. The bathing at this period was said to be excellent. The hours of bathing were between 6.00am and 1.00pm; the sexes were separated whilst bathing. For the poor of Eastbourne there was free open bathing east of the Redoubt by the Fishing Station. It was some years before the Council allowed bathing and changing on the beach along the Parades.

September 1887.

In a sailing race in September, the 17ft lugger 'Frolic' came second to the 21 ft cutter 'Spitfire' over a course of 6 miles, 'Spitfire' winning in the time of 1 hour 53 minutes. The 'Jubilee' a 19ft Lugger came third.

May 1888.

An interesting sailing race had taken place in May, with a side bet of £5 between 'Delphine'- Alleyn Sayers and 'Royal Albert'- Arthur Matthews (landlord of the Beach Hotel), over a 4 mile course. Sayers won the race. The 'Royal Albert' was 36 years old, having been built by William Simpson of Eastbourne in 1852.

March 1889.

Parade Inspector Gilbert gave his annual report for the year 1888 before the Council and licences issued were as follows: -

Sailing boats - 25
Rowing boats - 142
Boatman 1st class, Sailing & Rowing - 64 (a 1st class Boatman had to be proficient in both sailing and rowing)
Boatman 2nd class, rowing - 23 (2nd class Boatman rowing only)

Boat Stands & Capstan Stands,
Grand Parade - 13
Royal Parade - 9

Bathing Machines,
Ladies - 131
Gentlemen - 114

The total monies received by the Council for licences issued in 1888 were £56.11s.6d. Mr Gilbert's report stated "no fines and the conduct of Boatmen generally good". All existing licences were renewed for 1889.

George Gausden. Eastbourne boat builder.

May 1889.

The month of May saw the building by Mr George Gausden at his Eastbourne boat yard, of a racing lugger rigged yacht named 'Paradox'. Said to be unique to the yacht-racing world - there had been a previous lugger rigged yacht the 'New Moon' reaching a speed of 13 knots built by F. Tutt of Hastings in 1859, with whom Gausden served his apprenticeship. So he had a good master.

The yacht was for Mr. F W Leyborne-Popham, whose idea it was to have the yacht built. Popham became Gausden's partner in a fishing enterprise. Gausden built and Popham financed the building of a fleet of big Eastbourne fishing luggers. Popham resided at that time on the Royal Parade.

The 'Paradox' weighed 60 tons, was 70 feet in length, had a 20-foot beam and 10 feet of dropped keel; Foremast 64 feet, mizzen mast 75 feet high with a total sail area of 7,000 square feet. A Mr Storey of London was her designer. Normally a lugger sail had to be lowered when tacking but due to a special contrivance the lugger sail would dip round without lowering. The keel had 26 tons of lead. She had accommodation for 6 passengers, having a saloon and 4 cabins and was crewed by 20 men.

A large labour force commanded £100 per week in wages while she was being built. In June she was rolled from the yard in Beach Road (now a residential development named Sovereign Court) to the beach at the Fishing Station. From there she was launched by being pulled into the sea stern first by the steamer 'Lady Brassey' and taken to Newhaven for fitting out and rigging. Her total cost being £5-6,000. Her first sailing master was a Mr Hoskins of Bosham, her mate being Charles 'Bones' Hide and the crew made up partly of Eastbourne Boatmen.

In August of that year the 'Paradox' did not show well in any of her races. Her lugger rig was thought not up to it. So for all the expense and inventiveness she never made it as a racing yacht.

Mr. Popham whose idea it was for the lugger rig was a member of the Royal Thames Yacht and Royal London Yacht Clubs.

Popham did not give up on the principle of a lugger rigged racing yacht and June 1890 saw the launching of another racing yacht the 'White Slave' built again by Gausden at his yard in Beach Road, designed by Mr. W. Fife Jnr. She was 60 feet long and had a 14 ft beam with 40 tonnage. She had no centreboard but a keel of 30 tons 5 cwt. a foremast of 31 feet and mizzen of 77 feet, the sail area being 4,000 square feet. Having a crew of 11 and skippered by a Captain Tonkins of Penzance, 'White Slave' was christened at the launching by Miss Florence Gausden, aged 11 years, the daughter of the builder George Gausden. Like the 'Paradox' the 'White Slave' failed to impress as a racer and within a year or two she was converted to cutter rig.

George Gausden was born in Meads in 1847, going to St Mary's elementary school, Old Town and leaving at the age of 14 years. He was apprenticed to Mr Tutt, the Hastings yacht and boat builder. At the age of 21years on completion of his indentures he returned to Eastbourne and joined his uncle William Simpson, boat builder, who's yard was on part of which is now St Aubyn's Road. This arrangement was short lived and Gausden did some local fishing and then returned to Hastings where he joined the Brig 'Pelican' which carried coal and other cargoes along the South Coast. He then worked for James Hutchinson, boat builder of Worthing. After this he returned to Eastbourne and on his own account started boat building in Meads. He built boats for 3 years then moved to the site of the old Fishing Station, Seaside, building boats for clients along the South Coast from Folkestone to Worthing.

The lugger rigged racing yacht 'Paradox' built by George Gausden 1889.

With the building of the Royal Parade he moved to the site in the Beach/Sidley Road area known in the 1890s as Gausden's Yard. (It later became the Ice factory site.) Retiring in 1904, his business was taken over by Mr. Thomas Sisk.

Gausden attributed his success as a boat builder to the reliability of his men. He employed as many as 100 at one time, showing the boat building industry was then quite considerable.

Popham and Gausden eventually fell out and Popham moved to the Southampton area with his boats. In 1893 Popham obtained a court order directing Gausden to disclose accounts of monies received by Gausden on behalf of the partnership. Gausden appealed against this order, it being disclosed that an alleged total of £74,000 was involved between 1883-1891. The appeal was dismissed. Gausden nevertheless continued with his fishing interests as well as boat building.

In later life (1924 when he was aged 77 years) Gausden was asked if he had his life again would he do the same? He replied that he would do the same again, *"but would exercise a little more discretion and be somewhat less trustful of people in general"*. Of the Fishing and Boating classes, he could take their word and depend on whatever they said, with them it was a yea or nay. They were utterly and absolutely reliable.

August 1889.

Another sailing race involving Alleyn Sayers and Arthur Matthews in the August Regatta: -

Lugger rigged 18 - 25ft boats - 1½ minute per foot allowed for difference in length.
1st Alleyn Sayers 'Delphine' - 20ft.
2nd Arthur Matthews 'Royal Albert' - 22ft.
3rd William Hide 'Maud' - 21ft.

So 'Delphine' again defeated the 'Royal Albert' as in 1887.

Licenced Watermen's double sculls.
1st William & Edward Allchorn 'Village Flower'.
2nd Arthur Matthews & George Hide 'Princess'.
3rd John & William Erridge 'Bertie'.

Another sailing race in August between the 'Lord Randolph' owned by Mr Moore and the 'Little Mary' owned by Arthur Matthews, round the Lightship was won by the 'Lord Randolph' by 200 yards. A close finish after all those miles. Poor Arthur Matthews - second again.

October 1889.

Back in May the Council had posters displayed along the length of the Parades warning Fishermen and Boatmen not to clean fish on the Foreshore and Parades. Come October the Boatmen were still disinclined to obey. The Council placed an injunction on Fishermen and Boatmen prohibiting the use of the Foreshores and Parades for "baiting, landing, cleaning and hawking of fish and use of bad language" as many complaints had been received. The aforementioned had been an age-old tradition, a way of life (bad language?) and a source of income for the Fisherman and Boatman but was now restricted to the Fishing Station. It was good business to take the 'visitors' out fishing and the Council's injunction was to prove another 'battle' for the Fishing/Boating fraternity. The truth of the matter was that the owners of Hotels and private houses on the seafront objected.

Bearing this in mind, an article appeared in the local Gazette, July 1889.

"Numerous boats throng the beach from the Redoubt to the Wish and the class of boat ranges from the 'Skylark' Mockett's big excursion sailboat, to sailing and rowing boats of all sizes, down to the lightest skiff designed to carry one person.

Without exaggeration too, it may be stated that the Boatmen of Eastbourne are of a superior class, being very civil and obliging, and rowdyism, such as associated with many seaside Boatmen, is unknown. Trips to Beachy Head or Langney Fort, according to the state of the tide, afford a pleasant outing, while for those fond of going further out, a row or sail out to the revolving lightship some six miles out, will prove enjoyable. The fishing is excellent and plentiful. For instance in 1887, two visitors caught 98 lbs of fish off Langney Point in 4 hours".

Well that's a fine endorsement of the Boatmen of Eastbourne.

Chapter Two

1890 ~ 1899

April 1890.

April saw the building and opening of the 'Missions to Seamen's Institute' on land at the sea end of Beach Road adjacent to the Fishing Station. It was back in December 1888 when the Boatmen and Fishermen of Eastbourne held a meeting in the New Temperance Hall with a representative of the 'Missions to Seamen' with the intention of having a 'Mission' at Eastbourne. There was already one 'Institute' in the area for Navvies and Fishermen, built in 1881 in Sea Beach Lane (Now Beach Road sited where the 'Royal Naval Old Comrades Club is today) - The Vicar of Christ Church, Seaside, Rev. Robert Allen being the founder. It was called the 'Fishermen's Institute'.

Another 'Institute' in existence at the same time was the 'Fishermen's Mutual Association' opened by Mr Harry Stevens. Meetings were held in premises near Sea Beach Lane.

How long these 'Institutes' lasted is not known, but by 1888 it was obvious the Boatmen and Fishermen wanted their own 'Mission', henceforth the meeting under the Mission's representative Rev. C B Cooper. Present at that meeting were Mr Kensett, Richard Wood, William Wood, Charles Hide, John Mockett, Nick Jackson, Jesse Huggett, George Erridge, William Allchorn, Samuel Tutt, Edwin Matthews, Samuel Oliver, George French, Fred Huggett, Reuben Reed, John Erridge, John Hurd Snr. & Jnr., D. Foster, D. Matthews, S. Dyer, Edward Wood, Thomas Knight, H Tutt, William Hobby, William Godden and others. After discussion it was agreed to build the Mission. The following Committee was then put to the meeting and accepted: - Messrs. Jesse Huggett, Richard Wood, Peter Waymark, Fred Huggett, Thomas Boniface, Mr. Chandler (coast guardsman), Mr Yepp (missionary), Mr. Couchman (colporteur), Mr. Coleman, Mr Kensett, the Misses Bell, and Miss Seward.

Original 'Missions to Seamens' building 'The Bethel' built 1890. This later became Eastbourne Fishermen's and Boatmen's Protection Society (Aka The Fishermen's Club).

EASTBOURNE FISHERMEN'S MISSION

In publishing the subjoined Statement of Accounts, the Committee tender their hearty thanks to the kind friends who have enabled them to start the above Mission and are hopeful that much good will result from the special effort thus put forward in behalf of the Fishermen and Boatmen of the Town. There are no expenses connected with the working of the Mission save lighting, warming, cleaning, &c., those engaged in it gladly giving their services to help on the cause. The accounts show a small balance on the wrong side, which the Committee feel sure need only to be pointed out to be promptly met. It is the wish of the Committee, if funds permit, to supplement the work of the Mission by the provision of a Coffee-room and Reading-room, an adjunct which is felt to be greatly needed.

BALANCE SHEET.

Dr.

Subscriptions to April 5th, 1890	£134 8 6
Balance due to Treasurer	3 0 0
	£137 8 6

Cr.

Paid to Builder for Erection and Furnishing of Bethel...............................	£118 8 6
Sundry Expenses — Printing, Advertising, Lighting, Warming, Organ, &c.	16 18 11
In Bank April 5th, 1890.....................	2 1 1
	£137 8 6

C. B. COOPER, President.
REUBEN WOOD,
Secretary and Leader of Mission.
J. W. NICHOLLS, Treasurer.

First published accounts April 1890.

The Committee was formed to carry out the project and raise funds. This they did by advertising an appeal for subscriptions from the people of Eastbourne. In response to an application made to Mr Carew Davies Gilbert, he kindly gave a piece of ground on the beach for the erection of a Mission-room for the Fishermen and Boatmen of Eastbourne. By April 1890, an iron building had been erected and was in active operation. Painted on the roof in large letters for all to see were 'The Missions to Seamen's Institute'.

At the start meetings were held on Sunday afternoons and evenings and also Thursday evenings. All helpers and officers of the mission gave their services free, so there were no maintenance expenses other than lighting and heating.

The Mission building became known locally as the 'Bethel' perhaps in deference to the 'Institute' in Sea Beach Lane (Beach Road). The 'Bethel' was a teetotal, social and spiritual meeting place for the Seafaring Fraternity.

By 1892 it appeared that the 'Bethel' was not functioning too well, as a report in the Christ Church magazine for December of that year showed. *"It is with great pleasure that the church has secured the 'Mission to Seamen's Bethel', renting it from the Rev. C B Cooper and his Committee. A 'Reader' Mr D Giddens is coming to devote his whole time amongst the Boating and Fishing families".*

The Vicar of Christ Church was appointed Honorary Chaplain to the 'Bethel'. Fund raising continued and in a few months a coffee and reading room were added. The 'Bethel' evolved over the years under the stewardship of Albert 'Sam' Allchorn and Arthur Sayers into what is known today as the 'Eastbourne Fishermen's & Boatmen's Protection Society Club' (The Fishermen's Club).

There were local people willing to work on behalf of the Boatmen, Fishermen and their families. Apart from the Misses Bell, Miss Seward and Miss Moginie, there was Miss Laura Adams, the daughter of Rev. Samuel Adams of St. Mary's Parish Church, who would journey down daily to the 'Bethel', in those days being conducted on a religious basis. Miss Adams conducted the prayers and hymns for many years and was in charge of the coffee bar and organized concerts etc. She also visited the Boatmen and Fishermen's wives and children in their homes. Her charming personality and keen sense of humour made her popular even with the 'roughest diamond'. She died at a good age in 1940.

Eastbourne's First Motorised Pleasure Boat - 1890.

Mr. Harry Etches M.I.M.I. of Etches Brothers Engineers, 8-10 Langney Road, applied to the Council for a licence to operate a steam launch the 'Dora' as a pleasure craft off the beach at the Royal Parade for the coming season. 'Dora' had been purchased from a boating firm operating on the River Thames. A Capstan Licence was also applied for and in April 1890, the first steam launch pleasure craft was granted a licence. She was 22 feet in length with 6ft 6ins beam, an engine and screw. With this boat she was not dependent on whether the wind was in the northeast or northwest or no wind at all and she could make fast trips. The 'Dora' made a formidable competitor to the sailing pleasure craft. Accommodating 12 passengers, she was fitted with a foremast and sail in the event of an engine breakdown. So we had the very first Motorised Pleasure Boat on Eastbourne seafront. How long she operated is not known.

It was to be some 15 years before the combustible petrol engine would begin to take over from sail, but take over it certainly would.

That year of 1890 saw the community of Boatmen get together for a social cricket match the report was as follows: -

"On Monday, 16th July, the Married v Single Boatmen cricket match took place at the Seaside recreation ground. Daniel Waymark showed fine form by hitting 23 & 29 runs for the Married side. William Erridge did good business with the ball taking 9 wickets.

Teams:

Married: R Crouch, J Erridge, D Waymark, T Sayers, W Erridge Snr., W Erridge, A Sayers, C Hide, W Sayers and J Dove. 1st inns = 53. 2nd inns = 91.

Single: G Hide, W Delves, G Hurd, F Hurd, J Prodger, C Wood, B Erridge, H French, and G Sayers. 1st inns = 21. 2nd inns = 20.

After the game an enjoyable evening was spent by the Boatmen at the Victoria Hotel".

November 1890.

Life went on in the community, but not all-good news.

Old Thomas Sayers, a Boatman (the same one that did the Littlington trips) was summoned in November for failing to pay £1.16s due for his wife's maintenance in the asylum. Sayers said the order had been served on his wife who had put it on the fire. Not so he was told, his wife was in the asylum at the time. Sayers said he had been ill for 6 weeks and could not talk and he hadn't earned but a £1. Told that there were several boats with his name on them, Sayers said they were not his. He was ordered to pay maintenance of 3/- per week - Not much of a Christmas to look forward to for both Sayers.

Fishermen and Boatmen Dennis Breach, William Huggett and William Smith on Monday 24th November appeared at the Eastbourne Police Court summoned for an offence against the Bye-Laws - namely cleaning fish on the foreshore. All pleaded not guilty. The facts were that after having taken three gentlemen visitors out fishing they had landed on the beach opposite the Cavendish Hotel. Off went the gentlemen with their catch and the above were cleaning what was left when they were seen by Pc Cook. He stated they had caused the fish offal to be thrown on the beach. The three pleaded through their representative Mr. Dale Hart, that they had all rights and privileges to do so under 'legal custom'. It transpired that the case against Breach was not proceeded with, but Huggett and Smith were found guilty and both fined 1/- and to pay 13/6d costs each. Notice of an appeal was given and a subscription was later raised for the Boatmen's defence - a good round sum being collected.

March 1891.

A Committee of Boatmen and Fishermen proposed to the Council that tanks be placed on the Parades for fish offal to be deposited in - 8 in total. This idea was not well received by the Council (imagine the offensive smell and seagulls the visitors would have to put up with). Actually there was no trouble with the Fishermen over the cleaning of fish on the beach at the Fishing Station. The problem only arose when the Boatmen took out fishing parties off the Parades.

April 1891.

It was on Saturday 25th, at the Queen's Bench Division of the High Court - Mr Justice Day sitting, that William Huggett and William Smith, Licensed Boatmen and Fishermen of Eastbourne appealed against their conviction for cleaning fish on the foreshore - an offence against the Bye-Laws. Their counsel Mr Dale Hart claimed they had a legal custom to land and clean fish on the foreshore - the Council having no jurisdiction over the foreshore and as such it was not covered by the Bye-Laws. But Mr Justice Day said, a legal custom did not stand higher than an Act of Parliament and the Eastbourne Improvement Act of 1885. This gave the Council the right under section 143 to make Bye-Laws, one being that the cleaning of fish on the foreshore be prohibited. His Lordship felt this was a good Bye-Law and Huggett and Smith had been properly convicted - Appeal dismissed. So ended the saga and one cannot help feeling the old Sussex saying of 'We wont be druv' was very apt. With Eastbourne being the 'Empress of Watering Places' some customs had to change.

The 1891 summer season had been a busy one on the Parades, made bearable by the actions of the Chief Constable. He had been instructed by the Watch Committee at the beginning of the season to get tough with the expected large numbers of persons with stalls and stands for the sale of goods on the beach and Parades, also the excess number of entertainers all operating without permits. The Chief Constable and his men did their job well. This problem had been ongoing for many years. Previously in 1871 there had been a purge and looking ahead to 1894 the problem would arise again, only this time the Watch Committee would have a go at the Boatmen.

But staying in 1891, from the extracts of the Watch Committee minutes we see that in February, 'Old Screw' Reuben Wood, the owner of rowboat 'Palace' was told that if he used this rowboat again as a sailing boat (he could charge more money), proceedings would be taken against him.

Arthur Matthews applied to licence a steam launch and a new yawl yacht 'Royal Sovereign' being built by George Gausden. In July a licence was granted for a steam launch to carry 12 passengers and a licence for the 'Royal Sovereign' to carry 36 passengers. Another sailing boat 'Little Skylark' (owner not known) was licenced to carry 35 passengers. The Board of Trade were advised of all Pleasure Boats carrying more than 12 passengers, an inspection being required. There were two big sailboats operating off Eastbourne during this period - Joseph Mockett's 'Skylark' carrying 100 passengers and Ben Bates 'Britannia' carrying 140 passengers.

August 1891.

The end of August saw the running aground on the boulder bank to the west of the pier of the fishing smack 'Mystery' of Brixham. The wind was blowing a gale from the SSW, the tide was 3/4 ebb and a heavy sea was breaking over the bank. The sea knocked the 'Mystery' over the bank into the inner deep water and the crew of 4 men and boy took to their lifeboat. It was at this point that the Pleasure Boat 'May Morn' put off with 4 Licenced Boatmen aboard, Albert Hide, John Dove, Fred Hurd and William Smith (of the fish cleaning episode). Hide and Hurd boarded the deserted vessel 'Mystery' and being aware of a gap in the boulder bank steered her through it into the open sea. The Lifeboat 'William & Mary' having been launched, rowed up to the crew of the 'Mystery' in their lifeboat but of course they did not need any assistance. Hide and Hurd aboard the 'Mystery' could not manage the boat on their own so Cox'n Jesse Huggett put three of the Lifeboat crew aboard to assist and the smack 'Mystery' was sailed down to Dover. Her Brixham crew landed safely at the Fishing Station. The Lifeboat however did sustain some damage to her bow when alongside the 'Mystery'. A good day for salvage money for Albert Hide, Fred Hurd, John Dove, William Smith and also the Lifeboat crew, well earned.

January 1892.

The Council, with a view to adopting some new Bye-Laws covering Pleasure Boating on the Parades for the forthcoming summer season, invited a group of local Boatmen to a meeting held at the Library of the Leaf Hall. Boatmen present were; Reuben 'Old Screw' Wood, George 'Pincher' Hide, William 'Young Bollard' Hide, Dennis Breach, John Hurd, William Allchorn, Albert Hide and Edward Allchorn.

A proposal that the date when a boat was built and the builder's name should be given when licenced and that it be crewed by a minimum of two, met with total disagreement. A remark by 'Young Bollard' Hide was that *"the build and stability of a boat depended on who was aboard her and some boats were built for one crew only. It was not right to make them have two crew"*. It was also remarked that some of the boats could be 100 years old. Dennis Breach said, *"I think 'Old Chambers' (George F. Chambers - A local historian of that time and Local Councillor) ought to know that"*.

There was also a complaint from the Boatmen that the Council were slack in the issuing of licences and greater care should be exercised to whom they issued to. There were some, not from Eastbourne, who were not competent to man a boat.

The Boatmen of Eastbourne had been on the water all their lives, yet visitors would pass them and go to a man with no experience because he was cheaper. Dennis Breach remarked that you got *"house painters and sweeps"* acting as Boatmen. John Hurd said, *"Even 'Brightoners' have come here and had licences for a short time".*

Another Bye-Law intended that the Parade Inspector would hoist a red flag when, in his opinion, the sea was too rough to safely put to sea. 'Young Bollard' Hide questioned, *"What if it is a dead calm and you go off, will you be summoned?"* Dennis Breach and 'Pincher' Hide spoke in commendation of the Inspector Mr. Gilbert. Generally it was agreed that this was a good rule.

It was proposed that each boat had a metal plate affixed containing a list of charges. 'Pincher' Hide said, *"We have had them in the past, and they have done away with themselves. Why put the town to the expense of 140 plates at 7/6d each."*

It was also proposed that boats have the licence number painted on the bow - this did not meet with approval. Licence numbers previously had been on the plate but subsequently this had fallen into disuse. It was proposed and agreed that the Boatman Licence Number be on the ribbon of a hat. Previously Bye-Law 7 had required every Boatman to wear on his chest a badge containing his number and the words 'Licenced Boatman' - but this had not been enforced.

1892.

Charges for 1892 to be:
Open rowing Pleasure Boat.
With Boatman. Without.
One hour 2/- 1/6d.
Half hour 1/- 9d.
Less 'hour 9d 6d.
Sail Boats.
Not exceeding 10 persons. 4/- per hour.
Not exceeding 20 persons. 5/- per hour.
Not exceeding 10 persons. 2/- per half hour.
Not exceeding 20 persons. 2/6d per half hour.

A large sail boat like the 'Skylark' 6d per person per voyage.

A Bye-Law that required Boatmen not to stay at sea longer than passengers desired caused much amusement - "Not much fear of that" remarked William Allchorn. As a result of the discussions with the Boatmen, the Council did amend and adopt some new Bye-Laws in March 1892.

May 1892.

Extracts from the Watch Committee minutes for May showed Boatman Samuel Tutt had not paid his fees for the Year 1891, nor indeed the current year. His licence was refused and proceedings were to be taken if payment was not forthcoming.

June 1892.

In June an application for a Boatman 2nd class Licence by Richard Hide was granted and Francis Gilbert, Parade Inspector, agreed that Thomas, a son of William Hide be granted a 2nd class Boatman Licence.

The Boatmen complained that the large number of buskers and beach entertainers obstructing the beach and slipways were interfering with their livelihood. Furthermore Bathing Machine Proprietors must have rescue boats equipped and ready to launch when operating their machines. Of the operators it was further reported that George Luck had not numbered his machines and the hand ropes of machines belonging to Messrs Knight, Hide, Brown and Bennett were in bad condition.

John Vine was refused permission to have a 'Rocking Horse' on the beach. The Parade Inspector had also received a complaint about sailboats advertising commodities on their sails. This practice had to stop and the Inspector stated a prosecution was pending.

November 1892.

Beecham's Pills and Bones

'Bones' Hide clashed with the authorities when he was summoned to appear in court in November to answer a charge of exhibiting a 'Beecham's Pills' advertisement on the sail of his boat the 'Ilex' while laid on the beach at the Royal Parade - this being an offence against the Bye-Laws. A sail, coming within the meaning of 'a placard or board' for advertising, which was banned upon the beach if they were an annoyance to the public.

Charles 'Bones' Hide b.1849. d.1905. Boatman, Fisherman and Lifeboat Coxswain 1881-1884. Coxswain of the Sailing Yacht 'Skylark' 1883-1895.

The words on the sails of Bones' boat read, "Try Beecham's Pills" in foot high letters, and on the others "The World's Remedy" and "Worth a Guinea a Box" - The boat was kept on the beach all through the day, evidently for many weeks and did not go to sea. The proprietors of the hotels and boarding houses of the Royal Parade objected saying it was an intrusion on their view. 'Bones' receiving a regular income from the adverts and was quite happy for it to continue, but that was not to be and he was summoned.

The report states that the case was held with much amusement - 'Bones' being the character he was. He was introduced as a Herculean Boatman and Lifeboat Coxswain of the famous rescue of 1883. Representing 'Bones' was Mr Treacher, Counsel from Brighton paid for by Beecham's.

He obviously argued that the sails were not an advertising board/placard. But the magistrates held otherwise also saying it constituted a nuisance. One of the complainants, a Mr Ellis, said he did not object to the boat being there because it belonged to 'Bones'. Another point about the boat 'Ilex' was that it was not even registered as a Pleasure Boat. (That's 'Bones' for you!) The case was finalised by 'Bones' Hide giving an undertaking not to repeat the offence. He was fined 2s with 18s costs.

December 1892.

The year 1892 finished with an amusing Court case involving that (cantankerous) Fisherman/Boatman, Reuben 'Old Screw' Wood living on the Marine Parade. He was summoned for 'beating a carpet on the foreshore' contrary to the Bye-Laws on the 6th December.

Wood said he beat the carpet on the girders of the Pier. Pc Veness said the beating took place about 21 feet from the sea wall. Wood then produced a letter he had received from the Board of Trade in 1889 stating that they (the Police) had no power to interfere with the Corporation in regard to the removal of capstans above the high water mark. The Clerk said he did not see what that had to do with the matter in hand under the Bye-Laws pursuant to the Improvement Act 1885. The foreshore and sands were put on the level of a highway for the purposes of the order. Wood said the idea of the beach being a street was ridiculous and an old bird like himself was not going to be caught by such chaff as that. The point where the carpet was beaten was considerably below high water mark and he denied that the jurisdiction of the Corporation extended there. Only the Government had authority over the foreshore below the 'full' and these proceedings were taken out of spite. Wood went on to say that he had beaten carpets on the beach on other occasions since the passing of the Improvement Act. The Chief Constable then interjected and said that might be so and if he had been detected he would probably have been prosecuted. There had been several previous complaints of carpet beating on the beach. The Chairman said they had no choice but to convict as the Bye-Laws clearly prohibited carpet beating on the beach. Wood then said, *"Then notices should be posted up"*.

The Chairman: *"You will be fined 1/-"*. Wood retorted, *"I shall not pay! I have got two lawyers and you will have to get over them first"*. The Clerk to Wood, *"Have you any goods upon which a restraint may be levied?"* Wood: *"No, all belongs to the Missus. I shall not pay until the Board of Trade tells me I am liable."* The Chairman: *"It looks as if the law as to carpet beating has not been put into force before, but you are guilty and must not do it again."* Wood: *"I will not pay, you may do the other thing."* (We wont be druv). The Chairman; *"We don't intend to make a martyr of you."* The Bench then as an alternative to a fine ordered Wood to be detained in custody till the rising of the Court. (In 1927, it was recalled that 'Old Screw' Reuben Wood convulsed the Police Court with the remark that he suffered with 'Sky-Atics')

April 1893.

Moves were afoot to get rid of Parade Inspector Gilbert when in April 1893 the Watch Committee resolved that the Parade Inspector should be a member of the Local Police Force.

The full Council agreed, recommended and authorised the Watch Committee to make the necessary arrangements - but in May the matter was stood over sine die.

June 1893.

In June the Watch Committee did decide to appoint a new Inspector of Pleasure

Boats and Parades. They instructed the Town Clerk to advertise for a suitable person on a wage of £1.5s 0d per week and that Francis Gilbert be asked to tender his resignation. This, Gilbert refused to do and the matter stood.

February 1894.

It was resolved that the Parades, Boatmen, Pleasure Boats, Bathing Machines and the Fishing Station be placed under the control of the Chief Constable, with the Parade Inspector to assist him. (Turning the screw on Mr Gilbert?)

Mr Gilbert finally resigned in June 1895, after 20 years service (1875 - 1895), owing to advanced age and poor health. Police Sergeant George Burr was appointed Parade Inspector in his place - Mr Gilbert being retained on 20s per week for 3 months to assist Burr. So Mr Gilbert went on his own terms some 2 years after the Council had tried to get rid of him.

Sadly Mr Gilbert died in December 1895 aged 75 years, just a few months after retiring. He had led an interesting Service life. Serving in the Royal Navy from 1842 to 1857 aboard the ships, Camperdown, St. Vincent, Grampus, Castor and Caesar. The Castor took part in the suppression of the slave trade off Zanzibar. He was in the Naval Brigade in the Kaffir War and served in the Baltic Sea during the Russian War. From 1857 to 1875 he was in the Coastguard. Always in uniform until he became Parade Inspector. The Local Board, then the Town Council, refused to kit him out. But with the employment of Sgt. Burr, already a serving Police officer, a new era had begun. Being an ex-Naval man, Burr had his nautical experience to assist him in dealing with the Boatmen. (Perhaps a good idea to have a policeman as Parade Inspector - more authority? Did the Boatmen need a firmer hand?)

That could well have been the case as later in 1895, for touting on the beach, the Chief Constable cautioned the owner of the yacht 'Skylark' Joseph Mockett as to the nuisance caused by him in touting for passengers. A complaint from The Rev. Pennethorne was that Boatman Hurd had hired a boat to 6 boys aged 11 - 14 yrs. This caused the Chief Constable to suspend Hurd's licence. Also on occasions Boatmen were disregarding the red flag (sea too rough for boating) when hoisted by the Parade Inspector and so a notice board was to be put up.

The Chief Constable's involvement with Pleasure Boating required him to present before the Watch Committee an annual report on the state of Pleasure Boating. This included giving totals of 1st & 2nd class Waterman, Sailing Boat, Rowing Boat and Bathing Machine Licences issued. It also became the responsibility of the Police serving Parade Inspector to collect fees.

April 1894.

April saw the Council getting tough over the coming seaside season with a very anti-Boatman, bullying attitude. An order was put out by the Council under the Bye-Laws that all Boatmen be banned from plying for hire, touting on the upper and lower Parades and to only tout from the beach and sands. Complaints had been received the previous season of visitors being accosted every few yards by the invitation 'Boat sir?' (A sign that business was dropping off possibly brought about by the competition of the Steamers running from the Pier). The Boatmen being

Published by CARTER & Co., 17, Terminus Road, Eastbourne, with the kind permission of Messrs. Bradbury, Agnew & Co., L.T.D. Proprietors of "Punch."

FINIS!—THE END OF THE SEASON.

Sketch of Eastbourne Front by the late Mr. G. du Maurier, which appeared in "Punch."

Blind 'fiddler' James Collins and dog 'Rosie' 1895.

restricted to the beach and sands was quite impossible. The Boatmen themselves being civil to the visitors felt very hard done by but under the Bye-Laws the Council had the right to restrict them.

As a result of the above, up before the Watch Committee were Boatmen Frederick Hurd, Edward Ticehurst, Harry Novis, William Smith and John Berry for touting on the Parades and refusing to obey the Parade Inspector - their cases being put back to May.

Another nuisance facing the Council was the problem of busking and concert parties along the promenade and beach, as mentioned before a never-ending problem. It was the Council's intention to curtail the buskers and concert parties. One well-known busker at this time was an Irishman, the poor blind fiddler James Collins and his dog Rosie, immortalised by the artist Mr. G du Maurier in the

Eastbourne Beach Concert Party C.1900.

magazine 'Punch'. Collins had made his living playing his violin on the beach by the Wish Tower for many years off and on. Now having been warned off his pitch by the Police, he went to the local newspaper and made a plea through their columns to be allowed to continue or else it was the workhouse for him and his dog 'Rosie'. Collins did play on during that summer season but in the

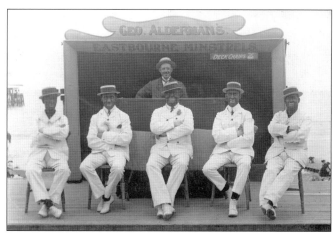

Eastbourne Beach Concert Party.

cold winter of 1895 he caught the flu and died at his home, No.1 Gilbert Road.

The Committee resolved that all applications for new Boatman Licences be submitted to them from now on. (A case of the Committee losing confidence in Mr Gilbert or giving him hassle, as they wanted him to resign?)

May 1894 - Touting.

The Council meeting for May and the Watch Committee in particular discussed the Boatman subject. It was reported that Boatmen Frederick Hurd, Edward Ticehurst, Harry Novis, William Smith and John Berry were reported by the Police for touting on the Parades, refusing to obey their instructions and for failing to obey the new licence provisions of touting only on the beach and sands. The proposal was to withdraw their licences. Councillors Wenham and Bennett, the champions of the Fishermen and Boatmen, criticised the Watch Committee's attitude to the Boatmen, stating that to restrict them to the beach and sands was to take the bread from their, their children's and wives' mouths. No community had ever regarded touting as a crime punishable with starvation. Strong words which the Mayor took exception to. Wenham went on to say our Boatmen were worthy of greater consideration and kinder treatment and it was impossible to tout from the beach. He accused the Watch Committee of oppressive behaviour and put an amendment that the Boatmen be allowed to tout/ply for hire from the lower parade. Councillor Bennett seconded this amendment saying the Council had a bullying attitude to the Boatmen. Alderman Haine also supported the amendment. (In fairness to the Council, a quite impossible situation had arisen over the crowding of the Parades with buskers, photographers, flower sellers, concert parties and of course the Boatmen of which there were 113 holding licences. The Boatmen had traditionally touted from all Parades, but this had all ended.) Councillor Wenham's amendment was passed and henceforth the Boatmen would tout only from the lower parade, which of course they did. The report against Hurd and others was withdrawn and their licences granted.

The aggravation caused amongst the Boatmen is best shown by a Court case involving Boatman John Richard Mockett. In May 1894, a report from the Eastbourne Gazette of the court case headed under 'A Boisterous Boatman' makes interesting reading. John Mockett, Boatman and labourer, a sturdy dark haired young man, was summoned for disorderly conduct on the Grand Parade.

Pc Compton said, *"On Sunday April 29th, at 3.40pm, I was on duty in plain clothes near the Pier gates. I saw Mockett who was walking to and fro, shouting at the top of his voice. He said, 'No Englishman can live in this ******* town now. If you want to live here you must be a ******* German, a ******* Italian, or a member of the ******* Salvation Army. They can shout and get £5,* (possibly alluding to the foreign buskers and Salvation Army band now allowed to play on Sundays?) *but Englishmen must go down on the sand and starve"* (alluding to the ban on touting on the Parades). Pc Compton cautioned him to which Mockett replied, *"I want them to hear me. This piece of flesh (taking hold of his tongue) was given to me on purpose to shout with."* Mockett continued shouting and was told if he did not desist he would be arrested. Mockett to Pc Compton in the courtroom said, *"You say I was shouting about. I was close by your side and was speaking to you simply."* Pc Compton, *"You were not speaking to me."* Mockett said, *"Sergeant Burr then came up and spoke to me like a dog. He said, 'What did you ask people to go into the boat for?'"* Pc Compton said, *"I never spoke except when I said, ' Steady on Mockett, that language won't do on a Sunday afternoon. You will get yourself disliked."* Mockett then said in court, indicating to Pc Compton, *"This man I think is telling a lot of stories, as to talking about the Salvation Army, I never said a word to him about it. I did tell him I was starving all the winter through, there being no fish. Surely when the summer comes along we can earn a shilling or two."*

Pc Compton, *"I don't know who you were speaking to. I said if you wanted to talk you must talk in a lower tone."* Police Sergeant Burr, *"I cautioned Mockett at twenty minutes past three. Inspector Stirling had left Pc Compton there to see that Mockett did not cause any disturbance. When I came to the pier before four, I had to caution him for using bad language and shouting about. He was not a Licensed Boatman at the time. His license had run out and he had not applied for a renewal. When I cautioned him he said, 'I could do what I d*** well liked."* Mockett said, *"After I got that party and shoved them off on the water, did you not come to me and ask me 'what is your number?' and I said, 'Beg your pardon I did not tout."* Police Sergeant Burr said, *"I stood against the Pier gates and heard you ask the lady and gentleman if they wanted a boat. I saw you push one of your brother's boats off."* Chief Constable Plumb (It appears a lot of police were in court) said, *"If Mockett had been licensed he is not entitled to ply on the Top Parade. The license says on the beach and sands. There is one conviction against the defendant for resisting the police in November 1891."* (This was a case of Mockett with others, some sent to prison, being abusive to the Salvation Army.)

The Chairman of the Bench regretted to see a man discharged from the Navy with a good character giving trouble to the Police. He was fined 10/- including costs. Mockett said he was out of work. He was granted time to pay, but soon produced the money. It is obvious that complaints had been received again about touting by the Boatmen on the Top Parade and especially by the Pier gates as the Paddle Steamers operated from the Pier Head.

The Watch Committee also granted certain licences for Photography and Concert parties. The following gives us an insight to what was happening on the Parades and

Beach and their locations: -

Performances on the Beach:
No.1. Stand opposite Lascelles Terrace to the 'South London Concert Party'.
No.2. Stand opposite Burlington Place to the 'Helvian Trio'.
No.3. Stand opposite Victoria Place to the 'Adolphus Keefe Nigger Troupe'
No.4. Stand opposite Sussex Club to 'Mr Granliegh' Photographic Stands.
No.1. Stand near the Pier to Mr Albert Owen.
No.2. Stand near the Wish Tower to Mr George Austen.
No.3. Stand opposite Hartington Place to Mr J A Waylett.
No.4. Stand Marine Parade to Mr C Cain.
No.5. Stand Royal Parade to Mr J Heard.

The Watch Committee recommended that the Corporate Seal of Eastbourne be affixed to Pleasure Boat and Waterman/Boatman Licences from the year 1894, which it duly was.

1895.

Several Boatmen came to the notice of the Watch Committee during the summer of 1895.

A complaint was made about the behaviour of Boatman Tutt and he was ordered to attend before the Committee. Another complaint was that the sailing yacht 'Britannia' had put to sea with only 3 crew instead of 4 (a big Pleasure Boat up to 140 passengers). Owner Ben Bates was informed not to repeat the offence otherwise proceedings would be taken. And finally, shouting on foreshore - a report against John Mockett, Thomas French, Charles Hurd and John Erridge Licenced Boatmen.

Dandy rigged Pleasure Yacht 'Britannia' 1890-1906 - owned and operated by Ben Bates on this site. Ted Sayers Pleasure Yacht 'Skylark' took over until C.1908. The rowboats in the foreground belong to George 'Pincher' Hide.

Crew of the 'Britannia' C.1895. Standing back from left - Jack Mockett, Ben Erridge, Richard John 'Paddyjack' Erridge, William 'Killcraft' Erridge. Seated from left. Henry Novis, Ben Bates owner - son of Ben Bates, Fred 'Ackerpay' Hurd.

Cautioned. A further report against Hurd for not wearing a badge whilst plying for hire, led to him being cautioned.

October 1895 - Illicit Beer Sales at Sea.

Ben Bates the owner of the pleasure yacht 'Britannia' (Licenced to carry 140 passengers, the largest pleasure yacht along the south coast - built by Messrs Kent of Hastings with a 48 feet keel, 30 tons, 4 crew), the captain Richard John Erridge and seaman Henry Novis were summoned jointly for having sold beer on board the 'Britannia' without having taken out a licence. The Inland Revenue prosecuted at the Police Court. A 'Packet Boat' Licence should have been taken out. The evidence was that back in July, when

Joseph Mockett's dandy rigged 'Skylark' 1890.

half a mile out on a short trip, a passenger asked for and was served a pint bottle of 'Bass's ale', being charged 6d. Several other passengers were also served with beer. Novis said he served the beer, but they were 3 to 4 miles off shore. Bates pleaded that he was not responsible for the sale of beer and he did not share in the profits. Erridge the captain said he was unaware that a licence was required. Novis admitted he knew he was doing wrong. The prosecutor said the practice of selling beer without a licence at sea off Eastbourne had been going on for some 15 years.

Pleasure yachts 'Skylark' and 'Britannia' C.1890.

Joseph Richard Mockett owner, Edwin 'Lord' Matthews captain, and Joseph Mockett Jnr. seaman of the pleasure yacht the 'Skylark' were also summoned for a similar offence. These being the first cases of the kind, the Justices were lenient and all were fined 10s each. They had all made money over the previous 15 years so 10s wasn't too much to be fined. As to whether any 'Packet' Licences were ever taken out, it is not known. The cost in 1895 was £5 per year or £2 per day.

April 1896.

The Parade Inspector had a busy time throughout the year of 1896, keeping the Boatmen in line and bringing applications and incidents before the Watch Committee. Starting with Boatmen John & Henry Tutt in April, being given 14 days to remove their old and worn out boats from the foreshore or face prosecution under the Bye-Laws. Charles Clark was refused permission to sell shrimps on the parade between the Bandstand and Pier and Boatman Dennis Breach was granted permission to operate from Boat Stands Nos.11 & 12 on the Grand Parade and Mr. A E Dumbrell to operate Boat Stand No.42 at the Royal Parade.

An interesting revelation made by the Inspector was that various Boat Stands were alleged occupied by Boatmen free of charge. After consideration the Committee decided that the Borough Surveyor prepare a revised foreshore plan showing numbers and positions of all Boat Stands and Capstans on the beach between the Wish Tower and the Great Redoubt. Also to implement an existing Bye-Law that all boats be numbered on the exterior of the stern.

(It appears that ex-Parade Inspector Gilbert may have been lax and that some old Boatmen may well have had free boating. Having cleared the beach/foreshore of the Grand Parade when it was developed, at no charge to the Local Board, they may have felt entitled.)

Boatman John R Mockett's application for a Boat Stand was refused. (He was a source of aggravation to the Parade Inspector and Watch Committee. Remember the court case over 'Touting'?)

John Dove 2nd class Boatman applied for 1st class Licence, it was refused.

John Mockett, John Erridge, William Erridge and Ben Erridge, were brought before the Watch Committee and warned for shouting on the foreshore. There was a complaint against the Parade Inspector over his conduct from Boatmen Richard Hurd and a Mr Savary.

June 1896.

Thomas Huggett of Sidley Road was fined 10s for plying for hire and acting as a Boatman without a licence on June 8th. Huggett stated that he did have a 1st class Licence in 1893.

July 1896.

In mid July it was Reuben 'Old Screw' Wood up before the Committee again regarding his conduct, slandering and threatening towards Parade Inspector Burr. Wood was cautioned as to his behaviour and told he could lose his licence.

11 householders on Grand Parade complained of shouting by men of the pleasure yacht "Britannia" on the foreshore - but the shouting had diminished since proceedings were taken.

'Bones' Hide in court again this time as an expert witness. 'An 1892 Bye-Law agreed by the Boatmen is ignored', so said the headlines in the local paper.

Seafaring men mustered at the Police Court on Monday 20th July 1896, to hear the case in which Benjamin Bates, the owner of the pleasure sailing yacht 'Britannia' was summoned for allowing his boat to unlawfully embark passengers when by reason of the state of the weather, the management of the vessel and embarkation or disembarkation might be attended with danger - an offence against the Bye-Laws. The Town Clerk Mr Fovargue prosecuted. Parade Inspector Burr gave evidence to the effect that on 30th June, there was a moderate SW gale blowing, the sky was overcast and the glass was falling. As a result of which, he hoisted the small 'red flag' which indicated: No Pleasure Boats of any description should put to sea. (There were a series of flags denoting different conditions under which Pleasure Boats could put to sea. A white ensign hoisted indicated: all boats can put to sea with or without Boatmen. A blue ensign hoisted indicated: that Pleasure Boats carrying from two to five persons are prohibited from going to sea without Boatmen. A red ensign indicated: that large rowing boats and sailing boats can put to sea with Boatmen.)

Parade Inspector Burr went on to say, at 2.30 pm on the Royal Parade he saw the 'Young Britannia' a rowboat, ferrying persons from the beach to the 'Britannia' anchored off shore. In his opinion the sea was too rough for this operation and a danger to persons and he warned the Boatmen involved. The ferryboat made three trips and the 'Britannia' upped anchor and sailed off towards Pevensey Bay. There were some 30 - 40 passengers on her. She returned to the east side of the Pier at 4.45pm and disembarked her passengers.

The "Britannia" a large boat of 30 tons, was licenced to carry 140 passengers and 4 crew. On this occasion Bates was on the beach, the crew being, Captain Richard John Erridge, Ben Erridge, Thomas Huggett and John Mockett.

Inspector Burr maintained the sea was too rough for rowboats to put off, especially the ferryboat and he warned Bates that the 'Britannia' went to sea at his own risk. He Burr, would not be responsible.

A witness William O'Halloran, 16 years in the coastguard at Hastings gave evidence that in his opinion the sea was too rough for boats to put off from the beach.

Mr Prince, defending Bates, said to O'Halloran, *"that not a single glass of water was shipped in the ferryboat, coming or going"*. O'Halloran replied, *"If there was no water shipped, there is no doubt it would be beautiful."* (Great laughter in court)

A witness Hamilton Seale living at 33 Marine Parade, served 26 years in the Royal Navy and a pensioner from 1870, gave evidence of his opinion that the sea was too rough to embark persons in the row ferryboat.

Samuel Barnard an elderly man, a bathing attendant in the employ of the Corporation at the Redoubt bathing station said in his opinion the sea was too rough for young children to bathe, but there was not the slightest danger to the ferryboat 'Young Britannia'.

Witness Thomas Patton deposed that on the day in question he went for a sail in the 'Britannia' and was ferried from the beach with about 13 others. It was a comfortable journey and the ferryboat shipped no water.

'Bones' Hide was then called as a witness and he said; *"I live at 2, Eshton Terrace and have been to sea for 30 years. During part of that time I was Coxswain of the lifeboat."*

Mr Prince, *"Rendered some good service more than once?"*

'Bones' replied gruffly, *"So I believe. In my opinion there was not the slightest danger in embarking passengers in the ferryboat on June 30th. If I had been in charge of the 'Britannia' I should not have ceased to ply for hire. I was master of the Skylark for 12 years (1883 - 1895). I never took any notice of the red flag and the then Parade Inspector Mr. Gilbert never took proceedings against me. I was on the Fishing Station. I think the red flag ought not to have been hoisted. We go when we use our discretion."* A question to 'Bones' *"It was not a moderate gale?"* Bones, *"A jolly sailing breeze, I should consider it was."*

Richard John 'Paddyjack' Erridge, aboard private yacht 'Silver Spray'.

Richard John 'Paddyjack' Erridge (master of the Britannia) said he had 25 years experience of the Eastbourne coast. On June 30th, Mr Bates was not in charge of the 'Britannia'. He took no part in the embarking of passengers. He, not Bates was in charge of operations that day. No difficulty was experienced in the ferrying of passengers or the sailing of the 'Britannia'.

The Bench retired to consider their verdict and on returning, found by a majority to convict in this case. After much discussion they felt they had to uphold the opinion of Inspector Burr, otherwise the public may disregard his authority. A nominal fine of 1/- and costs were imposed on Mr Bates. On the balance of things the Bye-Laws had to be upheld.

After the above hearing Thomas Huggett, Richard John Erridge and John Mockett members of the crew of the 'Britannia' were summoned for importuning and touting for hire on July 8th.

Parade Inspector Burr said they were shouting on the beach from 2.45 to 3.20 pm. They called out *"fast sailing yacht Britannia! The only yacht a-going. This way for sailing."*

The complainant was a Mr Neidermayer. *'I don't think the wind would affect some of their voices. The Steamers whistle and screech. I have no complaint about the Boatmen,'* said Burr.

Mr John Neidermayer said, *'I live at 23, Grand Parade. I heard the defendants shouting for 20 minutes or half an hour. I constantly receive complaints from my visitors. I have no animosity against the Boatmen, they are always civil. I have complained about the hokey-pokey man in Victoria Place. I lost a boarder last year through the shouting.'*

Mr Prince on behalf of the Boatmen said, '*We are charged with importuning this German gentleman, Mr Neidermayer.*' Mr Prince went on to argue that to shout was not to importune within the meaning of the Bye-Law. Shortly after this the Bench announced they would not proceed to convict.

August 1896.

The month of August was a busy month on the Parades for the Boatmen. From an individual's report it shows how things were. "*The front was in a state of high water and broiling heat. Far away out at sea the sails of many ships dotted the horizon, whilst alongside the pier was the Paddle Steamer 'Lorna Doone' and Ben Bates sailing yacht 'Britannia' was filling with people. The latter is a fine boat manned by a smart crew. She is claimed to be the biggest sailing yacht along the south coast, anyway she rules the waves at Eastbourne. Some say the Eastbourne Boatmen are a grumbling, uncivil set of men with very little religion and no manners at all. They have never been as bad as that. They are a rough and ready lot but I rather admire their unconventional way and sturdy independence (we wont be druv). It would be advisable for some of them to take lessons in politeness, but they are not all tarred with the same brush. In the space of a dozen yards I was accosted by three different Boatmen, all desired if I wanted a little boat. No, I did not want one. The first Boatmen said "Thank you," the second said, " Thank you, sir, God bless you." and the third spat a volume of filthy tobacco juice over my patent leather shoes. I fully believe it was unintentional.*

Along comes the Parades Inspector Burr, a big burly man with a severe aspect and a fair beard. A good looking chap with the gait of a sailor and the tramp of a policeman and an expression round his face that he will stand no nonsense. He is the gentleman who keeps the paper boys in order, looks after the morals of the flowers girls and runs in people up to hokey-pokey on the Parades. Not far from the 'Britannia' the nigger minstrels were holding forth to a crowded audience and in the Bandstand the town band was playing and a solemn little gentleman was going round with a hat for some 'brass'. West of the Bandstand were the Black Pierrotts. There are many singers on the beach this year but the Music Hall songs are not for everybody and the worthy old fiddler near the Wish Tower, never learnt the art of voice production". So we learn of what life was like on the Parades in the summer time, all those years ago.

Frank Smith - Boat builder, Boats Chandler 'Smith & Gibbs'. Sailing Master to Eastbourne Sailing Club C.1935.

August also saw a mini 'Whirlwind' on the beach at Eastbourne. It was about ten to one on the afternoon of Tuesday 4th, when a whirlwind which, though confined to a very limited area caused damage to several boats. The first gust nearly sank Alleyn Sayers's sailing boat "Pet" which was lying at anchor a

Lugger rigged sailing punt 'Pet' rebuilt by Frank Smith C.1935. The 'Pet' was last seen on Eastbourne Beach in 1947.

hundred yards from the shore. The mizzenmast was broken off. Three rowing boats also belonging to Sayers and lying near the groyne opposite to the Sussex Club were blown up into the air about 15ft and whirled along 'as if they were paper kites'. They carried towards the end of the groyne opposite the Victoria Place steps. Two of the boats 'Wave Queen' and the 'Dauntless' were so much damaged that they had to be immediately removed from the beach for repairs. The timbers of the third boat 'Sunbeam' were broken in one part and loosened. The force of the wind threw about a dozen people down. In addition to the boats mentioned, a rowing boat belonging to Joseph Mockett was turned upside down. The whirlwind appeared to have been confined to a space of about 2 yards wide.

Interestingly the sailing boat "Pet" survived to the 1920s when she was acquired, brought up to standard and sailed for many years by Frank Smith, sailing master to the Eastbourne Sailing Club and in business as Boat Builder, Chandler with Fred Gibbs of Latimer Road. 'Pet' was still to be seen on the beach in 1947.

The 'Total Abstainer' was the name of the bathing boat on hand for the Bathing Machines near the Wish Tower. Considering the amount of water the leaky old tub took in it was a very appropriate name - someone had a sense of humour as the Boatmen and Bathing Machine operators were generally known for having a liking for the hard stuff.

John R Mockett attended before the Committee in August to apply for a Boat Stand to the east of the Pier. Parade Inspector reported - no room on the beach. (Mockett really out of favour?)

All Capstan and Net Shop Licence fees at the Fishing Station had been paid in full for last year, 1895 and a bonus of 3 guineas was paid to Parade Inspector/Police Sergeant Burr.

October 1896.

An application from Boatman Henry Hurd to place a small sailing boat on the beach in front of Royal Parade, opposite Cambridge Road was granted. (Room for him but not Mockett?)

December 1896.

The year 1896 finished with a very severe storm in December. The Parades and Pier decking sustained some damage. For the most part the Fishermen and Boatmen had removed their boats to a respectful distance from the sea. The following report shows some never got away from damage: *Mr A.Dumbrell, landlord of the 'Prince of Wales'*

Seaside Road, states that his decked yacht, the 'Florrie', which had six hundredweight of ballast was moved by the force of the sea. Reuben 'Old Screw' Wood Snr. had two boats stove in and his capstan broken. Mr Gilham's sailing boat, 'Eva' was damaged and boats belonging to Dennis Breach were damaged. A boat used for fishing and bathing purposes by Mr. T Bennett, 'Old Tom, the People's Friend' was washed two feet off the edge of the parade. Mr Dumbrell and John Hide drew her back again. Dumbrell, who was wearing top boots, oilskin and sweater in spite of this, was wet through. At the Fishing Station men were on watch all night. Dawn brought the sight of a French fishing boat close in having sheltered under the lee of Beachy Head. This storm was also responsible for the Chain Pier at Brighton being swept away. The storm it was said was on a par with that in 1877 when the Eastbourne Pier suffered great damage. A loss of shingle was again suffered.

April 1897.

The Parade Inspector was again busy in the year 1897, laying various applications before the Watch Committee. Boatman John Hide, after referral to the Stands & Foreshore sub-Committee (formed to take some of the work load off the Watch Committee), was granted permission to operate Boat Stands Nos.12 & 71 on the Grand Parade. Edward Allchorn was granted three Boat Stands on the Marine and Royal Parades. It was recommended that additional slipways be provided for Boat Stands Nos.31 & 32 Royal Parade. It was resolved by the Committee that Boatmen Henry Mockett and Arthur Matthews, the son of the late Arthur Matthews (died 1893, landlord of the Beach Hotel), be granted stands for their boats for the coming Easter 1897, near the Grand Parade Bandstand - owing to alterations being carried out at their stands at Splash Point, then known as opposite the Queens Hotel.

Ben Bates requested permission to affix to the mast of his sailing yacht 'Ibis', a notice board 22" x 10" with the words *'To let or hire. Please apply to the crew of the yacht 'Britannia'*. This application was not granted.

June 1897.

Boatman John R Mockett requested to place a capstan on the foreshore between Victoria Place steps and the flagstaff on the Grand Parade (Carpet Gardens). The sub-Committee visited the site, being the first groyne west of Victoria Place steps. Not granted - but at least Mockett was now licenced to operate rowboats from the beach and needed a capstan to operate a bigger sail boat. Harry Allchorn applied for a Boat Stand on Royal Parade. The Parade Inspector stated that Allchorn's boat was a fishing boat, not fitted out as a Pleasure Boat and as a result he was given notice to remove it to the Fishing Station. No fishing boats were allowed on the foreshore in front of the Parades.

Mr H Head & Mr W Gillham, private boat owners, complained that their allotted Boat Stands were not safe and could they have their old stands back. Gillham was given a Boat Stand immediately west of St Aubyn's Road and Head granted a Boat Stand opposite No.50 Royal Parade.

Mr Mark Hookham was granted a Boat Stand opposite the junction of Cambridge Road and Royal Parade, subject to him clearing his fishing tackle off the beach. In June, the Boat Stand opposite No.50 Royal Parade was granted to Mr A Garibaldi previously allotted to Mr H Head, who had sold his boat to him. Mr Gillham requested to leave his boat on Boatman Richard Swain's stand. Not granted, as his new stand was safe. The Parade Inspector reported that Sidney Gearing had left his old fishing boat on the beach opposite Royal Parade, causing an obstruction at long tides. 7 days notice was given to Gearing to move, if not Gearing to be charged. A similar situation to that of Mr A Dumbrell who was given only 3 days notice.

Yet another duty for the Parade Inspector regarding private boat owners who could leave their boats upon the beach - this practice continued for many years.

August 1897.

A bathing fatality occurred in August from one of the rowing boats hired by John Hide. A report at the time tells us that a Mr J. Sinnott and his brother, at about 7 am hired a rowing boat named 'Duke of Devonshire' from Mr John Hide Jnr. at the Boat Stand opposite Howard Square. The deceased Sinnott was seen swimming at the Boulder bank close by the wreck of the 'Sea Flower' which shows at low tide, when with a loud shout he disappeared from view. John and Ben Hide immediately put off in a boat and searched the scene without success. Another boat to put off at the time was one manned by Boatmen Tom & Henry Boniface but they had no success in their search. Some two days later the body was washed ashore on the beach opposite Bolsover Road. The inquest recorded a verdict of accidental drowning. A witness to the drowning was Mr. J S Charlwood, watchmaker, of Langley Road, who regularly had an early morning swim. The Jewellery/Watchmaker firm of Charlwood still exists to this day in Langney Road.

The wrecking of the ship 'Sea Flower' took place in 1849. She was carrying a cargo of granite blocks and it is said they long remained in view and were a danger to boating. George Chambers the author of 'Eastbourne Memories' said traces of the hull of the 'Sea Flower' could be seen in the year of the publication of his book in 1910. Retired Boatman Brian Allchorn recalls, in 1970 skippering the 'William Allchorn' Pleasure Boat and going aground briefly on the granite blocks.

The rest of the summer on the beach kept the Parade Inspector busy bringing the following incidents before the Watch Committee.

A complaint from a Mrs Timberlaine stated that Boatman No.108 Thomas Huggett, alleged her son had thrown stones at his boat and Huggett had threatened to throw her son into the sea. Huggett was called before the Committee and expressed his regret at threatening the boy. Huggett received a caution.

Boatman No.103 Thomas Hallam, in the interest of the public had his licence revoked because he suffered from epileptic fits.

Boatman W A Smith was fined 10s for letting his boat go to sea without a Licenced Boatman in charge.

Boatman Henry Boniface was fined 40/- for overloading a Pleasure Boat.

A Mr Sewell complained that the Boatman Ted Sayers had demanded a fare for a full hours sailing. Sewell had only been at sea 35 minutes. Sayers stated that with ferrying out, sailing and returning a full hour had been occupied and that it was only at the request of several ladies in the boat that he had returned so soon. Furthermore he had not charged so much as he was entitled to by the Bye-Laws. The Committee found, no cause for complaint.

September 1897.

September saw an application by Harry Allchorn to place his licenced sailing boat on the stand occupied by Richard Swain on Royal Parade. Granted.

Boatman Dennis Breach applied for use of No.5 Boat Stand on the Grand Parade owing to the present occupier's absence abroad. Granted.

November 1897.

Applications were received from private boat owners Mr E P Barfield, A Owen & A E Dumbrill to place boats on the foreshore at Grand Parade and Royal Parade. Barfield & Owen not granted. Mr Dumbrill would be allowed to place his boat on the stand allotted to Mr George Merrick Hide opposite the Cavendish Hotel until end of March.

Boats allowed on the seafront during the winter months were also allowed to be pulled up onto the promenade during the long rough high tides.

April 1898.

Applications for Boat Stands, capstans and alterations to the same were regularly received and April proved no exception. Applications for the following are shown:

Henry Mockett to place his boats on part of the bathing ground east of the Grand Parade Bandstand allotted to Tom Bennett, Bathing Machine operator.

Capstan No.42 to Boatman Ted Sayers, No.84 to Boatman Joseph Hope and Boat Stands Nos.56 & 57 westward of the Marine Parade slipway to Hope.

Capstan No.58 eastward of the Marine Parade slipway was allotted to Mr Ben Bates for the year.

Boatmen Charles Hurd & Richard John Erridge were advised that Boat Stands Nos.64, 82 & 86 were the only ones vacant at present.

An application was received from William Smith requesting a Boat Stand on his arrival from South Africa. None available.

The Boniface brothers, Tom and Henry applied to operate a Boat Stand between groynes Nos.20 & 21. Their application was not granted. Luckier though was Boatman Jack Sayers who was granted Boat Stands Nos.65 & 71.

September 1898.

A Grand sailing race took place off Eastbourne under favourable sailing conditions. The prizes being 1st. = £8. 2nd. = £4. 3rd. = £2. 4th. = £1. There was a good breeze and a slight ground swell when the boats were got away. The course was a triangular one about 3 miles in length, which had to be traversed 3 times, the starting point being the Pier head. The members of the Committee who supervised the race were; Mr George Gausden, Mr H Emary, Mr Mark Hookham and Mr Godfrey, while Mr J Morris acted as starter, Mr P Evershed as timekeeper and Messrs H Emary and J Hurrell as judges.

The 8 boats that took part in the contest on a handicap basis were:

"Dauntless" owned by Richard Swain. ....5 mins.52 secs.

"I.C.U." owned by Richard Hide..............5 mins.7 secs.
"Nona" owned by Jesse Huggett.............3 mins.53 secs.
"Jenny Lind" owned by Edwin Matthews..........3 mins.45 secs.
"The Gannet" owned by Tom & Henry Boniface.....3 mins.22 secs.
"Alert " owned by George Sayers............3 mins.22 secs.
"Ibis" owned by George Bates.............3 mins.
"Willing Boy" owned by Ben Erridge.............. Scratch

On completing the course first time 'Nona' led, closely followed by 'Dauntless', 'Willing Boy' third and 'Jenny Lind' fourth. After the second circuit 'Dauntless' led 'Nona' next 'Willing Boy', 'Ibis' and 'I. C. U'. The other boats retired from the race. The last time round 'Nona' overhauled 'Dauntless' and thus secured first prize. 'Willing Boy' came third and 'Ibis' fourth. Well-done Jesse Huggett. Ben Erridge did well in 'Willing Boy' having started from scratch. It must have been an exciting race to watch.

October 1899.

Naked people on the beach under the cliffs at Holywell are nothing new, as today we have the 'naturists' and other types. Also back in 1899 the problem existed. They could be viewed from the sea as well as land. In October a complaint of the problem was brought to the attention of the Council. Not resolved though.

December 1899.

Boatman John R Mockett was in favour, being granted a Boat Stand east of the Pier.

A Bathing Machine stand was granted to Mr George 'Pincher' Hide who was licenced for 12 machines on his stand to the west of the Cavendish Hotel and on the Royal Parade.

Boat Stands Nos.55 & 56 were granted to Richard Swain and No.57 to Edward Allchorn.

Messrs. Sam & Ben Hide were offered Boat Stands No's. 21 & 22, the only ones available.

A total of 75 Waterman/Boatman and 175 Pleasure Boat Licences were issued. No other details available.

C1870 Eastbourne beach prior to western parades being built to Holywell.

Grand Parade c1900.

C1895 down on the sands.

C1889 high tide.

Hide family bathing machines, Grand Parade 1913.

C1870 Marine Parade looking east to old fishing station (now Royal Parade). Anchor Hotel now Albermarle Hotel.

Tom Bennett's bathing machines and horses c1900. Grand Parade east of bandstand.

The sands at Eastbourne c1920 pony rides.

1900 ~ 1913

A search of all known available records and material concerning totals of Pleasure Boating and Waterman/Boatman Licences issued, proved somewhat difficult for the years 1900 - 1913. Nevertheless, what has been found is shown from extracts of the Watch Committee minutes giving applications made, movements and transfers of the above.

April 1900.

An application by Mr C E Etchell to place his boat on the stand of Boatman Jack Elms was granted.

May 1900.

A letter from Reuben Wood Jnr. saying John Mockett declined to buy his boats and had sold them to Mr George 'Pincher' Hide and William Wood's Boat Stand was transferred to him and his son Lucas Hide. An application from Boatman Albert Hide ('Pincher' Hide's eldest son) for a Boat Stand was not granted, as none were available.

July 1900.

The Watch Committee resolved to purchase a 'White Ensign' to hoist on the Carpet Gardens, Grand Parade. The same month Boatman Reuben Wood Jnr. complained that Alleyn Sayers was using the Boat Stand allotted to him and he objected to him plying for hire between Victoria Steps and Grand Parade Bandstand. A prime site, that part of the seafront and amongst the Boatmen highly prized due to the fact that day visitors arriving by train usually made their way to the beach via Terminus Road and Victoria Place (now the top part of Terminus Road, Co-op corner to the Fish restaurant)

September 1900.

Saw the decision to provide the Parade Inspector with a Patrol jacket and greatcoat, in lieu of a tunic, both garments to have words 'Parade Inspector' on collar.

April 1901.

An application from Boatman Thomas Swain Jnr. for a Boat Stand west side of the new groyne opposite the Queens Hotel was granted.

May 1901.

Saw Boatman G Bellamy have his licence revoked. Boatman Ben Hide was given permission to place boat on Ben Bates stand and in August a letter from Tom Boniface stated that Ben Hide had given him permission to lay a rowboat on a piece of his spare ground and asked for the Committee's consent. Granted.

February 1902.

Saw the death of Richard "Dick" Swain, a well-known Eastbourne Boatman of an old Eastbourne seafaring family. At the time the following was reported:

Richard 'Dick' Swain's Boat Stand on Marine Parade C.1895.

"A very familiar figure has disappeared from the Marine Parade; we refer to Richard Swain a Boatman well known to visitors and residents. About a fortnight ago he caught a severe chill from which he died on 7th at his home 33, Seaside. The deceased was a Licenced Boatman and had his Boat Stand opposite the Albion Hotel, his jovial face and cheery smile rendered him a favourite with all who knew him. A son of the late Mr Thomas Swain, he was 59 years old, born 1843, and his opinions on all matters connected with boating and fishing always commanded respect. He had formerly been connected with the Newhaven-Dieppe cross channel service. He was the owner of the 'Dauntless', which had figured in several races off Eastbourne, and always secured a 'place'. The funeral took place at Ocklynge cemetery. Five of the coffin bearers were members of the old Lifeboat crew of the famous rescue of the "New Brunswick" off Birling Gap 1883. Swain was a member of that Lifeboat crew. The bearers were William Bollard Hide, Charles 'Bones' Hide Cox'n, John 'Trunkey' Colstick, William 'Alligator' Erridge and John 'Kruger' Prodger the old crew members and John 'Jack' Mockett.

Family mourners being: Mrs Swain (widow), Thomas Swain (brother), Mrs Briggs (sister), Philip Swain (uncle) and Miss E Swain (niece). Local Boatmen/Fishermen among the mourners were; Alleyn Sayers, George Bates, Jack Elms, E Brown, William Godden, Dennis Breach, Edwin Matthews, Harry Erridge, D Allchorn, Ted Clarke, George Allchorn, Harry Allchorn, George Erridge, John Erridge, E Shrivell, Charles and John Hurd and Henry Bollard Hide."

The following verse is from a poem written by J. Logan of Ilford, in memory of Richard Swain:

> No more upon the silver sand or round by Beachy Head,
> 'Mid sun or wind, you'll meet him now,
> who's numbered with the dead.
> No more he'll launch his skiff at morn
> and revel in the foam,
> For the Pilot of the Mystic boat has called the Boatman home.

April 1902.

An application from Mr William Allchorn for temporary permission to place his pleasure sailing boat 'Golden City' on the beach near Victoria steps was granted. (The start of a 90 odd year occupation of this particular Boat Stand.)

The Allchorn family had a long and continuous association with their Pleasure Boats occupying Boat Stands on or near this site. Certainly the 'Allchorns' would have been amongst the first of the boating fraternity to ply for hire off the Sea Houses in 1790. Then through to Marine Parade and finally the Grand and Royal Parades, some two hundred years providing sea going pleasure trips for Eastbourne's visitors and residents.

A proposal of the Parade Inspector that numbers be limited of 1st & 2nd class Waterman Licences issued to 1st class 64 & 2nd class 30 was agreed by the Watch Committee. This ruling could help the non-boat owning Boatmen gain more employment during the season. There was already a problem with some boat owners employing unlicenced persons to take charge of Licenced Pleasure Boats and the Watch Committee had to put out another ruling to stop the practice.

August 1902.

Boatman Thomas Sutton was arrested as a deserter from the Royal Navy and his licence was revoked. Rueben Wood was cautioned for not wearing a licence ribbon when plying for hire.

A Mr Fritz was allowed to place his private rowboat on the beach with the consent of the Boat Stand owner. (A bit of extra income for Boatman for keeping an eye open?)

Pleasure Boatmen also served as Lifeboat men

November 1902.

Saturday November 8th 1902 experienced one of the most perilous services of the Eastbourne Lifeboat. That afternoon a strong southwest gale was raging in the Channel and a ship, the S.S. Southport, of Cardiff, was in trouble off Hastings. The weather was too extreme for the Hastings Lifeboat to be launched so a call was put through to Eastbourne to launch the 'James Stevens No.6' Lifeboat under Cox'n Ben Erridge and 2nd Cox'n Tom Boniface and crew. She was launched off the beach at the Fishing Station with some difficulty at about 2.30 pm. Taking advantage of the wind the sails were soon set and despite the mountainous seas good progress was made and the

Eastbourne Lifeboat 'James Stevens No.6 with most of the crew of 1902. Ben Erridge Coxswain. 'Bones' Hide is seated 3rd from right. Some publications give this as the 1907 Lifeboat and crew - 'Bones' Hide died in 1905!

Lifeboat arrived off Hastings about 5 pm. The previously distressed vessel had regained control of her way and made off towards the east. Being unable to make headway back towards Eastbourne against the prevailing gale, Cox'n Ben Erridge decided to land at Hastings. Distinct danger attended the task as the seas along the shore were very broken and huge waves dashed wildly. But the Eastbourne Lifeboat crew were not easily scared, being a fearless and valiant bunch. The efforts of the crew were directed to bringing the Lifeboat to the leeward of the western arm of the harbour. The seas were truly terrific and on rounding the head of the western arm in her effort to gain shelter she turned broadside to the sea as the crew pulled hard. It was a battle against the elements, all witnessed from the shore by many hundreds of people. Cox'n Ben Erridge later said, *'The boat ran on a wave and was then on her beams end, she righted herself and that was when 2nd Cox'n Tom Boniface was washed overboard. I got a rope to Tom which he clung to for some 200-300 yards, the boat was then twice more knocked on her beams end but righted herself, this was when crewman Hurd was washed out of the boat and back inboard again, a miracle. I told the crew to pull back on the oars and hold on for dear life, which we all did. The boat took the next sea and was then washed high and dry on the beach.'* Boniface being exhausted had to let go the rope and was washed into the surf unconscious until pulled ashore with great bravery by Hastings residents. Cox'n Erridge said it was one of the most miraculous things he had ever experienced. No one expected to get ashore alive and that the boat would capsize at any time.

As to Tom Boniface, his rescuers said they tried to get him to grasp a rope but he was semi-conscious and drowning. They heard Boniface shout *'Father, Father'* and after managing to get him ashore Boniface later told them that *'he could see God as plain as he could want to, and when he held out his hand Christ took hold of it'* Boniface was very ill for some time after the incident and as a result of his experience he joined the Salvation Army and was forever nicknamed 'Salvation Tom'. The following poem was written by W. Thorne, telling a tale of 'Salvation Tom'

God's Care for Tom.

The sea was rough and stormy,
The waves were white with foam,
A Lifeboat went forward,
Amongst them was one called Tom.

He saw the raging tempest,
But he himself kept calm,
When alas, the waters took him,
But God took care of Tom.

He swam and struggled for safety,
To reach the boat again,
His strength he felt was going,
But God took care of Tom.

He knew that Christ was near him,
And did not feel alarmed,
He thought he saw his Saviour,
Whose love was shown to Tom.

He raised his hand to Heaven,
Said, "Father, here I am,"
When Christ's own hand was stretched forth,
And proved his care for Tom.

The God he has served so faithful,
Brought him through the dreadful storm,
And he lives to tell the story,
How his Jesus cared for Tom.

People all around well know him,
His fame abroad has gone,
And if you wish to know him,
It's "Tom Boniface" our Tom.

'Salvation' Tom Boniface received a weekly allowance from the RNLI for the illness resulting from his experience, however in January 1903, he received an agreed sum of 12 guineas as a final payment. 'Salvation Tom' died at his home, 42 Sidley Road on June 28th 1928 - forced to retire from his occupation Fisherman/Boatman. He had assisted his brother Henry for many years at their Boat Stand just east of the Bandstand and was well known to visitors. Tom was born in a cottage at Holywell, Meads. His father Edward Boniface was son of a lime burner of Holywell, the family having lived down in Holywell for many years. Tom was aged 15 years when along with his father and brothers James, Charles and Henry they went to live down by the original Fishing Station and took up a career of fishing and boating. Aged 19 years Tom married Elizabeth Chandler and the marriage produced 15 children, 12 surviving childhood. The 6 sons all took up fishing and boating and were at various times members of the Lifeboat crew. Tom, a member of the Lifeboat crew from 1884 served 22 years, many as 2nd Coxswain. Also known as 'Old Tom', there were some 37 grandchildren and 16 great grandchildren when he died.

Back to the incident, what an experience for the whole crew especially Charles 'Bones' Hide aged 53 years - not a young man. Interestingly there were three Lifeboat men in that crew who were in the crew of the famous 'New Brunswick' rescue of 1883. Including 'Bones', they were George 'Smuggler' and William 'Alligator' Erridge - brave men indeed. The crew's bravery was rewarded with a dinner and a monetary reward as follows: - £1.10s for the Cox'n. £1.5s to each of the crew.

There were 7 Erridge family members including Cox'n Erridge in the crew.

The crew were as follows:
Cox'n Ben Erridge.
2nd Cox'n Tom Boniface.
Crew:
John Mockett, George Erridge Jnr.
William Erridge, Alfred Erridge, Charles Boniface,
Richard John Erridge, William Simpson, Fred Huggett,
Tim Erridge, Charles 'Bones' Hide, Thomas Huggett,
George Erridge Snr. Ernest 'Chalky' Hide, Andrew Hurd.

The year 1902 brought aggravation from the Council for the Bathing Machine owners. They were compelled to remove their machines and move their shops that had been there for years from the Fishing Station, as they were not connected with fishing. (The Council were following the letter of the covenant that only persons and businesses concerned with fishing could use the Fishing Station.) The Bathing Machine operators were forced to move and went further east on the beach where today the Leisure Pool stands.

September 1902.

An accident happened to young Henry Venn aged 13 years of 105, Longstone Road, on the beach opposite Burlington Place. A sailing boat called "I.C.U." belonging to Richard Hide of Latimer Road was being launched when the handle of the windlass struck the boy Venn on the forehead and knocked him down. A wound was inflicted and blood flowed freely. The boy had been told to stand clear of the windlass by Boatman Dennis Breach, but the boy had ignored his warning. Boatman Edward Hide summoned Dr Bomford-Emmerson from Compton Street, who had the boy taken to Mr Senior the Chemist where the wound was dressed and the boy was afterwards taken home in a cab. This type of accident was always liable to happen when the public do not keep clear of mechanical apparatus on the beach.

The Annual Eastbourne Regatta took place in September 1902 there being a stiff breeze from the east and the sea choppy.

Some of the events are as follows: -

Sailing race.
Open only to Eastbourne Fishermen and Boatmen
Prizes - £10. £4. £2. and £1.
1st   "Star of the East"......H.Matthews.
2nd   "Sunbeam"................J Huggett.
3rd   "Mona".....................A Huggett.
4th   "Gannet"..................T Boniface.
5th   "Petrel".....................R Wood Snr.

On the first round 'Star of the East' led from 'Mona' by about a length followed by 'Sunbeam'. Eventually the winner got home by two lengths closely followed by the others boats after a fine race. 'Old Screw' Rueben Wood (no youngster) competing in 'Petrel'

Eastbourne Boatmen's Double Sculls.
Prizes - £3. £2. £1.
1st   "Primrose"..........J Dove & E Allchorn.
2nd   "Thistle".............EW Allchorn & D Allchorn.
3rd   "Shamrock"........G Erridge & J Elms.
4th   "Surprise"...........W Erridge & J Mockett.
5th   "Fairly-in-it".......J Sayers & H Sayers.
6th   "Little Wonder"..T Boniface & H Allchorn.

Won by six lengths, several lengths separated second and third.

The Mutton Worry Competition.
Won by J Mockett, 2nd J Huggett, 3rd G Erridge.
Muttons were given by Mr. C O'Hara & Mr. S Easton, local butchers.

January 1903.

Boatman Henry Novis was fined 5/- for being drunk on the beach and had his licence revoked. He had to wait until June when it was restored to him. Boatman J Collins was granted a Capstan and a Boat Stand Licence for 3 boats at Holywell chalk pit, (originally Gore chalk pit, now Holywell Retreat)

Boats at Holywell Retreat. (Pronunciation Holly-well)

September 1903. - The Lifeboat to the Rescue.

The 'Olive', the Eastbourne No.2. Lifeboat had her first service on Wednesday 9th September 1903. At about 5.30am, the Coxswain Ben Erridge, received information that the pleasure yacht 'Britannia' owned by Mr Ben Bates, was drifting and dragging her anchor just west of the Pier and was likely to become a wreck. The 'Olive' was got out of her boathouse and launched just in time to prevent the 'Britannia' being driven ashore. There was a terrific sea at the time and the 'Olive' held the yacht off shore until being able to land her at 10.30am. This was the first test the 'Olive' had during gale conditions and the crew expressed themselves as being very pleased with the new boat.

November 1903.

Boatman Ernest Penfold was granted Boat Stand No.14 vacated by Mr Dugwell.

1904.

1st class Boatman Licences for the year 1904 were increased from 64 to 66. Mr. Garibaldi was given permission to place his private boat on Boatman 'Gospel' Hall's Boat Stand. In May, Parade Inspector Walls, having succeeded Sergeant Burr, was promoted within the Eastbourne Police from Sergeant to Inspector. Sadly, Inspector Walls was murdered in 1912 whilst on duty with the Eastbourne Police.

Henry Mockett was granted permission to place a 'Crab' (an 'A' frame windlass) on Boat Stand No.4 and Boatman Jack Sayers given permission to use Capstan No 80 in place of No 75.

In August a letter was sent to the Watch Committee from Reuben 'Old Screw' Wood. It claimed from the Corporation 10/- for 4 years rent for part of the foreshore let to him by the Corporation for a Capstan and Boat Stand at the Fishing Station. He alleged it had been used by the Corporation for a bathing hut, raft and boat. The Committee did not entertain the claim.

1905.

The 'Old Screw' Wood saga continued through to May 1905 when the Town Clerk reported that Rueben Wood's boats had been removed from the Fishing Station foreshore to the Corporation yard, for failing to pay annual rent. Wood in return claimed damages of £21.15s for their removal. The Council repudiated his claim - a thorn in their side over the years and the Council it appears went for 'Old Screw' Wood.

In August Parade Inspector Walls put a report before the Watch Committee that Wood had not exercised proper skill and care in the navigation of a Pleasure Boat whilst being used to carry persons for hire. The Committee resolved that Wood was unsuitable to hold a licence and duly revoked it but added that the Committee were willing to transfer his licence to any competent person he may appoint to take charge of his boat. They then suspended the licence for his boat 'Petrel' as it was considered un-seaworthy, until examined by a competent boat builder.

Local boat builder Tom Sisk examined and remedied certain defects that had caused the boat to leak. Made seaworthy Sisk stated the 'Petrel' could now be used for hire by a 1st class Boatman.

The Committee approved this but in no way would they reinstate Wood's licence. Finally in November 'Old Screw' wrote to the Committee advising them that he had given up his Sailing Boat Stand to Ben Hide, and was retiring. So a lifetime at sea had come to an end.

A Sketch of an Eastbourne Longshoreman - Reuben 'Old Screw' Wood. *"I was standing at the Redoubt end of the sea wall, watching a school of porpoises rolling up the Channel. An old man with white hair and a mahogany coloured face strolled up his hands thrust deep in his trouser pockets. He was clad in a blue jersey and an old pair of cloth trousers. A heavy pair of sea boots and a dilapidated straw hat completed his costume.*

I knew him as 'Reuben'.

"Them's after herring, sir," he said, nodding towards the porpoises. "Do you often see porpoises in this part of the Channel?" I asked.

"Only when the herrin' and mac'rel is about, sir, and then not always. They comes from the north."

He paused and I thought I saw him smile. "Tell 'e what a gent I know did see out there a week or two back," he said presently.

"Well?" said I with caution, for I was still suspicious of the lurking smile.

"Sea sarpint!" He laughed outright then. I smiled and leaned against the sea wall railing.

"You're joking, of course?" I said.

"Well sir, what this gent did see was true as gospel. He came up to me one afternoon and he says "Reuben" says he, "I'll swear I've just seen the sea sarpint a swimmin' out yonder"

"You must be joking", says I - same as you says to me jest now, sir. "Well come and look for yourself, Reuben", says he."

"And was it the sea serpent?" I repeated as he paused.

"Well, maybe t'was and maybe 'twasn't" he answered enigmatically. "Leastways I warn't going to dispoint the gent by tellin' him as what he sees he didn't see."

It took me a minute to unravel the meaning hidden in the Longshoreman's last sentence.

Reuben had evidently laughed in his sleeve at the 'gent'. Afraid of being made a victim myself, I offered Reuben my tobacco pouch as I asked the next question.

"And was it really the sea serpent?"

"No more'n them porpusses was what went by jest now. 'Twas the same kind of sea sarpint as they be."

And then I saw his joke. As is well known, porpoises are sometimes seen swimming in file, when their backs appearing above the surface of the water suggest the idea of a big sea serpent. I had noticed the same thing myself five minutes before, though the simile had not occurred to me at the moment.

I was in the humour for killing time, but it struck me as being something incongruous that old Reuben should prefer to talk to me when he might, perhaps, be earning a shilling or two by taking out a party of visitors in his boat on the water. There were hundreds lounging on the Parades this fine afternoon, and there were dozens of Boatmen lolling against the railings of the esplanade, staring out to sea with folded arms, or with their hands thrust deep in their trousers pockets. I asked old Reuben the cause of so much apparent idleness on the part of his fraternity.

Reuben slowly removed the pipe from his lips.

"Well, sir, it ain't no matter of choice, I reckon" He said, "There are too many of us. The steamers take so many hundreds, they've broke the Brighton Boatmen. There are over a hundred Boatmen here I think. I'm the oldest. If I get people along o'me I never get 'em away from me. They always keep recommending more."

"How do you live when you get a bad season?" "I goes fishing sometimes. I have gone for long lines, and for hooking whiting and codfish. Sometime I fish for bass, but there don't seem so many of them now as there used to be. Times is changed for the worst, and reckon the Almighty has got some reason to find fault with us."

"Well if boating is bad and fishing is bad, how on earth do you manage to keep out of the Workhouse? Have you got any money saved?"

Old Reuben removed his clay from his mouth and solemnly winked, "Well, I has got a bit of a nest egg, sir."

From his manner there appeared to be something behind his answer, which he was willing to impart with pressure. I endeavoured to draw him out. "Enough to live on?" I asked.

"Well, my old woman, she does a bit o'washing, and I stays at home and turns the mangle o'wet days. The Almighty is good, sir, and won't let a sparrer want" and he winked.

There was a mystery in the Longshoreman's wink that was becoming irritating.

"Look here Reuben" I said, "you and I know each other pretty well by now. I

intend to go fishing tomorrow morning out in the Bay. Would you like to come with me?"

"O 'course, sir, five shillin' is five shillin'."

"Well tell me what you've got in your mind, and I'll make it ten shillings, and give you half now." I jingled the coins together in my hand.

"I ain't unwillin' sir, a gent's a gent, and if so be as you'll take your davy and say, mum's the words I don't mind a tellin' of 'ee."

"Mum's the word," I repeated. "Come, here's the money," I added, handing it to him.

He filled his pipe from my pouch again, and then began with his lips close to my ear.

"Yer'see, when boatin's bad and fishin's bad us have got to make a bit somehow in order to live, or how be poor chaps like us to get on? There be only one thing to do and we does it."

"And that is?"

He brought his mouth closer to my face, "Smugglin", and he chuckled.

"You don't mean to say", I commenced, when he interrupted me.

"Mum's the word, you said sir."

"Yes I haven't forgotten, but"- and my questions came fast. Old Reuben answered them in his own way. "There's only one or two of us as does a bit, and they be mostly old hands. Why bless yer soul sir, most of 'em think the game ain't worth a candle. Two years ago four men got copped down there" he pointed with his thumb to the waste shingle eastward - "With 26 lb o'bacca that hadn't paid no dooty, and now they're doing a stretch o'three year."

"So will you be Reuben, if you're not careful" I said.

"Not me sir, I ain't no such fool. I goes out fishin'" he winked - "with old Ben about sundown. We meets a French boat in the dark that has come out fishin' too, takes our bit o'bacca, pays our money, and is off to the fishin' ground in time to make a catch afore we runs home. Smugglin's in the blood I reckon. My father was a wonderful big smuggler, and so was my grandfather. About the time of the Battle o' Waterloo my grandfather used to go over to Boulogne and bring back a lot of lace and silk. He'd take off his clothes and wrap it round his body and I've heard him say as he sometimes had five or six pairs o' ladies' silk stockings on. I've carried a many tubs o' brandy when I was a boy."

"But where do you conceal your tobacco while you are bringing it over? Aren't you afraid of being hauled to and questioned?"

"Well, if we was they'd find nothink but fish and nets."

"And you hide it where?" "That's telling, sir; but we does hide it."

And at this point old Reuben would not say another word.

Reuben Wood was born in Hastings, Sussex in 1824 - a 'Chopback' (the nickname for a Hastings Fisherman). He was 80 years old when the above tale took place.

He was only 13 months old when he came to live in Eastbourne and lived his life here when not at sea. He was introduced to the sea early, for that journey from Hastings to Eastbourne as a baby was made by sea on a fishing vessel. Other branches of his family were connected with those early days of Eastbourne's history. Reuben Wood's grandfather on his mother's side was a signalman at Beachy Head during the wars with Napoleon. Two uncles were attached to the gun, which apparently in those days was kept on the Head to fire on the French Privateers, who came too close inshore. One of his grandmothers used to live in a cottage in Grove Road opposite the Town Hall, and came to a sad end by being burned alive.

For 65 years Reuben roamed the narrow seas from Lands End to Hartlepool. He has not only never had an accident himself, but no man in any fishing vessel of which he had charge or any passengers on his Pleasure Boats have ever suffered any injury.

Reuben made his first voyage with his father, who was master of his own fishing Lugger when he was aged 15, and with a crew of 5 hands went down to Plymouth. Several other trips of the kind followed and then the youngster began work for other boats. Though some of the time was spent sailing out of Eastbourne he also went to Brighton, and for three seasons - two herring seasons and one mackerel season- he sailed Brighton boats. Two of the trips took him to the North Sea, while the other was down Channel to Plymouth.

Reuben's father was drowned off the Isle of Wight in 1847. He was tossed over in gale of wind and Reuben succeeded the command and possession of his Lugger. For several years he sailed in this and other Luggers up to the North Sea and down The Channel. Stress of weather often compelled the small craft to put into port and in consequence, Reuben knew the whole coast and had been in practically every harbour between Lands End and Hartlepool. About forty years ago he gave up going away deep sea fishing and devoted himself to Longshore Fishing and hiring Pleasure Boats off the beach at Eastbourne. He owned many in his time. His services were in demand as a Pilot for vessels laden with coal, which were beached on the shingle opposite where St Aubyns Road now runs into Royal Parade. Some of these boats were locally owned but they mostly belonged to Hastings and Rye and thence made the voyage to Northumberland for coal. The coming of the Railway put a stop to that. Since Bye-Laws were introduced Reuben always had 4 to 8 boats registered. He held that there was more money made out of Pleasure Boats in the 1870s than in 1905 and said he earned more by Longshore Fishing than by hiring out boats. This present decrease (1905) in Pleasure Boating he attributed to the coming of the Steamer and still more to the increase of competition by the large number of Boatmen (over 100) now engaged on the beach. Reuben, since the Royal Parade was built had a Boat Stand there.

Reuben rejoiced in the name of "The Old Screw", a nickname that had followed him from youth when he screwed through a hole in some railings surrounding the present Ordnance Yard in search of a cricket ball. Reuben kept fit and healthy for his age. Sight and hearing just failing a little. He was not the oldest of the Eastbourne seafaring community - that goes to a certain old seafarer named Philip Swain, who at 84 years took a regular walk to Holywell or Langney. In far off days Reuben and Philip sailed together and never had a crossed word. "We've always been chums" said Reuben. Another 'Old Screw' tale was told of his seamanship and local knowledge of tides and the rocks round Holywell and Beachy Head. It was January 8th 1887 when the barque 'Calliope' went aground at Holywell. It was Reuben that piloted her to deep water and got the sum of £3 for his endeavours.

Shortly after Reuben's yarn he was summoned in September 1905 for unlawfully plying for hire and acting as a Boatman whilst not being licenced.

At court, Town Clerk Mr Fovargue prosecuting for the Watch Committee, said is was with regret but owing to his increasing years and to accidents his licence had been taken away at the beginning of the season. Subsequently the Parade Inspector had seen Wood plying for hire touching his hat 'Boat Sir' to hire out his rowboats. Wood was seen to hire his rowboat 'Mignonette' to two small lads. On their return to shore they had no help, resulting in the boat broaching too and becoming half filled with water and the lads getting drenched. Told by the Parade Inspector that he was no longer qualified to act as a 1st class Boatman and could not ply for hire, Wood obstinately said he would continue to do so. Wood had on other occasions been seen plying for hire and rowing his boats for his hirers.

A Mr Kirtland appearing for Wood said although 81 years of age, Wood was still fit and skilful to act as Boatman. He produced a certificate from Dr. Sherwood, which stated Wood was still able bodied and fit for work. Nevertheless Wood was told he could not operate as a Boatman. He could have his boats operated by a qualified Boatman but he could not assist in any way. Wood agreed to this and the summons was withdrawn. So sadly 'Old Screw' came to the end of his boating life on Eastbourne seafront. Or did he?

February 1906.

There was an application by Boatman George Penfold to change Boat Stand No.14 into a Capstan stand. This was granted and Boatman Ben Hide was allowed to exchange his Boat Stand No.10 for No.12 belonging to Boatman John Hide.

April 1906.

George 'Pincher' Hide was granted permission for 13 Bathing Machines on his site No.9 opposite the Cavendish Hotel, Burlington Place.

Boat Stands No.70 to Ernest Sayers and No.79 to Jack Sayers.

'Pincher' Hide's Boat Stand No.32 and Mr William Allchorn Boat Stand No.34, sited at Victoria steps opposite Victoria Place, asked for Capstan stands to be granted on these sites now occupied temporarily. Agreed but a permanent licence not granted.

Steam Motor Launch - A letter from Mr W.A. Semple requesting licences for one or two motor launches to carry 12-14 passengers and to ply for hire near the Devonshire Park. Application was not granted.

May 1906.

An application was read from Mr William Allchorn for permission to allow him to put both his sailing boats on the temporary Capstan stand allotted to him at Victoria Steps. He was willing to move at anytime the Committee desired. His request was granted. (The best site on the beach opposite the top of Victoria Place, Terminus Road, and one from which William Allchorn never moved and the Boat Stand is still there to this day.)

August 1906.

1st class Waterman Licences granted to Samuel Knight, Hurd and Egbert Bates.

1906.

Pleasure Boating under the control of the Corporation, by whom all tariffs were fixed as follows:

Sailing Boats:
30 ft or more long, first hour or less..10/-
Less than 30 ft...5/-
Every additional half hour or proportion irrespective of length......2/-
Single passengers in 'Omnibus' boats, first hour or less.................1/-
Every additional half hour or less..6d

The sailing yacht 'Britannia' owned by Ben Bates was the largest on the coast and made trips to sea several times during the day.

Rowing boats:
Boat with Boatman, first hour or less... 2/-
Every additional half hour or less.. 1/-
Boat without Boatman, first hour or less.....................................1/6d
Single additional half hour or less.. 9d
Single passenger in 'Omnibus' boat, first hour or less....................9d
Every additional half hour or less...3d.

October 1906.

The local paper on 31st October, reported the salvaging of the converted barge 'Gwalia' fitted out as a luxury yacht. She was on her way down Channel to Shoreham when gale force winds took her close to Beachy Head. Fearing she would strike the Lighthouse she was abandoned by her crew who made for shore in a small dinghy, which after they landed beneath the cliffs, drifted away. The Coastguard saw their plight and they were rescued by rope. Meanwhile the incident had been seen by Boatmen on the Royal Parade and within minutes Albert Sayers, Edward Allchorn, Henry and Ernest Sayers launched the boat 'Seagull' and got alongside the deserted 'Gwalia'. Ernest Sayers was left to take the 'Seagull' back to Eastbourne, while the other three boarded the 'Gwalia' and sailed her down off Dover where a Tug towed her into harbour.

The Lifeboat under Ben Erridge had been launched to assist but returned when she found the 'Gwalia' manned by the Sayers and Allchorn. A pretty sum in salvage money was earned. The 'Gwalia was originally built in 1878 as a 60 ton barge named 'New Zealand', 'Four Brothers' and finally converted to a yacht under her present name for the famous marine artist William Wylie.

1907 Regatta.

Held on 14th August at 1pm - a Sailing race for the Fishermen and Boatmen of Eastbourne took place. Twice round on a triangular course from off the pier head. Below are details of starters and boats:

Length of boat. (Ft In) Time Starting. (Min Sec)
1. 'Freddy' 15'0" M Hardy Go.
2. 'Daring' 17'0" W Allchorn 2m15s
2. 'Pet' 17'0" Alleyn Sayers 2m15s
2. 'Spitfire' 17'0" E Allchorn 2m15s
2. 'Little Jack' 17'0" J Prodger 2m15s
2. 'Flower of the Fleet' 17'0" J Prodger 2m15s
3. 'Jenny Lind' 17'6" J Erridge 45s
4. 'Dolphin' 17'9" T & H Boniface 22m5s
5. 'Gannett' 18'0" T & H Boniface 22m5s
6. 'Star of the East' 19'5" H Matthews 27m5s
7. 'Mallard' 19'10" B Bates 37m5s
8. 'Nona' 19'11" A Huggett 7m5s
8. 'Golden City' 19'11" W Allchorn 7m5s
8. 'Kathleen' 19'11" Geo Huggett 7m5s
9. 'Our Lassie' 20'6" J Huggett 7m5s

Result: 1st Star of the East, 2nd Mallard, 3rd Our Lassie, 4th Kathleen.

Waterman's Double Sculls. Eastbourne Licenced Boatmen only
1. 'Our Tom' T Boniface & H Allchorn
2. 'Primrose' W Boniface & H Boniface
3. 'Fairly-in-it' H Sayers & G Hookham
4. 'Teal' E Allchorn & E Sayers
5. '?' E Mockett & G Erridge

Result: 1st Primrose, 2nd Fairly-in-it, 3rd Our Tom, 4th Teal.

Lady & Gentleman's Double Sculls.
1st 'Dauntless' Mrs French & G French.
2nd 'Primrose' Miss Allchorn & J Hookham
3rd 'Fairly-in-it' Miss Sayers & W Ashdown

A Duck Hunt.

A boat rowed by one person, chased by a four-oared boat not less than 18 feet in length without a rudder rowed by four persons. Quarter of an hour chasing allowed.

Duck: W Boniface
Chasers: T Boniface, H Boniface, F Read and G Penfold. - Winner not shown.

Dog race on beach.
Won by 'Nell' - 7 dogs entered.

Paired - Oared race. (For boys under 16 years.)
1st 'Primrose' J & G Boniface.
2nd 'Wild Flower' H Novis & J Allchorn.
3rd 'Our Tom' W Sayers & A N Other.

April 1908.

Parade Bye-Laws - Perambulators on the Grand Parade.

Three nursemaids were summoned before the court for pushing their prams three abreast along the promenade of Grand Parade after being told by a Policeman not to do so. All three pleaded guilty. The Chairman of the Bench told them only two perambulators abreast were allowed along the Parades. The Parades were not made exclusively for nursemaids and perambulators. All three were dismissed with a caution. (What so! for cyclists, skateboarders, rollerbladers, motorised invalid carriages and the Dotto train)

The same year saw a case of prostitution on the Parades. In court a woman of Seaside Road was sent to jail for 14 days for soliciting on King Edwards Parade. She pleaded guilty. Her husband was also prosecuted for living off her immoral earnings and given 14 days in prison. There was obviously a market for it up the posh end of the seafront!

May 1908.

Tom & E Boniface were allowed to place a windlass on their Boat Stand No.22.

August 1908.

The 22nd Workmen's Regatta took place off the Grand Parade on August 5th supported by many business patrons including Carew Davies Gilbert and Sir John Ellerman, the shipping magnate.

A full programme of events took place. An advert in the programme stated that the firm of Ted Sayers, Licenced Boatman No.14 situated next

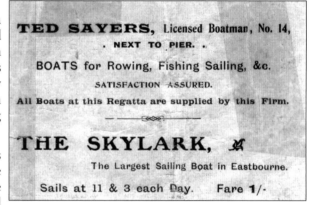

Ted Sayers 1908 'Skylark' advert.

Ferrying to the 'Skylark', Alleyn Sayers Row Boat 'Seagull' to the right. 1908.

to the Pier supplied all the boats at the Regatta.

Prominently displayed was the Sayers advert. *'The Skylark' the largest sailing boat in Eastbourne. Trips at 11am & 3pm each day. Fare 1/-.* So Ben Bates 'Britannia' no longer operated.

November 1908.

The Borough Accountant's report for November showed the following:

Receipts from Waterman Licences. = £5.4s. 0d
'Pleasure Boats' = £26 1s 0d
'Capstans & Net shops' = £15 0s 0d
(Receipts covered from 1st October 1907 - September 1908.)

The summer season of 1908 was not a very satisfactory one for the Boatmen of Eastbourne. The sturdy Boatmen of Eastbourne had experienced a very uneven season, they were like Mr Micawber waiting for something to turn up in the shape of better weather and patronage. While the Boatmen experienced considerable hardships, it must be admitted they were civil and well behaved. There was an absence of prevalent persistent touting unlike Hastings and Brighton, which the visitors did not like. The early part of the summer the weather was fine and business fairly good but there were few visitors. When the weather was not good in September there were a lot of visitors.

On the Eastbourne Parades that season there were 180 Licenced Rowing Boats, the licence charge being 2/6d each: 15 sailing boats plying, their owners paying 3/6d each a year. A total of 104 Licenced Boatmen were engaged. (Motor petrol driven Pleasure Boats were not yet developed and operating.)

As Reuben 'Old Screw' Wood said *'too many Boatmen on the front, the pleasure steamers claiming the attention of most of the visitors.'* In 1908, P & A Campbell had four steamers running from the Pier namely - 'Brighton Queen', 'Cambria', 'Glen Rosa' and 'Bonnie Doon' not forgetting 'Lady Rowena' making daily trips.

As to the names of the Pleasure Boats in 1908 some of the examples are 'Dreadnought', 'Silver Morn', 'Powerful', 'Red Rose', 'Dauntless', 'Happy Return', and the 'Anson St Clair'. (Remember her from 1880 when she was built for Edward Allchorn by the grateful parents of a boy he saved from drowning. The same boat? Yes, she would have been a well built boat and well maintained over the years.)

Winter for the Pleasure Boatmen.

During the winter months, most of the rowboats were stored in net shops and on the beach along with the big sail boats down at the Fishing Station where the main occupation for Longshoremen was fishing. Some Sail Pleasure Boats were restored to their fishing occupation and those that were strictly summer Boatmen just stored their boats away and undertook another occupation. That is not to say that Longshoremen didn't. It is known that work on the foreshore defences was undertaken by some of them. Inclement winter weather was the time for boat, net and tackle repairs and for all those other seafaring needs and of course, drinking in the Beach Hotel and other Pubs in the vicinity.

To say all Fishermen and Boatmen had a liking for drink is not true. Some were teetotal, religious and regular members of the 'Missions to Seamen's Institute/Bethel' situated on the beach at the top of Beach Road. A place where they could meet in comfort, away from the pub and partake of tea or coffee supplied free by volunteers who also took bible meetings for those Fishermen and their families that cared to attend. Of this community there was a natural jealousy amongst themselves. There are stories of arguments and fights among the families and the tale goes, that after the families had stopped quarrelling, their dogs started scrapping which started it all off again!

Among the Boatmen, competition was fierce for the best-turned out boats. To have the biggest boat on the front was all-important and to get the 'trippers' on their boat. But on the whole they were a close community ready to stand together in times of trouble, hard times and when at sea if one of their kind was in trouble, go to their aid.

With the coming of spring the Fishing Station would become a hive of activity; Rowboats were brought up to tip top condition, varnished and painted. Sail boats were rigged out as they had been from days of old, ready for the start of the season. (March or April as the weather allowed.)

A letter in the local paper from a person signed 'Nauticus' sang the praises of Eastbourne Boatmen.

Spring clean. Preparing boats for the coming season.

"Although our Boatmen have to work in all sorts of weather and are often subjected to superfluous questions, they are, nevertheless civil and obliging. The boats are very clean and seaworthy. The charges are very moderate, and the Boatmen give every facility for a days fishing if required. Most of them have a yacht, which sails every morning and afternoon. It is very hard on the men when the town is full of visitors and the weather is against them. Every boat costs no less than £10 and is a big outlay for people in a humble position in life."

1908 saw Boatman Henry Novis of Tower Street, in Court for failing to maintain his wife Esther and family. He was £51. 6s. 0d in arrears. Novis said he had not worked for 5-6 months but the Parade Inspector stated Novis had been working on the front and had earned £9 in August. Novis was sentenced to 3 months imprisonment. This upset his wife who asked the Justices not to send him to prison. The Justices said Novis had 12 previous convictions against him; he had behaved in a brutal manner towards her and had treated the court with utter contempt. Prison was the only course of action.

January 1909.

William Allchorn's application for Boat Stand No.4 was granted.

March 1909.

It was agreed that 2nd class Waterman/Boatman Licences be increased from 36 to 40, giving an indication that 'pleasuring' was not over yet. Boatman Sam Hurd was granted a Capstan Licence No.76 for his Boat Stand.

May 1909.

Applications from Harry Boniface for Capstan & Boat Stand No.17 and Albert 'Tuppy' Sayers for Capstan No.15 that Reuben Wood was giving up (retired at last?) were granted.

Interestingly the month of May saw what could be the first application for a Motor Boat Licence made by Boatman Harry 'Early Doors' Allchorn. It was not granted on this occasion but in all probability 1909 saw the start of the Motor Pleasure Boat operating from Eastbourne Seafront.

Converting from sail to motor took place and local boat builders soon developed and custom built Motor Boats for the local Fishermen and Boatmen. An indication of the heavier Pleasure Boat as the Motor Boat would be, is shown by an increase in applications for Capstan and windlasses all needed to deal with the launch and haul up on the beach.

February 1911.

The following came before the Watch Committee and the Parade Inspector said he had consent from the Boatmen for alterations to certain Boat Stands & Capstans. Edward Hide was granted Boat Stand No.1, Boatman Ben Erridge gave up his Boat Stand on Royal Parade to Samuel Hurd provided Hurd purchased his boats. Erridge then emigrated to Canada.

July 1911.

Henry Novis was again under suspension for drunkenness. Dr Willoughby appeared before the Committee and asked them to give Novis his licence back, but to no avail.

September 1911.

Albert French's application for a Motor Boat Licence was granted. He was allowed to use Messrs Sayers' Boat Stand No.28.

In September the Watch Committee discussed the question of the Boatmen using their Motor Pleasure Boats to tow rowboats. The Committee felt that it was a dangerous operation and stated it must cease forthwith. It was brought to their notice due to the steamer 'SS. Charlton' in May and 'SS. Hercules' in June, having both gone aground west of Langney Point after collisions near the Lightship. It transpired that pleasure rowboats rowed to the scenes were being towed back against the tide, one in particular being used by the local reporter of the Eastbourne

Gazette. The vessels aground at Langney offered interesting sightseeing spectacles and were a source of income for all the Boatmen. The owners of the Motor Boats namely: Henry Boniface Jnr. William Boniface, Henry Sayers and Ted Sayers petitioned the Watch Committee to be allowed to continue

Damaged SS. Hercules off Eastbourne. Hired rowboats. 1911.

the practice stating they were all fully competent seamen. Their petition was supported by the following Licenced Boatmen and Fishermen of the Borough: George Huggett, J P Huggett, W Godden, M Hardy, W Morley, James Boniface, Alfred Hurd, M F Hardy, W Gibbs, Reuben Reed Jnr. Henry Matthews, G Grooms, F P Huggett, Henry Matthews Jnr. Andrew Chester, J Huggett, John Prodger, H Erridge (Cox of the Lifeboat), Thomas Hide, J Sayers, E Sayers, E Allchorn, F Weakford, C Hurd, J Godden, J Allchorn, G Hookham, William Allchorn Snr. Tom Huggett, J W Hurd, E Penfold, George Erridge, William Erridge, William Allchorn, Alleyn M Sayers, Dennis Breach, John Hide and Edward Hide. But it was to no avail - the Watch Committee would not be moved and the practice ceased.

November 1911.

Boatman Alleyn Sayers objected to giving up one of his Boat Stands to W French. The Committee insisted one go to French, and it did.

1912.

Boatmen Thomas Boniface and George Huggett were among the first in 1912 to be granted Motor Boat Licences subject to the Corporation Motor Bus Engineer certifying their boats were satisfactory. The Engineer inspected all Pleasure Motor Boats for many years, even the big Motor Boats carrying over 12 passengers certified by the Board of Trade. The practice did end finally about 1970.

John S Gowland who had started a boat building business in 1911 and had his boat yard premises in Winchelsea Road, made an application for a Motor Boat Licence. This was denied, as he was not a Licenced Boatman. Over the course of the next couple of years other applications were made, but all were turned down. A boat builder for several years, Gowland turned out many a fine Motor Boat, one being the 'Estella' built in 1912 for the Hardy Brothers, Boatmen and Fishermen. (See page 153) The 'Estella' was driven by the 'Thorneycroft Marine' paraffin motor. Operating from the Royal Parade Boat Stand, 'Estella' gave sterling service for many years at 'Pleasuring' and as a fishing boat during the winter months.

George Huggett was granted Capstan Stands Nos.79 & 80 on Royal Parade to operate his Motor Boat. William Boniface was granted 2 Boat Stands and a Motor Boat Licence to operate east of the Pier. Applications from Mrs Mockett and Andrew Hurd for Motor Boat Licences were deferred.

The Pleasure Motor Boat certainly caused some controversy amongst the fishing only fraternity down at the Fishing Station. A petition was raised by 27 Fishermen protesting against these Motor Boats being used during the summer months for fishing purposes. Messrs. Huggett and Matthews attended in support. The Watch Committee considered the petition and a letter was read from Henry Boniface, owner of a Pleasure Motor Boat explaining what was done. When the weather was not suitable for 'pleasuring' but alright for fishing, the boats were used for such, maximising their potential. With this the Committee decided to take no further action and the Fishermen lost the day to the Boatmen/Fishermen. Perhaps the old ways died hard amongst the fishing only fraternity. Sail was still predominant at the Fishing Station in those days. One must remember that the covenant covering the use of Fishing Station was that occupants must fish for a living. This was carried out by the Boatmen who kept their boats at the Fishing Station and did cause some animosity between those that only fished and those that 'Pleasured'. Indeed the general situation at the Fishing Station was Boatmen/Fishermen to the west and Fishermen only to the east.

Further applications for 1912 were; Andrew Hurd granted a Motor Boat Licence. Mrs Mockett not granted. William Allchorn Jnr. granted Boat Stands Nos.26 & 27 and Edward Allchorn No.25. Capstan No.19 granted to Alleyn Sayers. William Boniface was granted Boat Stand No.20 lately occupied by William Wood.

June 1913.

Mr Lovely a Garage proprietor of Cavendish Road attended before the Committee and stated that Ben Hide desired to sell his boats. If he purchased them would the Committee grant him Boat Stands? The application was refused. Lovely then asked the Committee to consider the question of Licencing a 1st class Mechanic to attend to the engine of his Motor Boat, providing that he can pass the necessary test to qualify as a 2nd class Waterman/ Boatman. The Committee raised no objections; Lovely went on to tell them that he had bought a sailing boat from Ben Hide and made application to be granted his Boat Stand. With this a deputation of Boatmen attended before the Committee and objected to the transfer. Lovely's application was not granted. (He was not a bone fide Boatman. The protest was a good example of the Boatmen standing together to protect their living.)

Henry Sayers to occupy Boat Stands Nos.51 & 52 and William Sayers to occupy Boat Stands Nos.53 & 54. Fred Allchorn applied for a Boat Stand opposite West Rocks Hotel but it was not granted. George E Erridge granted No.58 as a Boat Stand for his Motor Boat 'Unique'.

August 1913.

Boatman Henry Sayers said he proposed to buy two Motor Boats. In this event, would the Committee grant licences? Deferred but later granted in September providing the Boats passed the relevant tests.

Miss Adams requested to place 3 notices on the Parades advertising a sale of work on behalf of the Fishermen's Institute. Denied by the Committee.

Collection of foreshore rents and Pleasure Boat Licences etc. The late Inspector Walls received £5 per season for collecting the above, the same to be paid to his successor Inspector Dann.

Chapter Four

1914 ~ 1932

January 1914.

Renewal applications from Mike Hardy and Ben Hide for Motor Boat Licences were both granted. It was agreed that the total 1st class Waterman/Boatman Licences issued be raised from 68 to 80 (a sign of a booming boating business). A first time 1st class Waterman Licence was issued to W McCormick.

Space on the beach was at a premium due to the many thousands of visitors coming to Eastbourne during the summer months. To accommodate them with deck chairs and to increase revenue for the Council run department, the Watch Committee had held meetings and eventually proposed to alter the Boat Stands and to completely remove some from the Grand Parade. Word got out to the Boatmen and as a result they, along with the Fishermen, formed a Society in January 1914 to fight these proposals. But more of that later.

The Committee recommended the following alterations to Boat Stands between the Wish Tower and the Pier: -

Firstly, that Boat Stand Nos.1, 2, & 3 belonging to John & Edward Hide, be placed between groyne Nos.33 & 34 instead of 34 & 35.
Boat Stand Nos.29, 30 & 31 be let to George Hide (son of 'Pincher').
Boat Stand Nos.32 & 33 to William Allchorn Snr.
Boat Stand Nos.46, 47, 48 & 49 to Mike Hardy.
Boat Stand No.50 to Harry Sayers.
Boat Stand No.51 to William Sayers.
Boat Stand Nos.67 & 68 to Jack Sayers.
Boat Stand Nos.71 & 72 to Mrs. Hide (widow of 'Pincher') and that Boat Stand Nos.34, 35, 52 - 56, 64, 69, 70, 73, 74, 79 & 80 be withdrawn.

Were the above the favoured few? Certainly they were from the old established Eastbourne Seafaring community, but there were others who were being moved off the Grand Parade and this would not do. The Society formed in January presented a united front against these proposals and in March, led by George Gausden, Albert 'Tuppy' Sayers and others, a meeting was held with the Watch Committee. The meeting became somewhat heated resulting in the Chairman, Alderman Duke and Alderman Rowe tendering their resignations - but nevertheless decisions were made between the Boatmen and the Committee. The month of May came and the following Boat Stand sites were agreed upon: -

Boat Stand Nos.1, 2 & 3 to remain between groyne Nos.34 & 35.

Albert Sayers was to retain Boat Stand No.69 on the understanding that if the Council needed to place deck chairs on it, they would.

Jack Sayers to use Boat Stand Nos.70 & 71 and to give up Nos.67 & 68. Mrs. Hide also to use Boat Stand Nos.72 & 73.

Notices to quit the following Boat Stands were withdrawn: -
Nos.29, 30, 31, 32 & 33 Mrs. Hide widow of George 'Pincher' Hide.
Nos.34 & 35 Mr. William Allchorn.
Nos.46 - 50 Mr. Michael Hardy.
Nos.51 & 52 Harry Sayers.
No.53 William Sayers.
No.64 Ben Bates.
No.79 Henry Matthews.

It was agreed that Boat Stands be withdrawn: -
No.54 William Sayers.
No.56 Thomas Boniface Snr.
No.63 Ben Bates.
Nos.67 & 68 Jack Sayers.
No.74 George Huggett.
No.80 Mike Hardy.

All private boats were to be placed on Boat Stand Nos.81 & 82 (Previously they had been allowed all along the Parades on various Boatmen's stands).

The above gives an idea of some but not all of the Pleasure Boat operators along the Grand Parade. Those Boatmen not affected by the alterations are not mentioned in the Watch Committee minutes. What a pity the foreshore plans are missing, they could help so much in identifying where the Boat Stands were in relation to their position along the Parade and of course marry up with the many photographs that exist of the Boats and Boatmen.

May 1914.

Boatmen William and Henry Allchorn were reported for shouting (touting) on the Parades and brought before the Committee and cautioned. Mike Hardy requested use Boat Stand No.49 as a Capstan. It was agreed and in June when he made a Motor Boat application for the 'Estella' it transpired that he had already obtained a licence from the Board of Trade therefore a second licence from Eastbourne Council was not needed. Jeffrey Allchorn was reported for continuously shouting on the Parades - He was cautioned.

The aforementioned problems between the Council and the Boatmen over the loss and moving of Boat Stands on the Grand Parade brought the Fishing/Boating fraternity together. United they formed the Eastbourne Fishermen's and Boatmen's Protection Society. The following explains it: -

From 1903 the Boatmen and Fishermen of Eastbourne had no Society to represent them. Previously for many years from 1839, the 'Eastbourne Fishermen's Compensation Fund Society' had represented their needs, but in 1903 this Society was disbanded.

1914 saw a solidarity meeting of the Boating and Fishing fraternity over a potential problem for the Boatmen. On Tuesday night 27th January, they met in the Beach Hotel to consider the proposal by the Town Council to alter the Boat Stands on the Grand Parade. Among those present were George Gausden boat builder, Ted Sayers, William Allchorn, John Hide Snr. & Jnr. William Simpson, Alleyn Sayers, Tom Swain, Ted Allchorn, John Hurd, Mike Hardy Snr. & Jnr. Tim Erridge, Henry Matthews, William Boniface, Penfold and others.

George Gausden was elected to chair the meeting. He told the Boatmen that the Council was considering moving some of the Grand Parade Boatmen east of the Pier. On a motion proposed by Alleyn Sayers, seconded by William Allchorn, it was agreed that a petition be raised to present to the Council but one further proposal was the all important resolution to form the 'Eastbourne Fishermen's and Boatmen's Protection Society'. It was duly formed and is still in existence to this day (known by the initials. E.F.B.P.Society). Officers of the Society elected at that first meeting were: -

President. Charles Jewell.
Chairman. Arthur Sayers.
Hon. Secretary. J Godden.
Hon. Treasurer. Henry Boniface.

With regard to the above some alterations were made but only with the agreement of the Boatmen and no Boatmen were moved to east of the Pier, honour being satisfied on both sides.

August 1914.

With the outbreak of War in August, a 'War Watch Committee' was formed. From 11pm on Tuesday 4th August 1914, a state of War existed between Great Britain and Germany and many Eastbourne Fishermen and Boatmen, members of the local Royal Naval Volunteer Reserve enlisted to serve their country

March 1915.

Fisherman/Boatman John 'Foot' Prodger saw the enemy at close hand. He was about 2 miles off Eastbourne tending to his whelk pots when a German submarine surfaced near him but made no attempt to molest him. He made his way quickly to shore and informed the Authorities. Prior to that incident there had been a lot of enemy submarine activity. The ship 'Branksome Chine' had been torpedoed off Beachy Head and the Eastbourne Lifeboat 'James Stevens No.6' attended to find that the crew of the attacked ship had been taken off by another vessel. Next day the 'Western Coast' was torpedoed off Eastbourne. Again, vessels in the vicinity had taken off the surviving crew. One up for us though - the captain of the steam ship 'Thordis' bound from Blyth to Plymouth, claimed to have sunk a German submarine off Beachy Head at the time of all the activity. His ships log entry told the following tale; '*8 miles off Beachy Head was seen the periscope of a submarine on the starboard bow. The submarine crossed his bow and took up a position forty yards off. The wake of a torpedo was seen and the helm was put hard over to starboard. It missed and the 'Thordis' ran over the periscope, there was a crash, and he saw no more of the submarine.*' - Well done the British Seamen.

Boatman Jesse Huggett Jnr. also witnessed the sinking of a ship. It was about 4pm in the afternoon; Jesse was on the Royal Parade beach with his Pleasure Motor Boat

'Royal Sovereign'. Looking through his binoculars he saw two steamers going eastwards when one blew up, a great cloud of steam and smoke ascending. He immediately put off in his Motor Boat with a crew of James Novis, Andrew Chester and Percy Jessop. They arrived about seven miles off where the steamer had blown up and spoke to the skipper of a Ramsgate trawler who told them that crew of the stricken ship had been picked up. Jesse Huggett and his crew must be admired for their courage - without a thought for their own safety they immediately put to sea to give assistance and hopefully save lives. They had no protection themselves just a wooden Motor Boat. That was the way of seafaring men. The Lifeboat had also been launched and Huggett met her as they returned to shore and told the Cox'n that the crew of the sunken ship were safe. (The Lifeboat returned with them.)

At 3pm on Sunday 21st March 1915, a German submarine struck again off Eastbourne sinking the steamer 'Cairntorr'. The Coastguard Station in Latimer Road was advised and they contacted the Lifeboat House. Double maroons were set off and the 'James Stevens No.6' was quickly launched under Coxswain Tim Erridge. The experience of William 'Laddie' Simpson, 2nd.Coxswain, is worth mentioning. Laddie was on the Parade west of the Pier with his wife Maria tending the family Bathing Machines and Pleasure Boats. Anxious to join his comrades, Laddie hired a taxicab and sped to the Lifeboat House. But to no avail as the Lifeboat was already on her way. On this occasion the Lifeboat had acquired the services of the Hardy family's Motor Boat 'Estella' to tow her to the sinking ship. Interestingly the Motor Boat 'Estella' is shown on a post card dated July 1915. (The sender writes *"The town is in darkness after 9 'o' clock not a street lamp alight"*) The Lifeboat with the Motor Boat arrived at the scene of the sinking and took aboard 18 crew members of the 'Cairntorr' and brought them ashore at the Fishing Station. Later they were boarded at the Albion & Albermarle Hotels and shown the greatest kindness by the Shipwrecked Mariners Society, being fed and clothed as the poor men had only what they stood in. Well done the crews of 'Estella' and the Lifeboat.

April 1915.

The fact that England was at War did nothing to deter the visitors and day-trippers to Eastbourne. Eastertide 1915 saw a large influx. On the Wednesday before, 1,000 visitors arrived at the Railway Station, on Thursday there were ten extra trains and on Saturday 2,000 passengers arrived plus normal traffic. The weather being inclement kept the numbers down! Hopefully the Boatmen had a good Easter.

July 1916.

The War certainly did not deter life on the beach. July saw a Mr. E Penney being given permission to leave his private Motor Boat on the Boat Stand belonging to John Hide, opposite Howard Square. (After the Committee had banned all private boats to Stand Nos.80 & 81.)

November 1916.

Boatman Edward Hide gave up his Boat Stand Nos.1 & 2 and at the age of 40 years enlisted in the Royal Navy for the duration of the War, as did many Eastbourne Boatmen of that age.

War Losses.

From 1914 onwards there of course came back the reports from the War fronts of our losses. Brave Eastbourne men of the three services losing their lives.

May and June 1915, saw the fruitless assaults on the Dardenelles in Turkey, where so many lives were laid down in the fighting for King & Country. Many of the Boating/Fishing fraternity paid the ultimate sacrifice, in particular those serving with the Royal Naval Division made up of: -

1st Royal Naval Brigade. 1st Bn. Drake. 2nd Bn. Hawke. 3rd Bn. Benbow. 4th Bn. Collingwood.
2nd Royal Naval Brigade. 5th Bn. Nelson. 6th Bn. Howe. 7th Bn. Hood. 8th Bn. Anson.
Great names from Naval history.

The Eastbourne men served mainly in the Howe, Hood and Collingwood Battalions. The Royal Naval Division was the brainchild of Winston Churchill, then First Lord of the Admiralty. There being a surfeit of volunteers for the Royal Navy and sea going ships being fully manned, it was decided to have a land fighting force of sailors. The Prime Minister at the time Mr. Asquith (his son served with distinction with the Naval Division) christened it "Winston's Little Army". Some famous names associated with it were the New Zealander, later General, Bernard Freyberg V.C. and the poet Rupert Brooke of Hood Battalion.

Of those Eastbourne men who had been serving with the Howe, Hood and Collingwood Battalions some were killed or missing in action going ashore as an Infantry Brigade.

A report in June 1915 of the attacks showed missing believed killed: -
Able Seaman George William Allchorn son of William Allchorn.
Leading Seaman Tom Hide, son of William Bollard Hide.
Leading Seaman W Diplock, son of Harry Diplock.
Able Seaman Luke John Hardy, son of Mike Hardy.
Able Seaman E Hunt, of Hydnye Street.

Leading Seaman Ernest Sayers, one of three sons of Ted Sayers, had been wounded.

Able Seaman Sydney Hide, son of Samuel Hide, died of wounds two days after the June attack, fighting with the Collingwood Battalion.

There were many more as the months went by and wounded servicemen began arriving in the town for convalescence and treatment. An Eastbourne postcard dated October 1915 stated *'Eastbourne is full of wounded soldiers, 3,000 here they say'*.

The Fishermen & Boatmen of Eastbourne stood the name of Sussex in good stead. Reports of their fighting abilities and courage under fire was read of by the people of Eastbourne in the local newspapers. Graphic stories of their heroism sent home in letters were read, eyewitness reports by Able Seaman Fred Hurd Jnr. local Boatmen and Fisherman, Howe Battalion, of the fighting at Gallipoli. Fred survived the War. How sad really, death was commonplace and on reflection what a waste of young lives, but that was how it was in those days. It is well worth taking the time to read the local papers for the War years. Reports of the Royal Sussex Regiment, Royal Naval Division, Royal Navy and other branches of the Services, they are all there. Sad stories of families losing not one, but several members.

The War did not stop Pleasure Boating or Fishing.

Fishing was restricted to daylight hours only in an area within a line drawn from Beachy Head to the Royal Sovereign Lightship, thence to Dungeness, thence to the North Folkestone Gate Lightship and from there to Folkestone Pier. With the able bodied men away, it was left to the older generation to carry on fishing and boating.

The War Watch Committee.

There is little to glean from the War Watch Committee minutes for the War years but what was found is as follows:

March 1916.

Boatman Tom Boniface was granted a Motor Boat Drivers Licence.

July 1916.

Boatman Fred Hurd Snr. applied for a licence as a steersman on a Motor Boat. The licence was granted subject to the condition that he was accompanied by a 1st class Waterman/Boatman when acting as a steersman. Hurd did not have a 1st class Licence, so regulations were strictly adhered to, as they should have been. It was most important that Pleasure Boats had a competent 1st class Boatman in charge.

May 1917.

R Bennett was given temporary permission to act as steersman in Mike Hardy's Motor Boat 'Estella'.

An interesting Government order of the War was the prevention of men over military age and also men rejected for military service from earning their living as Pleasure Boatmen unless they were boat owners. Although the Watch Committee had no jurisdiction over this order, the Committee at the suggestion of the Parade Inspector decided that Boatmen aged between 16 - 60 years, unless they owned Pleasure Boats, and not allowed to engage in 'Pleasuring'. They should nevertheless have their licences granted without payment. Then at least they could receive their licences regularly without having to forego them and have to reapply at the end of the War.

April 1918.

The Committee refused to grant a Waterman/Boatman Licence to Harry Hardy due to his extreme youth.

November 1918.

Come November 11th with the end of hostilities those members of Eastbourne's Fishing and Boating fraternity who survived, returned from their military service to pick up their lives again.

July 1919.

First time 1st class Waterman Licences were issued to James Hardy, James Boniface and George Boniface and 2nd class to Fred Erridge. Henry Boniface was granted Boat Stand No.20 on Grand Parade.

That year the Town Council held Peace celebrations on 17th July with a Regatta being part of the celebrations. Rowing, sailing and swimming were among events well supported by the local Fishermen and Boatman as well as an evening illuminated boat procession watched by thousands that lined the promenade. The boats were all prettily decorated most with Chinese lanterns. There were twelve boats in two sections of six drawn by Motor Boats lent by Ted Sayers. The winner for best-decorated boat was Fisherman Albert Addington. The procession went from opposite the Burlington Hotel to the Wish Tower and back. Then a mimic battle took place with fireworks - altogether a fine show. The organizers were Mr. W Ashdown and Ted Sayers.

September 1919.

A Boat Stand application received from Lucas Hide (on return from War service) for tenancy of Boat Stand Nos.29, 30, 31, 32 & 33 and to convert 32 & 33 into Capstans was granted. Luke a son of 'Pincher' Hide was picking up the family livelihood again.

There was an application by John 'Foot' Joseph Prodger of the old Eastbourne seafaring family, for Capstan Stand No.63 on the Royal Parade where the family operated Pleasure Boats between the Wars 1919-1939. The application was granted.

That same month the Council decided to take over ownership of all Bathing Machines operating on the beach - compensation to be paid to all active proprietors. Mrs. Elizabeth Hide had some 13 Machines that had not been operated through the War years owing to her son Thomas joining the Royal Navy in 1914, and being killed at Gallipoli in 1915. As she had not been operating the Council proposed to pay her less compensation. She complained and rightly so, that without her son she could not operate. The Council reconsidered and did pay but still on a lesser scale to other operators. The era of horse drawn Machines had gone and by 1922 the Council placed static machines and Bathing Stations established whereby opposite genders had their own changing areas with some behind canvas.

The No.1 Bathing Station situated east of the Redoubt continued until 1957 when the Council due to the 'mackintosh bathing' changing on the beach closed it. The No.2 static Bathing Station east of the Wish Tower stayed open and is still in operation today. Spare a thought for the fine Bathing Machine horses, commandeered by the War Department in 1914. Most never survived the War dying on the Western front. The late Fred Erridge related that their three Bathing Machine horses, Big Prince, Polly and Kronig were taken in 1914 but sadly never returned.

February 1920.

The Chief Constable reported to the Committee that Albert 'Sam' Allchorn (of the William Allchorn family) had applied for a 1st class Waterman Licence. *"He is only 22 years old, however, I ask for your directions?"* The Committee resolved there and then that the age to qualify for a 1st class Waterman Licence (Motor Boat only) be reduced from 25 to 21 years - Granted. (In previous years the Boatmen of Eastbourne had to serve a long apprenticeship as a 2nd class Boatman, as in general they came from the seafaring community and started at an early age on the beach.)

June 1920.

Meetings were held about an amendment to Pleasure Boat Bye-Laws to cover Pleasure Motor Boats and in June it became law.

A request by Tom Boniface to convert Boat Stand No.22 to a Capstan was granted.

(As the heavier Motor Boats were taken up, so more Capstans were applied for.)

Mr. W Strange Jones was allowed to keep a private boat on the beach at Holywell Retreat for 2/6d rent per year.

As the War was over the seafront became a peacetime environment again although it had remained open and busy during those years. The paddle steamer trips resumed from the Pier head in May 1920, after a break of six years - renewed competition for the Boatmen?

1921.

Over the coming years there was much interchanging of Boat and Capstan Stands between Boatmen and the usual applications for Licences. These early inter War years appear to have been a busy period for the Pleasure Boatmen and they saw the complete take over from sail to motor, whilst Row Boating continued with a fair calling for their use.

January 1921.

Fred 'Tinker' Novis was granted Boat Stand Nos.56 & 57 on Marine/ Royal Parade for 8 Pleasure Rowboats. 'Tinker' is said to have got his nickname from an ancestor Thomas Novis, who is recorded in the 1650 Parish records as a mettle man (a tinker). A well-known character as a Lifeboat man, Fisherman and Boatman, 'Tinker' operated his boats from the Marine Parade stand for many years and after the 2nd World War with his boat 'Waverley' built by Richard Lower of Newhaven. Indeed Godfrey Wynn journalist, in 1951 wrote an article in the 'Fair Country' magazine. Quote *"Fred Novis like all old salts has a tale to tell. A landmark on the beach with his fleet of Pleasure Boats. Fred tells that he can teach young ladies to row in 20 minutes. Being a charmer, one day a customer tore his trouser's seat on a nail in 'Tinkers' boat. Not a problem sir and took the customer across to a boarding house where the friendly landlady sewed up the trousers seat with the*

customer in situ. It being a Sunday and no tailors' shops were open. She saved his life that day. A brave man is 'Tinker' being machined gunned and wounded during the 2nd War while out in his fishing boat."

February 1921.

Henry Boniface and L Argles were given permission for 2 Capstan Stands on Marine Parade,

Boatman Fred 'Tinker' Novis, Marine Parade 1930. Row Boat to winter quarters.

opposite the 'Sandon Boarding House' and Boniface to transfer his Boats & Crab ('A'frame windlass) from Boat Stand No.22 to No.4 Grand Parade. Boatman Jack Tuxford's application for Capstan Stand No.63 to transfer to him from Jack Prodger and vacant Boat Stand Nos.85 & 86 to Jack Prodger were granted.

J. J. PRODGER & SONS,
LICENSED BOATMEN
Nos. 59, 65, 146.
Motor Yachts CHILDREN'S FRIEND and OCEAN'S GIFT.

Private and Fishing Parties
CATERED FOR.

Stands : ROYAL PARADE, near Redoubt.

Private Address :

35 SEAFORD ROAD :: EASTBOURNE

Royal Parade Boatmen.

Boat Stand applications were received from Jack Sayers and Mike 'Jersey' Hardy. The former asked for the transfer of Boat Stand Nos.67 & 68 from Hardy and Boat Stand Nos.70 & 71 from Sayers to Hardy. This was granted.

The Pleasure Grounds Committee considered all the above applications, as was now the case. They then advised the Watch Committee of their findings.

In his annual report the Chief Constable told the Watch Committee that the number of 1st class Waterman/Boatman Licences issued should be raised to 100. This was agreed. It appears that 'Pleasuring' after the War was good or could it be said employment was scarce and many tried their hand at Pleasuring with large numbers of visitors coming to the town?

September 1921.

Sayers Bros. application for an additional 'Crab' (windlass) for Stand No.38 on Grand Parade was granted.

Several applications for Motor Boat Licences by non- residents were not granted.

Boatman Harry R Tyrrell was given permission to place his boat upon the Stand occupied by Albert Sayers subject to an annual acknowledgement of 2/6d.

The Prodger Family

Boatman John 'Foot' Prodger was granted Capstan Stand Nos.83 & 84 at Royal Parade to go along with previously granted Stand Nos.85 & 86. So continued an association with Royal Parade along with his sons Harry and Jack Jnr. that took them through to the late 1930s with their Pleasure Boats 'Children's Friend' and 'Oceans Gift'. ('Oceans Gift' was used regularly during the winter months

Boatman Harry Prodger.

Prodger Boatman Hat Tally.

Royal Parade Boatmen. Left - right. John 'Foot' Prodger, Fred Hurd? George Prodger, John 'Jack' Prodger. C.1930.

to carry on the family calling of fishing). Son Harry tragically lost his life in 1932 due to a motorcycle accident. With the coming of World War II the family ceased to 'Pleasure' and surviving son Jack Jnr. carried on fishing for many years until selling his Net Shop. But he did not retire from the beach, he was still a regular at the Fishing Station, lending a hand and making trawl nets for the younger generation of Fishermen. His skill and knowledge of his calling were passed on to the new generation and he could be seen on the beach not long before his death aged 90 years in 1996. From the extended Prodger family of Eastbourne Jack - as his forebears had done, served on the Eastbourne Lifeboat. His Grandfather John 'Kruger' was a crew member during the famous life saving exploit in 1883, when the Lifeboat 'William & Mary' was hauled overland to Birling Gap and launched to save the lives of the crew of the 'New Brunswick'. 'Kruger's' son John 'Foot' also served the local community when in April 1900, he and two others went to the assistance of two police officers who were dealing with what can only be described as a 'riot'. Overwhelmed, the officers

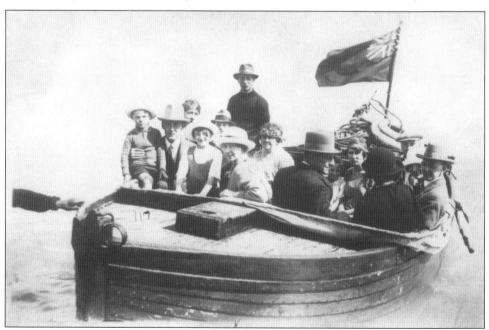

Prodger Pleasure Boat 'Children's Friend' - 'Jack' Prodger standing centre. C.1930.

were hard put and but for the intervention of 'Foot' could well have suffered serious injury from an ugly crowd of some two hundred rioters outside the Railway Station. Stepping in to assist in the arrest of the ringleaders 'Foot' Prodger and the two other men had their bravery recognised by the presentation each of a suitably engraved silver topped cane walking stick from the grateful police.

Tyrrell Pleasure Boat Royal Parade C.1890.

Interestingly 'Kruger', son 'Foot' and Jack Jnr. were all christened John Joseph. The Prodger family go back in Eastbourne to the very early days, no doubt associated with smuggling and the like, carrying with them nicknames 'Flummy' 'Juicy' and 'Crickets' to name some later Prodgers'.

March 1922.

The Watch Committee discussed Motor Boat adverts. A growing tendency among Motor Boat owners to increase their number of 'notice boards' advertising trips and fishing excursions on the Parades was causing problems to the free passage of promenaders. The Parade Inspector was instructed that one board per operator would suffice.

An application by Fred 'Tinker' Novis for Capstan Stand No.55 was granted.

It was also in March that F Jessup (Jessop) was granted Boat Stand Licences to share Nos.1, 2 & 3 on the Grand Parade opposite Howard Square. These particular Boat Stands had been operated by a branch of the Hide family from the 1840's prior to the development of Grand Parade C.1860, then held by George and later his son John Hide and later vacated in 1925 by Boatman Edward 'Ted' Hide son of John. 'Ted' carried on with his fishing occupation, and retained his Boatman Licence and was active at the family Boat Stand site assisting Harry 'Early Doors' Allchorn, who ran the Rowboat Stand, (Jessup having given up), up to the 2nd World War. Ted's Rowboats were sold in 1925 - some to William Allchorn and some went up to St.Neots where they were employed as riverboats. The Pleasure sailboat 'Bill Bailey', built as a sprat boat, was kept and used for fishing by 'Ted' through to the mid 1930s.

The 'Hides', Fishermen to a man from very early days in Eastbourne, took to 'Pleasuring' and Bathing Machines back in the 1780's at the Sea Houses and Marine Parade. Indeed, John the father of the above George, in 1816 also became 'letter receiver' (Post Office) for Sea Houses.

In 1913, two old Eastbourne Boatmen were interviewed and their tales reported in the local paper. The following gives us an insight into those early days on the seafront: -

Grand Parade Boatmen with Hide Pleasure Boat 'Bill Bailey'. Edward 'Ted' Hide second from right. John Hide extreme right 1913.

"If you walk east from the famous Wish Tower along the bottom Parade at Eastbourne, you will almost at once come across two of the oldest Boatmen still working in any seaside place.

Their names are John Hide and Dennis Breach, and it is easy to pick them out. Hide, whose number is 13, wears a black bowler hat over his thick, curly white hair, his face is fringed with white whiskers, and his person is 'round'. Breach, who is short and spare, is clean-shaven, and wears his registered number 5 on the band of his straw hat.

To look at them you would not think their combined ages total 150 years, but they do - or that they have been 'boating' as they call it, at Eastbourne for 115 years between them, but they have.

John Hide, who is seventy six, two years older than his friendly rival Breach, first started telling people that it was 'a nice day for a boat, sir,' in the year the Crimean War began, 1854, and he has gone on doing so ever since.

Boatmen father and son. Edward 'Ted' Hide and John Hide 1912.

"I've never missed a summer," he told me - and for a man of his age his memory is excellent and his vitality is remarkable - Hide said, "but boating is not what it used to be". "I'll tell you why. The present generation is soft and slack. Compared with my Grandfather and father, the young man of today has not got much 'go'. Once upon a time gentlemen used to come down at seven and eight 'o' clock in the morning and go for a row or else fishing. Now a days there's none of that. Why, now the young people haven't got up from breakfast much before ten. They waste half the morning in bed, and haven't got time for boating. Besides there are more amusements at the seaside in these days."

"The best year I ever remember having was 1894. King Edward was down at Eastbourne then, and March was as good to us as August that season. No, he never went boating himself, but I've taken out some

Grand Parade Boatmen. Left Edward 'Ted' Hide other unknown 1900.

swells in my time."

"There were the Queen of Greece's children, for instance. Her majesty spent several summers with her family in Eastbourne, and they were always down on the beach. She used to sit against one of the breakwaters while they bathed or went for a row, and she always had a smile and a pleasant 'good morning' for you."

"No, I never expected them to pay more than anyone else. Why should I? Our prices are fixed by the Corporation - eighteen pence an hour without a Boatman, two shillings an hour with one; and that's what they paid me."

Dennis Breach, who became a Waterman in 1857, had a rather more 'intimate' experience to tell me of how he took Princess Royal (the present Empress of Germany's mother) for a row.

"Coming back we landed on some rocks, and there was nothing for it but to carry the Princess ashore. She 'had' her arm round my neck but didn't kiss me!"

Both Hide and Breach are natives of Eastbourne, but whereas the latter was 'something of a traveller' before he became a Boatman, having lived in Cornwall and Devon for a time and also been a North Sea fisherman, the former has rarely been away from the town, except on fishing expeditions.

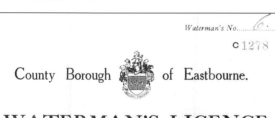

'Waterman's (Boatman's) Licence 1st class, issued in 1939 to Edward 'Ted' Hide aged 64years.

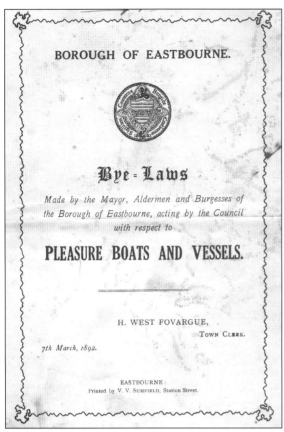

BOROUGH OF EASTBOURNE.

Bye=Laws

Made by the Mayor, Aldermen and Burgesses of the Borough of Eastbourne, acting by the Council with respect to

PLEASURE BOATS AND VESSELS.

H. WEST FOVARGUE,
Town Clerk.

7th March, 1892.

EASTBOURNE:
Printed by V. V. SUMFIELD, Station Street.

Pleasure Boats Bye-Laws issued 1892.

Almost on the spot where they now stand looking for custom, Jenny Lind the world famous Opera singer called the Swedish Nightingale, used to have a cottage called Cliff Cottage built by Mr. White, carpenter & builder of South Street. "She used to sing indoors with the windows open," Hide told me, "and many is the time I've stood outside and listened to her. I knew she was a great actress, and I reckon hearing her sing was about the best free entertainment you could want."

When the two Boatmen first started they had two boats apiece and there were only eight other Boatmen on the front. Now they have twenty-two boats between them and there are about 108 Licenced Waterman on the Parades. All their boats are named, one of Hide's being called 'Bill Bailey'- because, as he laughed, 'she always comes home'.

John Hide and Dennis Breach took part in the first Regatta ever held in Eastbourne, and it is a coincidence that the former finished first, the latter second in their race" John Hide married Fanny Coppard of Holywell House, (pronunciation Hollywell) Meads in 1866, and from 1870 took over the licence and later purchased the freehold of the 'Pilot Inn' Meads. He ran this successfully along with his Fishing and Pleasure Boating interests until 1901 when he sold the 'Pilot Inn' but still kept an interest in fishing and boating until his death in 1918.

March 1922.

The increase of Pleasure Motor Boats, were showed in the Committee reports, namely: -

Motor Boat renewal licences were issued to 1st class Waterman. Nos.3, 67, 69, 114, 120, 142, 167 & 216 and 2nd class Waterman Nos.87 & 117. Also two new Motor Boat Driver Licences were issued.

April 1922.

The Pleasure Boating season was already in full swing according to 'Non Aquatic' writing in the local paper. He complained about the touting by Boatmen from St. Aubyns Road to the Wish Tower where there is one continuous line of touting

Boatmen calling 'a jolly day for a row, sir' or 'have a trip in the prettiest craft in Eastbourne'. This person called on the Council to make it a proviso of their licence that they do not tout. Well, this showed that the seafront was busy and hopefully the Boatmen were doing good business.

The foregoing complaint brought forth several letters to the local paper in defence of the Boatmen. High praises were sung of them *'they are an attraction to Eastbourne. They are very civil and polite, they are part of the seafront scene.'*

The Licenced Boatmen of Grand Parade wrote a witty response *'as pore Boatmen wot as had is day on the Eastbourne front for donkies years and coz fathers as been brawt up in Eastbourne ever since it wos a little village and coz fammly as catered for Eastbourne anual visitors with lettin them as our boats to injoy thereselse on the watter and get good elth and good boats too'* etc, so it went on in a witty way ending by suggesting that 'Non Aquatic' go camp on the top of 'Snowdon' to get away from the world. Another writer said, *"There was much value in the Boatmen, they add charm to the front and over the years have been on hand to save many a person from drowning"*.

May 1922.

Motor Boat Licences were granted to Watermen Nos.146, 74, 61, 125 & 192.

Rowboat Licence to No.134 and 1st class Waterman Licences to Nos.21 & 71 - All granted. Further additions continued through the season, plus 2 Motor Boat and 5 Rowboat Licences issued.

June 1922.

The Town Clerk and Watch Committee chairman met Mr. A C Forman, solicitor for the Eastbourne Fishermen & Boatmen's Protection Society and 3 representatives of the Boatmen. The problem was the current Boat Stands & Capstan Stand Agreements. In a number of cases the occupiers had not signed them on the grounds that in their present form the agreement did not give security of tenure. Mr. Forman raised objections to the Capstan Agreement. It was agreed that the Agreement should provide for the removal of the Capstan itself and any other property or thing attached thereto only, in lieu of the words "and any other property or thing erected or placed by the occupier thereon" at present contained in the agreement.

Of the Boat Stand Agreements, Mr. Forman stated that as the Boatmen have to be licenced each year by the Watch Committee before they can ply for hire, it would meet his objections if the Agreements were made so as to run concurrently with the individual Boatman's Licence. This action was approved. (All Boatman Licences issued, always ran to expire 1st April every year)

With regard to the Capstan Agreements, it appears not only on the non-payment of rent the Capstan could be removed, but other property belonging to the occupier. The Council also omitted from this new Agreement on payment of rent the following words " that the occupier shall be undisturbed in his possession of the site and shall be at liberty to transfer his interest in the same under the agreement to any party or parties, subject to the approval in writing of the Corporation" which had been contained in all previous agreements.

An application by Boatman John 'Foot' Prodger to have railings cut at his Capstan

No.85 on the Royal Parade was granted. Messrs. Hardy Bros. made a similar application for Capstan Nos.70 & 71 but this was not granted.

With the Royal Parade having railings along its length, difficulty was experienced gaining access to Capstan and Boat Stands. Prodger seems to have set a precedent to some degree as after his application several more Royal Parade Boatmen applied for 'rail cuts' as their applications read. Some successful - some not. Fred Hurd's application for a Boat Stand at present belonging to Mike Hardy was granted.

July 1922.

The modern day surfers are really nothing new. Back in 1922, the Boatmen of Eastbourne were surf running ('Hooker running' as it was known to the Boating fraternity) in there skiffs (Rowboats) and had done so for years. When the weather was too rough for boating they would 'Hooker run' when the tide and wind created the rollers that made it possible. Thrilling the crowd going out and riding in on the crest of the rollers. It must have been quite exciting to watch and an excellent way for the Boatmen to raise money for the local Leaf Homeopathic Hospital in Marine Road. On Thursday 6th July, Boatmen Alleyn Sayers Jnr. Harry Boniface Jnr. Fred Hurd, Joe Boniface and Albert Wood took part in 'Hooker running' entertaining a large crowd by their antics. On the promenade with collecting boxes were ladies Miss Orpin, Miss Hoadey and Boatmen Bill Sayers, Jack Elms, Tom Harris and Bill Wood. £5.12s.8d was collected and thankfully received by the Matron.

August 1922.

Messrs. Sayers of Grand Parade on the evening of 15th August hired the rowing boat 'Widgeon No.66' to a lone Scottish man. He offered to pay for the hire but was declined by Sayers as the normal practice was to pay on return. As it turned out they never got payment. The man failed to return and after several days fruitless searching of the Channel the boat was found empty by a passing steamer and taken into Plymouth. The body of the man was discovered two weeks later washed ashore at Bexhill, having committed suicide by drowning. So Sayers got no money for the hire and had the expense of getting their boat back from Plymouth.

March 1923.

Tom Sisk, boat builder, was given permission for 2 Boat Stands on the beach. Nos.48 & 49, temporary only. Boatman Lucas Hide made application to cut railings opposite the Pier steps to help him pull up boats during long tides. This was granted. William Allchorn made application for permission to have a Capstan upon his Boat Stand No.34, Victoria steps. Also granted.

May 1923.

A proposal (which was subsequently turned down) by Mr. Argles to form a Yacht Club on Boat Stand Nos.1, 2 & 3 opposite Howard Square.

June 1923.

Boatman Henry Boniface made a request to operate new leased Motor Launches 'Kohinor' and 'Royal Sovereign' carrying 89 passengers each. It appears that the Council advised the Board of Trade, for they received notification back by telegram. It stated that the Motor Boats may ply for hire during daylight hours and fine weather between and from Eastbourne to Beachy Head and Pevensey and Hastings, keeping within the three-mile limit. Passenger certificates were issued by the B.O.T on the understanding that the Parade Inspector exercised supervision and prevented plying for hire during unsuitable weather conditions and ensuring all conditions on the certificates were complied with. Safety being paramount then as these days with the Pleasure Boats. The coming of the big motorised boats was in its infancy and needed monitoring.

Boniface family Motor Pleasure Boats. 'Royal Sovereign' and 'Kohinor' C.1920.

Later that year the Committee met a deputation of Boatmen from the E.F.B.P. Society opposing the Board of Trade's directive that Eastbourne Licencing Authorities should fix, as regards boats licenced by them, the plying distance, which in no case should exceed 3 miles from starting

point. This incensed the local Boatmen who licenced their smaller boats with the Council and after much discussion they won the day. Beachy Head lighthouse trips over three miles?

'Railing Cut' - Samuel Hurd applied to have rails cut upon the Royal Parade for convenience of Boat Stand No.75. Granted subject only to being replaced at any time. John 'Foot' Prodger applied for Capstan Stand No.82 at Royal Parade, which was granted. In August, Mike Hardy again requested to cut the rail on Royal Parade. This time agreed but to be replaced at the end of each season.

February 1924.

Willowfield School was given permission to place a boat for boys on John Prodger's Boat Stand at the Royal Parade.

March 1924.

A request to place a 'Pay Box' on the beach was granted to Henry Boniface. (The first recorded instance of a 'Pay Box' erected on a Grand Parade Boat Stand).

May 1924.

Transfer of Boat Stands & Capstan Stands - William Allchorn requested a transfer from Lucas Hide the present occupier, for Capstan Nos.32 & 33 and Boat Stand Nos.29, 30 & 31. This was granted (Previously occupied by George 'Pincher' Hide Lucas's father, up to 1910), as was Messrs. Sayers Bros. application for Boat Stand Nos.42 & 43 that had previously been occupied by Lucas Hide. (Groyne immediately west of the pier, so ending another Hide family association of Pleasure Boating going back to the 1780's.)

George Merrick Hide to give 'Pincher' his real name was born in 1840, the second son of George and Mary Ann Hide and younger brother to John Hide. A character on the beach and around the town during his lifetime, 'Pincher' was something of a businessman - A Fishing and Pleasure Boat owner, Bathing Machine operator,

1880. George 'Pincher' Hide - Boatman, Fisherman and Bathing Machine Operator.

1886. Grand Parade. 'Pincher' Hide and Paul Paul's Pleasure Boats and Bathing Machine Office opposite the Cavendish Hotel.

Pub landlord 'Anchor Tap' and for many years from 1880 Sussex Fisheries officer. Being married to Elizabeth Huggett, there were 9 children from the union. The elder daughter Mariah marrying William 'Laddie' Simpson of the Boat building, Fishing and Pleasure Boating fraternity.

So we see the expansion of the William Allchorn 'Pleasuring' business having acquired the above, given control of the beach immediately facing the Victoria Place steps. With Sayers Brothers acquiring the other Boat Stands of Lucas Hide, they now had possession of the two groynes immediately west of the pier.

Mike Hardy was granted Capstan Stand Nos.72 & 73 at Royal Parade.

'Pincher' Hide's Bathing Machine Office for Ladies and Children 1908.

'Pincher' Hide's Bathing Machines 1908.

The Hide Bathing Machines. Seated centre rear - Mariah Simpson (nee Hide) with daughter Olive. Standing right - Lucas Hide son of 'Pincher'.

Grand Parade in groyne immediately west of the Pier, the Hide Motor Pleasure Boat 'Spitfire'. Standing in boat Boatman William 'Laddie' Simpson C.1920. Sayers boat behind.

June 1923.

Sam Hurd was granted Boat Stand No.74 previously Mr. Tom Bennett's. Henry Boniface was granted Capstan Stand No.18 on the Grand Parade. As with the Allchorn and Sayers Pleasure Boat businesses so with Boniface, the need to expand and compete. These three boating families emerging as the foremost on Grand Parade.

July 1923.

A collision at sea occurred when a single sculler (Rowboat) was run into by a Motor Boat steered by Boatman Tom Boniface. No action was taken over the incident.

1924.

William Allchorn & Sons, Pleasure Boat proprietors in 1924 had in their employ a humorous Boatman named Fred Hurd. At the Allchorn Boat Stand he would daily write witty verse on a display board, one example being *'It takes 11 muscles of the face to smile, 32 to frown, so why waste energy? Keep smiling'*. Fred was for many years a well known Fisherman and Boatman, coming from the old Eastbourne family of that tradition. This was the Fred Hurd who served in the Royal Naval Division during the 1914-18 War and had written regularly to the local paper reporting his experiences. The above brings to mind the tale of an Eastbourne Boatman at sea in his Rowboat with two nervous ladies who were concerned about rocks. The Boatman assured them that he knew every rock, when at that very moment the boat struck a rock. He finished by saying *'and that's one of them!'*

January 1925.

Albert 'Tuppy' Sayers was granted a Boat Stand opposite the 'Sandon' Boarding

House 29a, Marine Parade. ('Tuppy' still going strong, a lifelong Fisherman/Boatman. He was a crew member of the Lifeboat 'William & Mary' that launched from Birling Gap in the famous rescue of the crew of the stranded ship 'New Brunswick' in 1883.)

February 1925.

Boatman Albert 'Sam' Allchorn the youngest son of William Allchorn was granted Boat Stand Nos.10, 11 & 12 on Grand Parade. As part of the Allchorn family business 'Sam' also had his own Rowboats and operated them from the above.

June 1925.

It was agreed by the Committee that Boatman Albert French could have Boat Stand Nos.1, 2 & 3 on the Grand Parade previously occupied by Frank Jessop. (Evidently the proposal of Mr. Argles back in May 1923 to form a Yacht Club on the stands never materialised.)

September 1925.

Boat Stand No.48 and Capstan Stand No.49 Marine Parade, were granted to Fred W Hurd. Ernest Sayers took over Boat Stand No.63 from Boatman Jack Tuxford.

The Committee paid £2.17s damages to Nelson Prodger for damage caused to his boat by the Police using it to recover a drifting Rowboat used in a suicide at sea in November. The recovered Rowboat belonged to Fred Hurd who offered to pay half of the damages to Prodger.

April 1926.

Reverend F B R Browne, headmaster of St. Andrews School, Meads was given permission to keep his sailing boat on the beach at Holywell Retreat.

May 1926.

Boatman Alleyn Sayers was granted permission to place a hut on the beach. Similar in size to a bathing cabin to keep fishing gear etc. instead of in boxes for Pleasure Boat fishing, on condition that he pay 1/- per year rent.

June 1926.

Tom Sisk Boat builder, made an application for 2 Boat Stands on the beach opposite Albermarle Hotel in lieu of his StandsNos.46 & 47 immediately east of the Pier being unsafe due to the shingle being washed away. The application was granted.

A new Motor Boat Driver Licence was granted to John 'Jack' Prodger, son of 'Foot' Prodger.

1 Rowboat Licence each granted to Tom Sisk and Harry Boniface.

July 1926.

Transfer from Tom Boniface to Henry Morgan Boniface of Boat Stand No.21 Grand Parade.

Licenced Boatman Alleyn Nelson Sayers was convicted of being drunk and was cautioned by the Committee.

Eastbourne Regatta September 1926.

The first Regatta to be held after the 1919 Peace Celebrations was held on Saturday, 4th September 1926. The weather was glorious but a stiff breeze made sailing difficult there being only two finishers in the sailing race. It also affected the swimming and rowing to some extent. Thousands of people watched from the beach, promenades and Pier. The stiff breeze and a strong current caused some excitement in the ladies single sculls. One competitor was carried some way out to sea and was brought back by the Committee's Motor Boat.

In the Motor Pleasure Boat race the passengers had quite a lively time and most had a good wetting in to the bargain. Although no close finishes in any of the races, interest was still maintained, especially in the events of the 'greasy pole' and 'mutton worry'. There was also the 'Tub' man Biddy Stonham from Hastings. The Regatta concluded at about 6 pm.

The Eastbourne Fishermen's and Boatmen's Protection Society were responsible for the running of the Regatta. Chairman of the Committee Mr. A Robertson, paid tribute to Mr. Arthur Sayers for making the event a success.

Results:

Single scull race. 'Sykes' Challenge Cup (Boys under 14).
1st N.Hurd.
2nd S Pratt.
3rd S Luck.

Others - R Jasper, L Dunn, T Garcia, F Crowhurst and C Page. Hurd won by a distance of ten lengths having taken the lead on turning the buoy.

Private Motor Boat Race. Eastbourne Pier Co. Ltd. Cup.
1st J Macfarlane in 'Gem'
2nd J Shipstone in 'Quest'
3rd A Couchman. Motor dinghy.

Winners time 57 mins. Only 1 min. difference in the first two boats home.

Boys 100 yards Swimming Race.
1st W Barnsley
2nd H King
3rd R Stevenson.

Waterman's Singles Scull Race. Mayor's Challenge Cup.
1st H M Boniface
2nd J Boniface
3rd E H Sayers.

Also competed F Novis, A F Brown, T Allchorn, W Sayers, E Sayers and H Hardy.

Competition was keen in this event. The winner pulled well throughout and won by 20 lengths. E H Sayers ought to have finished second but pulled up before he reached the finishing line, letting through his nearest opponent.

Amateur Sailing Race. Murray King Challenge Cup.
1st A Davis in 'Yvonne'

2nd A Wyatt in 'Stella'
Only two finished.

Others that started. L P Flude 'Saucy Jean', A Jones 'Water-Witch', W H Smith 'Maudelania', C Bond 'Friend of Mine', W Lamport 'Smiling Morn' and Willowfield School 'Willow Spray'

Eastbourne Motor Fishing Boat Race.
1st F Erridge 'Dawn of Hope'
2nd T Prodger 'Flower of the Fleet'
3rd G Erridge 'Ben-Ma-Kree'

Winners time 2 hours 10 minutes.

Also entered M Hardy 'Colleen', T Prodger 'William & Violet', J Huggett 'Reaper' and H Boniface 'Kathleen'.

Motor Pleasure Boat Race. (Licenced) Eastbourne Pier Co. Ltd. Challenge Cup.
1st Hardy Brothers' 'Sunnyside'
2nd Harry M Boniface 'Silver Spray'
3rd William Allchorn 'Skylark'

Time 1 hour 49 minutes. There were 20 entrants.

Ladies & Gentlemen's Double Scull Race.
1st W Ashdown & Miss E Allchorn.
2nd S G Sayers & Miss Simpson.

Surf Riding. (Motor Boat towing rider on plank)
1st E Diplock.

Many dropped out of this race, sea too choppy and Motor Boat not fast enough to pull the plank.

Police Swimming Race in Uniform.
1st P C Comber
2nd P C Lawrence
3rd P C Arnold.

Mutton Worry.
1st P Huggett.

Climbing Greasy Pole.
1st F Foard.

Waterman's Doubles Scull. Gildredge Challenge Cup.
1st T & W Allchorn
2nd Sayers' Brothers
3rd E H Sayers & H M Boniface

February 1927.

William Allchorn asked permission to place a ringbolt in the sea wall at Capstan No.26 He was to supply the ringbolt, which was to be fitted by the Borough Surveyors Department. Permission was granted. Boatman Albert French was granted permission to have railings removed from his Boat Stand at Marine Parade opposite the Albermarle Hotel.

June 1927.

Fred 'Tinker' Novis, Boatman, hired his Rowboat 'Wild Rose' to a male person. It was later that 'Wild Rose' was found adrift 'empty' off Eastbourne. The body of the drowned hirer was found down by the Aeroplane sheds at Langney Point by W. Morley whilst he was shrimping.

August 1927.

William Prodger, Chief bathing attendant at the Redoubt, dashed into rough seas and saved the life of a male swimmer who had ignored the red Warning flag. Prodger had been at the Station since 1907 - except for the War years 1914 -18 spent in the Royal Navy.

In September 1930, Prodger was instrumental in saving life when W.Huggett, Corporation Boatman brought ashore an unconscious man he had pulled from the sea. Prodger gave artificial respiration for an hour before the man came around. All in a days work?

Messrs. Sayers Bros. Pleasure Boatmen said it was the worse season for boating weather since 1903.

April 1928.

Nelson Sayers' revoked Waterman Licence was returned to him.

Boatman Nelson Prodger of Meads made an application on behalf of Mr. Roy Faulkner (husband of Winnie Barnes, actress who lived at Wiercombe Cottage, Holywell) to keep his Motor Boat and small winch on the Boat Stand occupied by Albert French at Holywell Retreat. His application was granted.

Eastbourne Boatmen. Whaler boat race winners 1928. Left - right, Tom Allchorn, Ned Sayers, Jack Tuxford. Standing at back Andrew Chester, Harry Boniface and Harry Erridge.

May 1928.

4 Rowing Boat Licences were granted to Albert 'Tuppy' Sayers and an application by him for Boat Stand Nos.74, 75 & 76 at Royal Parade previously held by Samuel Hurd was granted.

Messrs. Pragnell Boat Builders were granted Boat Stand No.69 at the Royal Parade.

June 1928.

An application by Sayers Bros. of Grand Parade to erect a 'Pay Box' hut was granted. A new 2nd class Boatman Licence was issued to Albert Lusted.

July 1928.

The Royal Navy Beaten.

A great win for Eastbourne Boatmen in July. An exciting whaler race took place off

Eastbourne against the Channel Fleet Squadron whaler champions H.M.S. Cambrian. Over a set course the Eastbourne Boatmen were worthy winners with Cox'n Jack Tuxford, crew Tom Allchorn, Ned Sayers, Andrew Chester, Henry Morgan Boniface and Henry Erridge.

July also saw the rescue of a lone boy in difficulties in a sailing canoe off Eastbourne by Boatmen Fred Hurd and George Prodger in their Rowboat.

Having relinquished the leases on the large Pleasure Motor Boats, 'Kohinor and Royal Sovereign', Henry Boniface leased Pleasure Motor Boats 'Sussex Maid' and 'Sussex Queen'. It was on Saturday 7th July that the Pleasure Motor Boat 'Sussex Maid' had just put to sea with 80 passengers aboard, when her engine caught fire. Fortunately all returned safely to shore. Although there was no damage to the boat, the engine was extensively damaged.

Boatman 'Bill' Boniface.

The Pleasuring business proved bad for Boniface that summer as the following shows: -

"Further ill luck occurring in August, when Boatmen Henry Boniface, Stanley Smith and crew, Fred Richardson and Herbert Wood nearly lost their lives at sea. With Henry Boniface in charge of the Pleasure Motor Boat 'Sussex Queen' and Smith in

Grand Parade. The Boniface Boat Stand. To left is Allchorn's Boat Stand 1924.

charge of 'Sussex Maid' both undertaking a towing contract of an old naval barge each from Portsmouth to Fulham, London. When off the Nore both the 'Sussex Queen' and 'Sussex Maid' lost all power and drifted for two days, the men being without food or water. They were all in a bad way when the keepers of the 'Nore' lightship spotted their distress signals. The Southend Lifeboat was launched and took the Eastbourne men ashore who were in dire need of sustenance. The Pleasure Boats and their tows were taken into Southend. After repairs and being unable to complete the tow, Boniface, Smith and the crews returned with the Pleasure Boats to Eastbourne."

January 1929.

There was an unhappy sequel to the above in January when Henry Boniface appeared at the County Court to answer a judgement summons regarding non-payment of debts. It was reported at the time under the heading 'Fisherman's Bank'

Q. *'Haven't you been in work since September?'*
A. *'I've done a lot of work. I'm always at work, but don't get anything for it.'*
Q. *'Haven't you got a fishing business?'*
A. *'No.'*
Q. *'Did you get anything for it?'*
A. *'No sir, only trouble. I've got money owing for fish supplied, but people could not pay me. I'm on the rocks.'*
Q. *'But you might worry your debtors?'*
A. *'I do worry them but it's a bad time of the year.'*
Q. *'Have you got money in the bank?'*
A. *'My bank's at home on two legs. I keep it as a pet. I lost everything last year when I lost some barges I was taking to London.'*

Boniface was ordered to pay 10s per month for 3 months then £1 a month thereafter.

Henry Boniface and family did continue Pleasure Boating up to the late 1930s and some time after the 1939-1945 War.

Having previously mentioned the Boniface family and 'Salvation' Tom it is worth showing an article written by Grandson Tom Boniface for Sussex Life in May 1975.

Grand Parade. Boniface Motor Pleasure Boats 'Sussex Maid' and 'Sussex Queen' 1927.

"As a member of the now depleted Boniface boating family. I feel I must give the following observations on my family.

The men of the Boniface family were all Fishermen and Boatmen, earning their living by fishing in the winter and by Pleasure Boating 'up the front' as

they would say during the summer months.

My grandfather Tom, was a staunch Salvationist and it is said that while 'in the ring' at the Salvation Army pier head meeting he would say that 'getting washed out of the Lifeboat made him see the ways of the Lord, and I can vouch that he was a very religious man, and in the context would not work his boats on a Sunday.

Grand Parade beach. The Boniface family.

His sons were Henry (Lifeboat coxswain), Jim, Joe (bowman) and George (my father, mechanic). Jim and Joe all put in many years service with the Lifeboat here. Jim commanded a fire launch on the Thames during the War.

I must mention Henry Morgan Boniface MBE, boat owner and Lifeboat man who became Fishery Protection Officer for the South East Region, and has a very honourable distinction of having a new Fishery Protection vessel named after him. He was awarded the MBE for his organisation of 'small craft' for the evacuation of troops at St. Valery, France, during the Second World War. Naturally the sea is in my blood, so I spend my free time at sea, angling. But alas I have to tell that for some years now the Bonifaces have not plied their boats for hire 'up the front' nor have they fished, for they have all departed this world." T. Boniface.

The death occurred in January, of 55-year-old George Hookham, Fisherman & Boatman of 74, Latimer Road. He was brother to builder Mark Hookham; brother in law to Ted and Harry Sayers and partner in the well-known Pleasure Boating firm of Sayers Bros. George was a former crew member of Eastbourne Rowing Club and was in the crew of 1897-9 that beat all comers.

Touting by Boatmen. A never ending complaint from the public last season over shouting by Boatmen plying for hire was discussed by the Watch Committee 'They must not call out in such a way as to annoy people' and a Bye-Law change would be considered if the practice caused further complaints during the coming season. The E.F.B.P. Society were to advise their members. No further action to be taken on this matter by the Committee. (Competition amongst the Boatmen for Business? Business dropping off could possibly have been the reason?)

April 1929. Saving life at Sea.

Fred Allchorn, skipper of a Pleasure Motor Boat returning from a trip to the Lighthouse at 4 pm Tuesday, 16th April, effected a swift rescue of 3 men from the perils of the sea. The boat had capsized and the men were thrown into the sea and had to hang on to the upturned boat. Fred was about a 1/4 mile away and went full speed to the rescue. All were recovered in good health and taken ashore.

May 1929.

There was a report of an un-licenced Speedboat operating from the Pier. Police were requested to investigate. It appeared that the Hon. Mrs. M Bruce had been operating and in July formerly made an application for a Motor Speedboat Licence to operate from the Pier. Her application was refused. So no Speedboats yet at Eastbourne.

July 1929. Regatta.

A Waterman's Regatta was organized by the Eastbourne Fishermen's & Boatmen's Protection Society at the instigation of the President, Mr. Roy Faulkner. Due to his generosity there would be no financial drain on the Society's resources. There were two races, one for Pleasure Boats and one for Motor Fishing Boats. The proposed rules were, the Pleasure Boat race to start from the beach each launched with passengers aboard from their respective places of hire. The first turning buoy of the course was off the Pier head, the boats then proceeding towards Beachy Head crossing the finishing line at Holywell.

The fishing boats to start off at the Pier head and race under engine and full sail. Each to tow a small boat from which respective crews would abandon their fishing boats and row ashore to a point on the beach. There they would discharge a cargo, return to their fishing boat and then cross the finishing line at Holywell. Fishing boat crews would be dressed in full sea going kit.

On the 17th July the two races took place under handicap conditions the course being extended from the Pier to the Lightship and finishing at Holywell. Fishing boats were permitted to proceed in any manner they desired, row, sail or by motor. To test seamanship each vessel had to proceed to a point near the shore at the foot of Beachy Head and anchor on the rocks. The three man crew each had to place a sack of beach stones in the boat towed behind each vessel, row ashore, land them and return to the fishing boat to carry on the race. The course covered 7 miles.

The finish was close run, the result being: -

1st 'Ocean's Gift' - Jack Prodger.
2nd 'Nona' - Tom Prodger.
3rd 'Commodore' - Jimbo Huggett.
4th 'Ben Macree' - George Erridge.
5th 'Vindictive' - Andrew Chester.
6th 'Flower of the Fleet' - Will Prodger.
7th 'Princess Mary' - Fred French.

The winner received a Cheque and a Pennant bearing a Dolphin. 2nd & 3rd received cheques.

The Pleasure Motor Boat race was over a 10 mile course and was to be for the Presidents Trophy and Pennant. The trophy was a beautiful model of a Galleon, hand made in beaten silver on a plinth. The Pennant represented 'Cock of the Walk' on a green background. There were silver cups for 2nd & 3rd.

The keen nature of the handicap race may be understood from the fact that the winning vessel 'Skylark II', was first to start, the second home 'Enchantress' was the last to get off the mark and there was only half a minute between them at the finish. Amongst the others there were also exciting finishes.

1st 'Skylark II.' - William Allchorn & Sons.
Skipper - Jack Tuxford. Engineer - Arthur E. Sayers. 1hr. 16mins. 15secs.
2nd 'Enchantress' - William Allchorn & Sons. 1hr. 16mins. 45secs.
3rd 'Silver Spray' - Henry Morgan Boniface Jnr. 1hr. 18mins. 25secs.
4th 'Eastbourne Queen' - Sayers Bros. 1hr. 19mins. 20secs.
5th 'Britannia I' - Sayers Bros. 1hr. 20mins. 20secs.
6th 'Britannia II' - Sayers Bros. 1hr. 20mins. 24secs.
7th 'Albion' - E. Sayers. 1hr. 21mins.
8th 'Eastbourne Belle' - William Allchorn & Sons. 1hr. 21mins. 10secs.
9th 'Albion II' - E. Sayers. 1hr. 21mins. 40secs.
10th 'Skylark III' - William Allchorn & Sons. 1hr. 23mins. 30secs.
11th 'Britannia III' - Sayers Bros. 1hr. 25mins. 14secs.
12th 'Sunnyside' - Hardy Bros. 1hr. 25mins. 31secs.

What a splendid sight for the people of Eastbourne and visitors to enjoy. The Fishermen and Boatmen all dressed as pirates, cannibals etc. and put on a good show. Collections were taken in aid of the Society's Distress & Disaster fund for the Longshoremen of Eastbourne who suffer loss of boats, gear and injury - a worthwhile cause. It was hoped that a Regatta would become an annual event and it did for some years, run by the Fishermen and Boatmen themselves.

Later that same month Eastbourne's Seafront was to experience a freak squall. During a visit to Eastbourne by the battleship H.M.S. Nelson, a most strange sea movement occurred. It was on a Saturday evening and the Pleasure Boats were busy with trips when, with a sudden heavy squall the wind rate increased accompanied by a very high sea swell.

The following was related by Boatman Arthur Sayers: "At the time, we were landing people from our boats and many of them were walking along the plank walkways to get ashore, these were about 18 inches high. Suddenly the water seemed to come from nowhere and gradually lifted itself to the level of the planks, then to the peoples knees, and finally to their shoulders. Very frightening. The Boatmen of course initially went to their assistance and got them ashore to safety. That there was no mishap was due to the co-operation that exists among the Boatmen of Eastbourne. On turning to the Pleasure Boats, we found that the boats, planks and running gear were washing towards the Pier.

All this happened in about 2 minutes. We made a rush for the boats and eventually made them and the gear secure. Then strangely as we attempted to get ashore we found ourselves high and dry on the sands. The sea had receded very quickly. All anchors were moved out to sea to get the boats off and afloat. Then the water came in again quickly reaching our armpits. It receded and we eventually got the boats clear and to sea.

All the Pleasure Boats at sea then went to the aid of several Rowboats, their occupants being very distressed. Allchorn's 'Eastbourne Belle' rescued 3 Rowboats. Jack Prodger's boat and crew got 9 safely ashore.

The Pleasure Boats coming in from H.M.S. Nelson had anchored and taken shelter by the Pier. It was here that Allchorn's 'Enchantress', heavily loaded with people, snapped her first anchor in two halves. The second anchor and chain were let go, and half the stock of that was broken too, but she hung on until the tempest died down." Mr. Sayers went on to say at least 70 people were actually pulled from the water. Luckily the boats only sustained minor damage. All together an extremely frightening experience!

August 1929.

Messrs. Pragnell boat builders were granted a Motor Boat Drivers Licence, necessary when running engine trials on new built Motor Boats.

In addition to unpredictability of the sea & weather, the Pleasure Boatmen also had to put up with drunken members of the public. One such

R. Pragnell & Sons. Boat builders, Eastbourne.

occurrence happened in August, when Boatman John Henry 'Sausage' Grooms was assaulted on the beach. The facts went like this: Grooms was running a boat load of people ashore when a man in a Rowboat obstructed his boat, ignoring requests to give way.

The man in the Rowboat was 'beered' up. Getting ashore this man then punched Grooms hurting him quite badly. Boatman Henry Erridge saw the assault and went up to the man and said, *"Why did you hit that man?"* The man replied, *"I'll fight all of Sussex."* Erridge said, *"You couldn't fight pussy."*

Erridge later related, *"Being of Sussex breeding. I went for him. We had a bit of a rough and tumble, then he said he had had enough. The way the man had hit young Grooms was unmerciful."* The crowd was very hostile to the man whose name was Fendley. He was arrested and on appearing in court was fined £2 plus 8s. 6d costs. With a good hiding from Henry Erridge he was doubly punished.

September 1929.

The Silver Spray Hydroplanes Ltd, made an application to run Speedboats through the next season.

A complaint was received about Rowboats and bathers. Rowboats were not permitted near Bathing Stations and problems arose when bathers strayed outside the limits of Bathing Stations.

Boat Stand No.64 situated at Marine Parade previously occupied by the late Mr. Benjamin Bates was transferred to Ernest 'Chinaman' Sayers. With the passing of Ben Bates, Eastbourne lost the man who owned and ran the big sailing yacht 'Britannia' for the years off the Grand Parade 1890 to 1900. Still involved in 'Pleasuring' he ran Rowboats off Marine Parade until shortly before his death.

November 1929.

'Chris Craft' Passenger Boat Company made an application for permission to ply for hire from a point on the Pier for the next season.

This brought a protest from Eastbourne Fishermen's & Boatmen's Protection Society not to allow the above 'Chris Craft' operation. The Watch Committee decided to defer a decision until next year. Come January 1930, a decision was taken not to grant a licence.

Henry William Novis had his Boatman Licence revoked for the 3rd time due to drunkenness.

As opposed to the previous season the Boatmen of Eastbourne enjoyed a satisfactory season owing to the fine weather that blessed Eastbourne.

March 1930.

The Committee discussed a memorandum from the Board of Trade that Eastbourne Motor Pleasure Boats did not comply with certain conditions (details not shown in the minutes). It was resolved by the Committee that Mr. Ellison, Borough Engineer, was to examine all Licenced Motor Boats and submit a report before licencing by the Committee. This practice continued for many years.

First time 1st class Boatman Licences were granted to Nelson Prodger and Francis Rowland Pragnell.

A 2nd class Licence was granted for Ben Erridge.

Motor Boat Driver Licences were granted to Nelson Prodger, Francis Rowland Pragnell and Ben Erridge.

Mr.Pennyman of Trinity Mansions Hotel was given permission to place his private Motor Boat 'Spitfire' on the beach occupied by William Allchorn & Sons. The Committee seemed to have rescinded its decision to keep all private boats to the east of the Pier.

Motor Pleasure Boats 'No sail' C.1930.

September 1930.

George Prodger received Capstan No.77 from old Henry Matthews who had given up Pleasure Boating.

1931

Come March and April, this was the busy time for the Boatmen preparing their Motor Pleasure Boats for the summer season and the big Pleasure Motor Boats undergoing their Board of Trade inspection. It was a hive of activity down at the Fishing Station, seeing the Rowboats undergoing scraping and varnishing bringing them up to the high standard, as only the Eastbourne Boatmen knew how. Come the start of the season and they were a sight to behold. 'Ship shape and Bristol fashion'. Sadly now all gone.

April 1931.

A first time 1st class Waterman Licence was issued to Robert Hunt. Bob skippered the 'Sussex Queen' for Henry Boniface for a time. He was also occupied as a Fisherman down at the Fishing Station, becoming a well-known character amongst the seafaring fraternity.

May 1931.

As with previous years, the Chief Constable gave a report on licencing. It showed

the transfer of Boatman George Prodger's Rowboat Licences on his retirement.

Stand Nos.28 & 29 to John 'Foot' Prodger, Nos.32 & 33 to Frederick 'Tinker' Novis, No.48 to William Allchorn, No.59 to Edwin 'Ned' Sayers and No.60 to Bernard Sayers. So another of Eastbourne's seafaring men leaving the beach.

Boatman George Prodger.

A pint of beer saved George Prodger's life so the story goes, told by Fred 'Mucky' Erridge. George Prodger Boatman of Meads had an allotment up at Holywell. Working it one day he decided to go to the 'Pilot Inn' Meads, for a pint as it was a warm day. On returning to his allotment George was amazed to find it had slipped into the sea. After that George always said, *'that pint at the 'Pilot' saved my life.'*

July 1931.

The Eastbourne Fishermen's and Boatmen's Protection Society erected an Arch on the Royal Parade not far from their Club premises in honour of the visit of His Royal Highness the Prince of Wales in July. Attending the Lifeboat House the following had the honour of meeting him: -

Coxswain Mike Hardy, 2nd Coxswain Jesse Huggett, Jim Hardy - bowman, Ernest 'Glaxo' Sayers, William Allchorn Jnr. Fred Allchorn, Henry Thomas - 1st engineer, George Boniface - 2nd engineer, Jack Tuxford. Extra hands and shore staff - Fred

'Tinker' Novis, Alec Huggett, Henry Boniface, Andrew Chester, Eddie Hardy and Tom Boniface. Also presented were surviving members of the old '1883 crew' John 'Trunky' Colstick, the Erridge brothers William and George, and William Bollard Hide. Other Fishermen/Boatmen were J Delves, Jack Mockett and old Mike Hardy, father of young Mike the Cox'n.

September 1931. Motor winch on Boat Stand.

An application by William Allchorn & Sons. was made in September, to erect a motor winch on their Boat Stand at Victoria Steps. The motor was a 'Novo' manufactured petrol driven 10 hp - all gears enclosed in a metal case complying with the Board of Trade directions. This Motor was said to run practically silent. Winch size. 4' 6" x 4' 6" x 4' high. This application was granted in October.

With regard to the motor winch being fixed on the beach at Victoria Steps, the exhaust pipe was placed in a cage under the beach in such a way that hardly any noise or noxious fumes were apparent. So we see Allchorns leading the way with the first winch of this type on the seafront.

E H Sayers bought George Penfold's boats and took over his Boat Stand No.13. another of Eastbourne's old family Boatmen gone.

March 1932.

First time 2nd class Waterman Licences granted to Frank E Smith, Raymond Searle. Edward Prodger and Nelson Hurd.

Speedboats.

As the Watch Committee had rescinded its previous ban on Speedboats, a deputation went before the Committee from the E.F.B.P. Society to protest at the granting of Speedboat Licences. To no avail though, Speedboats were here to stay for some time.

Speedboat regulations were drawn up in time for an application to operate Speedboats from the Pier and beach. The beach site was occupied by Henry Boniface, who was to be paid £6 10s per week by the Company using his Boat Stand, namely the Silver Bullet Speedcraft Ltd. Speedboat Licences were to be considered for boats, 'Silver Bullets I, II & III', but various other applications were refused including one named 'Scootaboats'.

May 1932.

The month of May saw Messrs. Allchorn make an application to place a Ticket Hut on their Boat Stand at Victoria steps. This was granted by the Watch Committee and referred to the Entertainment & Pleasure Ground Committee who now had responsibility for the Parades and Pleasure Boating.

June 1932.

New Motor Boat Driver & 1st class Waterman Licences were issued to David Green, Frank Ward and Kenneth How.

A new Pleasure Boat Licence was issued to Tom Sisk for the rowing boat 'Wild Wave'.

So the summer of 1932 saw the Pleasure Boating income compensating those Longshoremen who suffered losses through the winter with their fishing.

But Pleasure Boating was on a slow decline from earlier days. Every year saw a reduction of income especially among the Rowboats. An old Boatman told of the dying out of rowing. Young people did not go rowing, it was too much like hard work. With the increase of Motor Boats giving the maximum amount of leisure time at sea with the minimum of effort, he put forward the theory that perhaps the decline was due to the majority of residents not being Eastbourne born and bred.

While they had civic pride in the town of their adoption, they had not been brought up on the water, and perhaps the spirit of those who had been associated with it for generations was lacking?

Certainly the Regatta had fallen by the wayside. No Regatta had taken place for 2 years and Eastbourne at that time did not boast a Rowing Club.

In June, Silver Bullet Speedcraft Ltd. was granted the first Speedboat Licence to operate off the beach and Pier head. The Speedboat to carry 8 passengers, was not allowed to go under the Pier and must be 450 yards off the shore before attaining full speed. At that time Henry Boniface and E Horne also made application for Speedboat Licences but were refused.

The Silver Bullet Speedcraft Ltd. operated the summer through and this caused something of stir.

November 1932.

Come November, Messrs. French & Novis, Boatmen representatives of E.F.B.P. Society stated a certain application for a Speedboat Licence was in no way associated with the Society. (A member making application through the Society without their knowledge?)

December 1932.

A letter was received by the Entertainments & Pleasure Boat Committee from E.F.B.P. Society, stating that they will not run Speedboats next season, (no record that they did) but the Committee did receive an application from Messrs. Allchorn for a Speedboat Licence for the next season. The Society protested against running Speedboats from the beach as they would interfere with other Pleasure Boats. Speedboat Stands should be away from Pleasure Boat Stands and if none were available no licences should be granted. (The Society appeared at odds with fellow members - Messrs. Allchorn.)

1933 ~ 1965

January 1933.

In January, a Speedboat Licence was granted to Messrs. Allchorn for a fee of £25 with the proviso that $\frac{1}{2}$d royalty on each passenger carried be paid to the Council. Protests by Allchorns were to no avail - the royalty was to stand.

The Board of Trade did not control Speedboats and Council rules stated that one man only was needed to control a Speedboat when operating. The E.F.B.P. Society demanded that two men were needed (understandable as Pleasure Motor Boats required 2 men per 12 passengers), but the Committee found against the Society.

March 1933.

A first time 2nd class Waterman Licence was issued to George Frederick Punyer.

Messrs. Sayers Bros. made an application for a small hut of the same size and style as that already owned by Messrs. Allchorn, namely 4' 6" x 4' 6" x 6' high for issue of tickets in connection with Boating. This was granted.

April 1933.

The Chief Constable's report for April on Pleasure Boats recommended the issue of existing licences for Motor Boat Nos.10, 67, 69 & 167. New licences were issued to Motor Boat Drivers John Hill and Walter Stapley.

May 1933.

Mr. A French made application to run 'Silver Bullet' Speedboats from a Stand between the Pier and Wish Tower. This was not granted because Messrs. Allchorn were already operating on Grand Parade. However, French was given permission to run from a Stand on Marine Parade opposite the Albermarle Hotel.

More Speedboats.

The year 1933, saw the Watch Committee eventually decide to grant 3 Speedboat Licences for that season. One boat, 'Alacrity' to Messrs. Allchorn and 2 boats to Silver Bullet Speedcraft Ltd. Licences were subject to a royalty payment of $\frac{1}{2}$d per head of passengers taken up on the foreshore with a minimum payment of £25

Henry Boniface took over the running of Silver Bullet Speedcraft Ltd. for that 1933 season but had an unsuccessful operating year and in September, Speedboat 'Silver Bullet I' sank in heavy seas. She was riding at anchor just offshore when she was swamped. Eight days later she was raised by grappling hooks and chains and brought ashore.

'Silver Bullet II' luckily was beached when the bad weather struck. Boniface never recovered from the above bad luck and in May 1934, Silver Bullet Speedcraft Ltd went into liquidation with a net loss of £222. It had been a disastrous season for Boniface with a sinking and numerous breakdowns plus bad weather and competition from Messrs. Allchorn. Bros, who successfully operated their Speedboat 'Alacrity' until the start of the 2nd World War.

Bad luck seemed to dog Boniface. He suffered back in 1928 when his boats 'Sussex Maid' and 'Sussex Queen' broke down and were nearly lost off the Nore, and the ensuing debts continued.

June 1933.

An application by E.F.B.P. Society for a collection to be taken during their 'Decorated' boat display to be held on 5th July, also to collect during the Regatta on 26th July. Both were not granted - it's hard to see why.

June 7th saw the visit to Eastbourne of a sailing replica of HMS Victory; a photo of her at sea off the Pier head was taken from the bows of Allchorns Pleasure Boat 'Skylark'.

During the summer of 1933, Pleasuring as it was known was still continued by some of Eastbourne's fishing families - Allchorn, Prodger, Boniface, Hardy, Novis, and Sayers among others. Of those that just fished, Chester, Huggett and Wood were prominent. At the Fishing Station the general rule became Pleasure Boating shops to the west side, fishing only to the east up to Tanhouse groyne.

August 1933.

Tributes were paid at the funeral of an old Eastbourne Fisherman and Boatman.

78-year-old William Allchorn's funeral was on 28th August 1933. The service was held at Christ Church followed by an internment at Ocklynge cemetery.

William Allchorn - Son of founder.

With over 50 years in the Pleasure Boat business, he was a founder member of the Eastbourne Fishermen's and Boatmen's Protection Society, whose members lined the path to the Church.

Chief mourners were, the Widow, sister - Mrs. Bailey, sons - Harry, Fred, Will, Jack, Tom and Albert, daughters - Edie, Flo, Annie and Beattie, nephews - Edward, Joe, David, Alfred and Arthur Allchorn.

Other mourners included, G Prodger, Mike Hardy, Jack Huggett, Tom Huggett, Fred Hurd, Jack Tuxford, Albert Sayers, William Erridge, J Bowler, T Prodger, G T Erridge Snr. G H Erridge, T Pollard, J Bell, C Foy, M Andrews, Jim Hardy, Alec Huggett, E Hardy, Harry Boniface Snr. E Gearing, Fred Novis, Tom Boniface, Jack Hurd, John Prodger Snr. John Prodger Jnr. Ted Sayers,

Alleyn Sayers, William Bollard Hide, Charles Wood and Nurse Beck.

The Allchorn Family & Pleasure Boating.

'Safety and Pleasure' for their clients were paramount for over 133 years and could be said to have been the family motto of the Allchorn family.

Allchorn is a name in Eastbourne that goes back hundreds of years - Fishing and Pleasure Boating and then finally solely Pleasure Boating off the beach at Eastbourne.

Back in 1833, Fisherman Edward Allchorn along with his brother Samuel were gallant crew members in Eastbourne's very first Lifeboat 'Good Samaritan'. They went to the aid of the sailing vessel 'Isabella' wrecked on 20th February saving 29 lives.

Boatman William Allchorn - grandson of founder with a happy client. Shark caught off Birling Point August 1913. Length 4ft 2". Weight 45 lbs.

From eyewitness reports of the incident, the 'Isabella' ran aground on the Boulder bank off the Wish Tower having lost her rudder. With a heavy sea running the 'Samaritan', under the command of Adam Hamilton on this first service, launched and on getting alongside the 'Isabella' was amazingly ordered by her Captain Wildgooss to stand by. Adam Hamilton did as ordered and he and his crew could only watch as the 'Isabella' was driven by heavy seas to run aground at Walls End, Pevensey Bay.

Allchorn's Speed Boat 'Alacrity' C.1933.

It was only then that Captain Wildgooss requested the Lifeboat to take off his passengers. Under extreme conditions this was done, eleven persons being taken to shore. The Lifeboat 'Samaritan' then returned and took off the Captain and crew of the 'Isabella'. All told, a fine first service by Adam Hamilton and his crew - Samuel, William, Thomas and Samuel Jnr. Knight, John, James and George Hide, John, William and George Simpson, Edward and Samuel Allchorn, George Cox, James Hutchings and Thomas Mitchell.

A passenger's experience of the wreck of the 'Isabella' and his criticism of its Captain Wildgooss is related in the Times newspaper, March 1833 - well worth reading.

The Royal National Lifeboat journal for March 1937, carries a story of the Allchorn family, related by Mrs. Caroline Allchorn (nee Breach), aged 100 years - born May 1836, the daughter- in- law of Edward Allchorn.

In an article by Mr. John Vine (born Eastbourne 1811) in the Eastbourne Gazette

1929 and a picture of some family members and crew following success in a regatta. Top right, Tom Allchorn. Centre, from right Jack Allchorn, Sam Allchorn, Will jnr and Will snr. Seated Fred Allchorn.

Allchorn Family 1929.

1888, he writes *"The First Lifeboat, we had was much more staunch than many of the Lifeboats of today. She was called the 'Good Samaritan' and given to the town by Jack Fuller of Rose Hill. Being built of timber grown on his estate and constructed by William Simpson of Eastbourne".*

Boatman Reuben 'Old Screw' Wood stated in September 1905, *"The Lifeboat 'Samaritan' was sold out of service in 1863 and turned into a river Pleasure Boat on the river Thames."* So she ended her life giving Pleasure.

The Allchorn family served the Institute and Eastbourne bravely and unstintingly through to the 1960s. Tom Allchorn serving with distinction as Coxswain and on two occasions being presented with the Lifeboat Institute's bronze medal for bravery.

A SHOT of the crew of the Enchantress. First left, Jack Allchorn, third left Fred Allchorn, fourth left, Tom Allchorn, sixth from left Sam Allchorn. Bottom right (seated) William Allchorn. In the suit is the Hon Gerald Lascelles.

Allchorn Family C.1930 Pleasure Boat 'Enchantress' lost at Dunkirk 1940.

The following excerpts are from a report of an interview with Brian Allchorn, published in the Evening Argus, March 2003, by Douglas d'Enno: -

"When Brian Allchorn retired in 1996, a family tradition of Pleasure Boating spanning 135 years came to an end.

The work had been hard and hours long but seeing the enjoyment it gave so many, young and old alike, had made it a fulfilling occupation. The business was started by Brian's great-grandfather Edward Allchorn in 1861. The railway brought in holidaymakers in great numbers and created a market. Brian says, "In my grandfather William's era, Motor Boats first started coming in (c.1910). They were not terribly reliable but, unlike the sailing boats, could at least go out in calm weather." "My grandfather, William, died in 1933. My father Albert - always known as Sam, took over the business with his brothers and the firm became Allchorn Brothers." Before the War, (1939) there were five brothers and six boats. Each boat had a skipper and engineer. We had the Enchantress, Eastbourne Belle, Skylark, Golden City (ex Lifeboat James Stevens No.6), the Iona (a small fishing smack really) and a Speedboat Alacrity. We had rowing boats as well some built by Tom Sisk, a superb local boat builder."

"It was busy, of course, we always worked seven days a week. Working evenings in the earlier days with the boats illuminated with lanterns. In 1940 we got a call to take the boats to Dover and the boats went to Dunkirk. We lost the Enchantress and Sayers Brothers, another boating firm lost the Britannia, its biggest boat on par with Enchantress. When the other boats came back the Eastbourne Belle was covered with shrapnel, which took a while to pick out. Barely a week later the boats got called on again to go to Newhaven. Nobody knew what was happening; my father simply being told to take them there. We didn't see him for four days. The boats were towed across to France with others to help get the 51st Highland Division off the beach at St. Valery-en-Caux."

"At Eastbourne double rows of concrete block dragons teeth were built on the beach as a defence. They worked along the coast with this defence, the beaches were mined and the boating trade was finished for the duration of the War. My father was sent to Coventry to work in engineering and my brother Colin and I were evacuated to Nailsworth, Gloucestershire, for 4½ years. After the War the boats started up again. All five brothers came back safely and no more boats were lost. A replacement vessel for the Enchantress was built in 1948, also called Enchantress. After the restrictions of the War years, trade was brisk. There was nothing much else for visitors".

"To go round the lighthouse in those days cost 4/- (20p) and was about a 50 minute trip. It was 2/- for a Channel trip. We worked from the beach, using a landing stage constructed from the old Eastbourne Lifeboat launching carriage. In the end the wheels collapsed and we fabricated new ones. It took us two winters as work on these was in addition to our normal, fairly tight maintenance schedule. The Golden City (ex Lifeboat) had been converted for Pleasure Boating but because of her design - tending to go through the waves rather

Allchorn advert C.1930.

Allchorn Motor Pleasure Boat 'Enchantress' 1932.

The engine of 'Enchantress' 1934.

than over them - she wasn't a success."

"After the War, I couldn't get a job in engineering so worked at the council bus depot as an apprentice painter/sign writer. Then I did 2 years National service in the Royal Navy. Then within the year, the old man decided he wanted me to work with him on the seafront and I started in March 1951 as engineer in the Eastbourne Belle. I served for 2 or 3 years with my uncle Fred as skipper. I think the boat carried about 38 passengers. The money was coming in and Dad had decided to go in for bigger boats. One was built at Newhaven by Cantell and named the William Allchorn. She was completed in July 1950 and carried 100 passengers. She is still operating to this day. It was boating's heyday really. With fine weather and when the tide was right, people would be queuing up. We used to have quite a few regular customers who would come down every year. You couldn't lose if you played your cards right".

"The Sayers Brothers had two big boats built in the 1950s, the Southern Queen and Eastbourne Queen. They traded until 1964 when we bought them out lock, stock and barrel. We sold the Eastbourne Queen and kept the Southern Queen. We put a lot of work into her and she is still operating to this day."

"My brother Colin, worked with me after the older generation retired. He was a chippie and did the woodwork whilst I did the engineering. We ran the business between us until he moved to Spain."

Allchorn Pleasure Boats under maintenance at Fishing Station 1934.

"It was a way of life, very fascinating in many ways when you look back on it. But there weren't many spare moments, believe you me. At the end of the season you would get a holiday - October was our holiday month."

"Some fishing was done during the winter maintenance period: Herring-drifting at night

October to December, sprat-drifting from November to February (Lord Mayor's Day being the traditional start) and long lining during the entire period, back of the Royal Sovereign Lightship. With long exposure to the elements and the work of clearing and re-baiting lines up until 9 to 10 at night in readiness for the next day, long lining was almost universally loathed."

Allchorn brothers with ex-Lifeboat 'James Stevens No.6' acquired and put into Pleasure Boating, renamed 'Golden City' 1936.

"With Pleasure Boating, Health and safety were important and more and more rules came in. The Marine Safety Agency (one time Board of Trade) would send its people from London to survey our boats, when stripped down and then later when reassembled and running. The inspections were pretty thorough. You then got your annual certificates. The Agency would also do spot checks during the year. When retired, I had a letter of commendation from the inspectors. We had a good name with them and the public. It was a nice note to go out on."

'Golden City' in service 1937.

"Others are now running the Pleasure Boats. Yet were it not for the solid foundation laid down by four generations of Allchorns, the landing stage might well be standing unused on Eastbourne beach."

'Southern Queen' ex-Sayers Brothers Motor Pleasure Boat - acquired by Allchorn's in 1964.

Allchorn's Motor Pleasure Boat 'William Allchorn' built by Cantells of Newhaven 1950.

September 1933.

September also saw the death of another Boatman namely Albert French aged 66 years of Southdown House, Silverdale Road, a member of an old Eastbourne

A young Brian Allchorn with uncle Fred C.1950.

Allchorn Boatmen. C.1960.

Business rivals and friends - Albert 'Sam' Allchorn on left and Ernest 'Glaxo' Sayers at the Fishermen's Club.

seafaring family. He was interred in Ocklynge cemetery. He served 22 years in the Royal Navy retiring in 1911 with the rank of Chief Petty Officer. Re-enlisting in 1914, he saw action at the Dardenelles and the Battle of Jutland. His son Fred, Royal Naval Brigade, was killed in France. After the War he resumed Fishing and Boating, owning a number of boats. His pleasant manner made him a popular person amongst his fellow Boatmen on the beach.

Mourners were, Widow and family, Boatmen Jack Allchorn, Harry Boniface, Tom Prodger, Ted Hide, W Howell, Henry Morgan Boniface, Fred Novis, W Morley, Robert Hunt, W Edwards, J Belsham, Len Hide and Jack Tuxford.

One of Eastbourne's evergreen retired Longshoremen celebrated his 80th birthday in September - Henry 'Old Dusty' Matthews. It was said - like an old soldier, they never die and seldom fade away.

A board announcing his birthday was displayed on a boating pitch on the promenade. A Fisherman and Boatman all his life, 'Old Dusty' had retired and sold his Pleasure Boat a year ago.

'Old Dusty' resided beside another veteran of the sea, Albert 'Tuppy' Sayers in his 72nd year. They had sailed together on many a fishing expedition. 'Tuppy' still operated his Rowboats on the beach and had the distinction of being a member of the famous 1883 Birling Gap Lifeboat rescue. Both 'Old Dusty' and 'Tuppy' were good adverts for the Eastbourne sea air!

November 1933.

For misconduct, 1st class Waterman Arthur Brown appeared before the Watch Committee and was fined 10s and cautioned. Silver Bullet Speedcraft Ltd owed £50 to the Corporation for last season's fees and the two Licenced Speedboats. The Committee was told one was a hulk on the beach. It was ordered to be seized.

January 1934.

An application was made to the Council by Messrs. Allchorn to be released from their agreement regarding royalties of ½d per carried passenger for their Speedboat. The decision was that they must carry on paying.

February 1934.

Angry members of the Eastbourne Fishermen's and Boatmen's Protection Society had a meeting at the Fishermen's Institute. Presiding were vice-president Roland Pragnell, Chairman H Ashcroft and Secretary W Butterworth. The problem was over the Council's introduction of Pleasure Floats for hire on the beach during the last summer season and the intention to make it permanent. It was taking a living from the Boatmen.

Ernest 'Glaxo' Sayers said, *"20 to 30 floats are being used at a time with Pleasure Boats lying idle."*

Fred 'Tinker' Novis, *"Eastbourne has the finest boating station along the south coast, but no trade, it is a case of no boats today, but floats."*

Jack Sayers, Boatman of Royal Parade, *"Floats were on his pitch, they were heavy things with advertising boards. Pleasure Boats are not allowed to advertise."*

Harry Allchorn, *"Living has gone since the floats arrived. I have seen at least 64 floats. They are allowed off when the sea is rough but Pleasure Boats are not allowed. The Council run the floats and flout their own rules. I suggest the floats be put between the Wish Tower and Holywell,"*

Jack Elms, Boatman, *"I was in my Pleasure Boat and had to pick up two ladies from the floats, they were too far out."*

The Society resolved to view with dismay the decision of the Town Council to allow floats to be used to the detriment of the Boatmen. The Longshoremen had a hard winter, and requested consideration be given to dis-continuing the floats. The request fell upon deaf ears, the Council deciding in March, to again allow floats on the beach. Other towns had them (but they didn't have Boatmen like Eastbourne!!)

Harry 'Early Doors' Allchorn commented, *"It's no good for us to fight against it, the Council has to keep abreast of modern times. They will affect us of course."* So there we have it. Another nail in the coffin leading to the demise of the Rowboat.

March 1934.

New licences were issued to the following: -
1st class Waterman George Henry Erridge and William J Kent.
Additional Motor Boat Licence renewals Nos.21, 27, 47,124 & 167.

May 1934. Rescue by 'Britannia'.

With a strong SW gale blowing off Eastbourne on 21st May, the yacht 'Comet' signalled for assistance. Sayers Bros. Pleasure Motor Boat 'Britannia' under skipper Jim Boniface and crew immediately put off and assisted the 'Comet' by towing her into Newhaven harbour. All told, a fine example of seafaring men ready to give assistance to another in trouble on the sea - plus a chance of salvage money! Sadly the 'Britannia' was to be lost at Dunkirk.

June 1934.

Harry Ekins was transferred from 2nd class to 1st class Waterman.

Albert Simpson and Arthur Blackman were issued with first time 2nd class Waterman Licences.

April 1935.

Additional licences issued.
1st class Waterman. No 62.
Motor Boat Licence Nos.5, 6, 21, 27, 36, 47, 67, 69, 124 & 167.

Fred Novis who had a fleet of 12 rowing boats opposite the Queens Hotel made an application to cut the railings by his Boat Stand. This was granted and then referred to the Entertainments & Pleasure Grounds Committee.

May 1935.

An application by Fred Novis showed that to enable him to remove his boats from the beach, 3 fixed rails needed replacing with 3 movable rods. This was agreed and the costs were to be borne by the Council.

June 1935.

Nos.10 & 12 Speedboat Licences were renewed. (Messrs. Allchorn running two boats? no details known.)

First time Motor Boat Driver Licences issued to Alfred Nelson Hurd and John Henry Grooms.

Speedboat No.12 Licence (Alacrity) held by Messrs. Allchorn. They again requested to have royalties done away with. Denied by Council and to remain as last year.

Boat Stand Nos.39 & 40 and Capstan Stand Nos.35, 36a, 37, 38 & 39a were transferred to Sayers Bros. thus increasing their holdings on the beach. Along with Allchorn's they were becoming the main Pleasure Boat businesses.

July 1935.

2nd class Waterman Licences issued to George Grooms and Charles Standen and 2nd class Waterman Rowing Boat Licence issued to William Morley, of 23 Bexhill Road.

September 1935.

Eastbourne Fishermen's and Boatmen's Protection Society held their first Boatmen's Ran-Dan race in September. (A 'Dan' being a flagged buoy attached to fishing gear at sea.)

A total of 12 boats entered, crewed by members of the Society. Ran-Dan Rowboats had a staggered crew of 3, 1 portside, 1 starboard, 1 port and Cox - The starboard rower had two oars, the port rowers had one each.

The crews adopted local nicknames and pseudonyms and all with much din and uproar had great fun.

The racecourse was from the Pier to the Great Redoubt.

Starting at 7.00pm - Starter, H Ashcroft. Umpire, G French. Judge, A Dyer. Official Boatman, Fred 'Tinker' Novis.

Result.
1st 'Bonnie John' - B Addington, N Hurd, E Andrews. Cox - Tim Erridge.
2nd 'Britannia' - C Reed, A Welfare, Tishy Huggett. Cox - Gammy.
3rd 'Nightingale' - J Bassett, N Sayers, C Pain. Cox - B Holmes.
4th 'Active' - Tut Tut, J Erridge, R Steers. Cox - Sausage.
5th 'Royal Sovereign' - Tupenny, W Reed, H Howell Cox - Bones Hide.
6th 'Forget-me-not' - Farmer Clark, H Erridge, G Punyer. Cox - H Hobday.
7th 'Elsie' - Ron, E Knight, F Richardson. Cox - Laddie.
8th 'Little Edith' - N Wilkinson, M Boats, A Wood. Cox - Mike Hardy.
9th 'British Queen' - Henry Allchorn, A Elms, H Strudwick. Cox - J Prodger.
10th 'Orphir' - Titty Huggett, J Allchorn, J Dunn. Cox - Quack.
11th 'Marjorie' - Uncle Mo, Jenkin, T Walsh. Cox - Eyebrows.
12th 'Sunbeam' - S Milton, G Erridge, T Wood. Cox - Fudge.

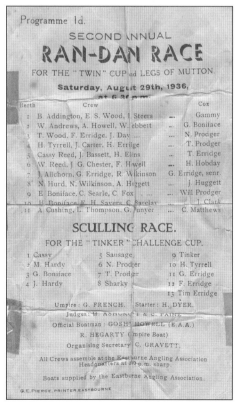

Ran Dan race winners August 1936 - 'Cassy' Reed, John Bassett, H 'Feathers' Ekins and Cox Tim Erridge.

1936

The Ran-Dan race 1936, followed a different course, starting at the Pier then to a line of buoys in line with Cambridge Road, turn and go under the Pier to a line of buoys in line with Victoria Place, turn back through the Pier to finish opposite the Queens Hotel. The winners on that occasion being Boat No.5 - crew Cassy Reed, John Bassett, H 'Feathers' Ekins and Cox - Tim Erridge.

A single sculls race was also held over a shorter course, and a report of the race was as follows: *"'Tinker' Novis held a good place until catching a 'crab', Tim Erridge broke a rowlock. Jim Boniface won, Nelson Prodger came second and Fred 'Tinker' Novis in third place. A collection was taken on behalf of the Eastbourne Hospitals and a jolly evening was spent at the Fishermen's Institute."*

Programme 1d.

SECOND ANNUAL
RAN-DAN RACE
FOR THE "TWIN" CUP ad LEGS OF MUTTON.
Saturday, August 29th, 1936,
at 6.30 p.m.

Berth	Crew		Cox
1	B. Addington, E. S. Wood, 1. Steers	...	Gammy
2	W. Andrews, A. Howell, W. ebbett	...	G. Boniface
3	T. Wood, F. Erridge, J. Day	...	N. Prodger
4	H. Tyrrell, J. Carter, H. Errige	...	T. Prodger
5	Cassy Reed, J. Bassett, H. Elins	...	T. Erridge
6	W. Reed, J G. Chester, F. Howell	...	H. Hobday
7	J. Allchorn, G. Erridge, R. Wilkinson	G. Erridge, senr.	
8	N. Hurd, N. Wilkinson, A. Higgett	...	J. Huggett
9	E. Boniface, C. Searle, C. Fox	...	Will Prodger
10	H. Boniface, E. H. Sayers, C. Barclay	...	J. Clark
11	A. Cushing, L. Thompson, G. Punyer	...	C. Matthews

SCULLING RACE.
FOR THE "TINKER" CHALLENGE CUP.

1 Cassy	5 Sausage	9 Tinker
2 M. Hardy	6 N. Prodger	10 H. Tyrrell
3 G. Boniface	7 T. Prodger	11 G. Erridge
4 J. Hardy	8 Sharky	12 F. Erridge
		13 Tim Erridge

Umpire: G. FRENCH. Starter: H. DYER.
Judges: H. ASHCROFT & C. PAINE.
Official Boatman : GOSH' HOWELL (E.A.A.)
R. HEGARTY (Umpire Boat)
Organising Secretary: C. GRAVETT.
All Crews assemble at the Eastbourne Angling Association Headquarters at 6.0 p.m. sharp.
Boats supplied by the Eastbourne Angling Association.
G.E.PIERCE, PRINTER, EASTBOURNE.

Ran Dan Race Entrants 1936.

February 1936.

Speedboat 'Alacrity' - Messrs. Allchorn requested a reduction of royalties (i.e. $\frac{1}{2}$d per passenger with payment of a minimum of £25 per year.) The Committee were sympathetic on this occasion and resolved to reduce royalties to a total of £12 10s per year. (So, after a few years they managed to get a reduction. Good old Sussex persistence paid off in the end)

Additional licences were issued for Motor Boats Nos.5, 67 & 125 and a new 2nd class Waterman Licence issued to Ernest Samuel Wood.

April 1936.

An application for a motor winch by Sayers Bros. on their Marine Parade stand was granted. (By now several motor winches were in use due to the heavier Motor Pleasure Boats and for ease of labour).

A new 1st class Waterman Licence was issued to Tom Wood.

June1936.

Speedboat 'Alacrity' owned by Messrs. Allchorn had its licence renewed for the year under same conditions. £12 10s royalties.

July 1936.

Additional Motor Boat Licence Nos.6, 21, 27, 36 & 37 were issued and a new Motor Boat Driver Licence issued to Tom Wood of 237, Northbourne Road.

September 1936.

A new 2nd class Waterman Licence was issued to Michael Frederick Thomas Hardy.

April 1937.

A report of renewal for the following licences: -
Rowboat Nos.1, 22, 62, 79, 128 & 141.
1st class Waterman Nos.4, 10, 30, 32, 38 & 54.
2nd class Waterman Nos.93, 94, 96, 107 & 119.
Motor Boat Driver Nos.21, 24, 26 & 38.
Motor Boat Nos.36 & 37.

Fred 'Tinker' Novis made an application for a portable slipway for his boats. This was granted after he submitted a rough drawing.

May 1937.

Licences were issued for Rowboat Nos.40, 77, 96, 104, 117, 162, 178,182 & 183 and 2nd class Waterman Licence No.84.

Coronation Celebrations.

It was Coronation Year and the Eastbourne Fishermen's & Boatmen's Protection Society played its part in the celebrations held in Eastbourne. Club members Albert 'Sam' Allchorn, Ernest 'Chinaman' Sayers, Henry Boniface and Fred 'Tinker' Novis were on the sub-Committee in charge of Aquatic Sports and the Illuminated Boats Procession.

On 12th May, Coronation Day, in the Grand procession through the town and along the seafront, the Club entered a magnificent float portraying 'With Captain Scott to the South Pole'.

At 9.30pm a procession of 'Illuminated Boats and a Mimic Battle' took place between the Great Redoubt and the Wish Tower.

Entrants for registered Fishermen and licensed Boatmen were: -
Sayers Bros. - All Electric.
E. Sayers - Fairy Lights.
Fishermen's and Boatmen's Club - Capt. Scott.
F W Novis - Paris by Moonlight.
W Allchorn and Sons - Decorated Lifeboat.
Chief Marshals: Messrs. A Allchorn and H Sayers.

On Friday 14th May, Children's aquatic sports, sculling and paddling races were held on Prince's Park Lake.

Officials being drawn from members of the Club were G French, F Nickson, G Erridge, T Boniface and F Novis. The Greasy pole master was Professor Tom Prodger.

A 'Battle Royal' was organized by the Fishermen's and Boatmen's Society which took place at 3.30pm

On Saturday 15th May, club members competed for a Coronation Cup in a Ran-Dan race. Single and double sculling races and fun events including the Greasy pole followed this.

The Coronation Cup race was a close run thing. Of the 9 entries the winning crew were: - Bert Addington, Jesse Chester, Fred Erridge with George Erridge - Cox.

Another Ran-Dan race for Licensed Boatmen also took place. This time the winning crew were: - Tom Allchorn, Nelson Hurd, Boniface with William Allchorn - Cox.

The crowds on the Parades were well entertained.

In aid of charity, these Ran-Dan races went on for the years up to the 2nd World War.

Boatman Jesse Chester on left C.1930.

June 1937.

Additional licences for Motor Boat Nos.10, 21, 27, 47, 69 & 124 were issued and new licences issued: 1st class Waterman to Nelson Hurd and Motor Boat Driver M F T Hardy.

September 1937.

A Motor Boat Driver Licence was issued to Ernest Wood.

April 1938.

Additional licences were issued - 1st class Waterman No.38, Motor Boat Driver No.38 and Motor Boat Nos.10, 67 & 69.

Regarding the Speedboat Licence No.12 for 'Alacrity', Messrs. Allchorn made a request to cease payment of royalties without luck - the payments to continue.

The same month Messrs. Sayers, Pleasure Motor Boat 'Britannia' was hired to recover a body from below Beachy Head. During the recovery operation damage was sustained by the boat and as a result Sayers were paid 16s 6d compensation.

June 1938.

Ernest Sayers requested to keep a Motor Boat on his Stand opposite the Albion Hotel. Granted.

September 1938.

Sayers was granted Capstan Stand Nos.18 & 19 recently held by Henry Morgan Boniface who left the town to take up a position as Fishery Officer for the East Sussex Coastal Area. (From the Eastbourne seafaring Boniface family and a Lifeboat crew member, he had a wealth of experience in the Fishing and Boating occupations and for many years carried out his duties with diligence and commanded much respect from the seafaring community.)

March 1939.

From the records of the minutes of the Entertainments & Pleasure Ground Committee, a complaint had been received about boating tackle left lying around the beach by the Boatmen at the end of the season. The matter was passed to the Chief Constable to deal with. He resolved that he would see it removed at the end of each season.

New 1st class Waterman Licences were issued to Frank Smith & Albert Wood and 1st class Waterman Licence No.72 was renewed for the ensuing year.

May 1939.

Chief Constable's report for Licencing - Existing licences in respect of Motor Boat Nos.10, 36, 41, 47 67 & 124 were issued.

The placing of a private sailing boat on the foreshore on Harry Allchorn's Boat Stand was agreed, and a Rowing Boat Licence application by E H Sayers to place on his stand was agreed.

June 1939.

Motor Boat Licence No.5 was renewed and a Motor Boat Driver Licence was issued to George Frederick Grooms.

July 1939.

Renewals of existing licences for Motor Boat Nos.21, 27 & 69 were granted.

George Grooms business card.

September 1939.

The renewal licence for Rowing Boat No.86 was agreed.

The War Years.

With the outbreak of War in August 1939, the Eastbourne Fishermen's and Boatmen's Protection Society elected a War Committee.

Chairman - Ernest 'Chinaman' Sayers.

Committee Society members - Albert 'Sam' Allchorn, William Allchorn, William Boniface, Jesse Huggett, Harry Erridge Snr. Edwin' Ned' Sayers and Mike 'Jersey' Hardy.

Associate members - Bill Andrews, T Mills, B Mepham and R Austen.

Blackout measures were put in hand, Silver cups placed into the Bank and enquiries put in hand regarding moving of the Society premises to St Anne's School during the War years in case of emergency. A stirrup pump was purchased for use in the event of a fire and £500 invested in War bonds.

The War years saw many of the Boating and Fishing Community on active service. Some lost their lives early in the War when H.M.S. Royal Oak was torpedoed in Scapa Flow, also the sinking of H.M.S Courageous and armed Merchant cruiser Rawalpindi. Boatman Jesse Chester lost his life serving aboard H.M.S Afridi.

With the country on a War footing it was in December 1939 that the Council decided to hire a boat for use by the local Police, in order to test whether the lights of Hotels and other buildings along the entire length of the Parades were properly blacked out. A boat was hired from Messrs. Allchorn at 5s per week in order that Parade Police could examine the position from the sea. The boat also proved useful to examine objects at sea which could not be distinguished by shore telescope.

May 1940.

It came to be, that the Boatmen and Fishermen of Eastbourne who could not enlist played an important part in serving their country on two occasions.

On May 30th an order came from the Admiralty at Dover for Eastbourne selected Fishing and Pleasure Motor Boats to proceed to Dover immediately for an evacuation of British forces from Dunkirk, France.

It was 9pm when Eastbourne's little squadron set sail. Sayers Bros. sent boats the 'Britannia', 'Eastbourne Queen' and 'Grace Darling'. William Allchorn & Sons sent 'Enchantress' and 'Eastbourne Belle'. Henry Boniface sent 'Coronation' and the fishing boat 'Commodore'.

Manned by their Eastbourne crews they arrived in Dover at 6am, fully prepared to sail across the English Channel to take part in the evacuation and 'do their bit'. Ernest 'Glaxo' Sayers on his return to Eastbourne said, *"We fully expected and wanted to take our boats across, but the Navy would have none of it. They commandeered our boats and that was that. They'll not get better boats, Tom Sisk and Roland Pragnell built them well."*

Sadly they were the last voyages for the 'Britannia', 'Commodore' and 'Enchantress' as they were all lost off Dunkirk.

June 1940.

Just a week later, Eastbourne Fishermen and Boatmen sailed in an armada from Newhaven to take part in a gallant action at St.Valery-en-Caux, Brittany, when an attempt was made to evacuate 2,000 British troops.

This time some intrepid Eastbourne men sailed their own open deck vessels across, others were manned by naval ratings. Spending two days off St.Valery they did indeed rescue some British and French soldiers.

The Eastbourne boats taking part were: - 'Mizpah', 'Amaris', 'Golden City', 'Britannia III', 'Olive Joyce', 'Lady Doris', 'Our Lassie', 'Hibernia', 'Albion', 'Ocean's Gift', 'Nona', 'Three Brothers', 'Hawfinch', 'Silver Spray', 'Ocean Spray' and 'Star of the East'. Eastbourne men also crewed the Brighton boat 'Fair Irene'.

The men who took part in the operation off St.Valery were Henry Erridge, Henry Boniface, Victor Crick, Albert Addington, George Henry Erridge, George John Erridge, Jack Allchorn, Edwin 'Ned' Sayers, Albert 'Sam' Allchorn, Ernest 'Glaxo' Sayers, William Sayers, Frederick Allchorn, Nelson Prodger, Nelson Sayers and Bevan Thornton.

In 1947 these men were honoured with certificates of merit and the boats each a bronze plaque bearing the legend 'St.Valery-en-Caux 1940'. Some of these plaques can be seen to this day displayed in the Fishermen's Club, Royal Parade.

The War Committee agreed in March that members of Marine Hall, Longstone Road, could hold religious meetings on the foreshore opposite the 'Sandon Boarding House' Royal Parade, from May to September on Sunday evenings. In July they agreed the issue of renewal for Licences 1st class Waterman Nos.4, 11 & 60 and Motor Boat Drivers Nos.26 & 48.

Records are sparse for the War years but it is known that all 'Pleasuring' stopped, as Eastbourne was in the front line and very invasion prone during those early years of the War. The seafront was closed to all. Barbed wire defences were erected along with a military presence and guns pointing seaward. It remained this way for the duration.

For the Boatmen with their boats laid up, other occupations called for those unable or too old to serve their country. But serve some did as Wardens of one sort in other Wartime civilian occupations. For those with fishing boats, they were able to follow this calling under certain restrictions, but not without danger. For example in June 1942, off Eastbourne, three times an enemy aircraft strafed a fishing boat containing the crew of Jack Huggett, Fred 'Tinker' Novis and Mickey Andrews. Huggett received shrapnel wounds to his shoulder, Novis was wounded in the shoulder and legs while Andrews had severe injuries to the stomach and leg, sadly losing the leg. What an experience - unarmed and at the mercy of the enemy.

December 1942.

From the War Committee minutes - An application by Edwin 'Ned' Sayers of 28, Latimer Road for transfer to him of Net shop No.53 at the Fishing Station presently held by Albert 'Tuppy' Sayers who was giving up due to advanced age. Edwin Sayers was a bona fide professional fisherman and owner of a large amount of fishing gear as well as owner of a number of small Pleasure Boats. Application was granted.

April 1945.

With the War nearly over in Europe an early application was made by Fred 'Tinker' Novis of 31, Seaford Road, to grant him a licence to operate 11 Rowing Boats and 1 Motor Boat. He fully understood that the Regional Petroleum Officer would not grant the issue of petrol for the Motor Boat. But Novis desired to obtain a licence so that if the release of petrol was long delayed he could adapt the Motor Boat for rowing. All his boats had been inspected by Police and Parade Inspector and found seaworthy. If licences were granted he would have to obtain permission of the Senior Naval Officer I/C Newhaven before operating the boats. The application was granted.

An application was also received from Albert 'Sam' Allchorn of 25, Carlton Road on behalf of Messrs. Allchorn for the opinion of the Watch Committee as to policy of granting licences for Pleasure Boats in the 1945 season. The firm operated boats that ran on power paraffin, but a quantity of 12 gallons of petrol per month was required to start the engines. Before boats were operated they had to be submitted to a Board of Trade examination. Allchorn desired guidance over making future plans to operate. It was understood the Ministry of Fuel would not at that moment issue petrol for Pleasure Boats. That was the situation just prior to the end of the War in Europe. All the Boatmen must have been itching to get started again on making a living but not only that, it was a way of life denied them for some 5 years.

The following information gives a good example of their need to start again. Applications for operating, Boats, Boat Stands, Capstan Stand, Waterman and Motor Boat Driver Licences must have kept the Council officers and Police busy.

The End of the War in Europe.

May 1945.

George F Grooms applied for Net Shop Nos.32 & 45 and Capstan Stand No.26a at the Fishing Station, also Boat Stand Nos.48 & 50 - All to be transferred to him, having purchased the Boating business from Frederick Hurd. The application was granted.

So young 'Sausage' Grooms continued a family tradition through his father William 'Sausage' Grooms who had fished and Pleasure Boated from Eastbourne beach since the early days. William 'Sausage' Grooms served his country well enlisting in the Royal Naval Brigade and being severely wounded at Gallipoli 1915. He was lucky to survive that horror. Young 'Sausage' plied his Rowboats for many post War years from the Royal Parade.

July 1945.

Net Shop No.41, Capstan Stand No.43 and Boat Stand Nos.23, 24 & 25 opposite Victoria Place - An application by Mr. William Allchorn (grandson of William Allchorn 1855-1933, and son of Edward Allchorn) for transfer to him of the above previously granted to his father who died in 1943. The Town Clerk reported that Mr. William Allchorn has been employed in the Motor Omnibus Department since 1925 and wished to retain his Corporation employment. He also wished to continue the business carried out previously by his father, which he would supervise in his spare time. In view of the terms of the agreements under which the Corporation held the Fishing Station on trust for the Fishermen of the County Borough of Eastbourne, the Town Clerk pointed out that as Mr. Allchorn would not be obtaining his living from Fishing, the tenancies of the Net Shop and Capstan Stand could not be transferred to him. (This was the case with all Boatmen. They had to fish if they wanted to rent Net Shops and Capstan Stands at the Fishing Station, which they did during the winter months usually some full time. Some made a few token trips, but fish they had to. In all truth the Council had from time to time been lax with this rule over the years)

The Committee interviewed Mr. Allchorn and Parade Inspector Arnold. After further consideration a decision was reached. With regret they were unable to grant the application.

Existing licences were issued in respect of Motor Boat Nos.6, 7, 10, 36, 47, 67, 69 and Rowboat Nos.51, 58, 82 & 83.

Boat Stands & Capstan Stands.

An application was submitted from Mr. Ted Hide, who was at present serving in the Royal Navy, for the transfer to him of any Capstan and Boat Stand previously rented by his father, the late Edward Hide.

P S Arnold Parade Inspector responded that there were now no such stands and it was resolved that Mr. Hide be informed. So an attempt by the Hide family to get back into Boating failed.

Also in July, the Police Chief Superintendent gave an annual report to the Watch Committee on licensing, in place of the Chief Constable.

A new Licence for 1st class Waterman and Motor Boat Driver Albert F Addington was granted.

Fred 'Tinker' Novis stated that in regard to his application for 11 Rowboats and 1 Motor Boat, the Motor Boat concerned was previously named 'Britannia' and had now been renamed 'Bonny Charlie'. The boat was to be used just for Fishing Parties as it did not conform as a Pleasure Boat and was in fact a Fishing Boat. Licences were granted for the Rowboats only. Permission was given to keep 'Bonny Charlie' at his Boat Stand opposite the Queens Hotel.

An application was made by Albert 'Sam' Allchorn of 25, Carlton Road, for tenancy of Boat Stand Nos.23, 24 & 25 on Grand Parade. The application was made on behalf of Messrs. Allchorn who already rented adjacent stands. Edward Allchorn, now deceased, formerly rented the Stands applied for. So the stands previously denied to Mr. William Allchorn were granted to the family firm made up of his uncles and cousins. Further control of the prime sites at Victoria steps passed to Messrs. Allchorn.

Mr. C A Meadows' application to place his private boat on the Boat Stand occupied by E A Sayers at Marine Parade was rejected. It was now the policy not to allow private boats on licenced Boat Stands. (A loss of income for the Boatmen who would have kept on 'eye' on the boat)

September 1945.

Insurance of Boats - The Town Clerk submitted a letter that had been received from the Phoenix Assurance Co. Ltd. offering to insure the proprietors of Pleasure Boats against 3rd party claims. Premiums for Rowing Boats carrying 6 persons was 7/2d, Motor Boats carrying 12 persons £1.6s.5d, the indemnity for one accident being £5,000. It was resolved that conditions be included in all licence agreements for Pleasure Boats and Pleasure Vessels issued under Sect.94 Public Health Acts 1907, that an Insurance policy must be taken out.

Speedboats.

An application was made by Capt. W Ford for permission to operate Speedboat Services from Eastbourne beach for the season 1946, from a point on the beach between the Victoria Court Hotel and West Rocks Hotel. This was granted subject to standing regulations and provided boats were only operated from Marine Parade between the Queens Hotel and a point 50 yards west of the Albion Hotel, which was the section now reserved for Speedboats.

In December, Capt Ford made application for all 6 Speedboat Stands on the beach reserved for Speedboats. The Parade Inspector recommended that 4 Boat Stand Nos.59-62 be granted as sufficient. The Committee were prepared to grant the above with No.61 to be used as a Capstan Stand.

Capstans Nos.14, 15, 42 and Boat Stand No.16 were granted to Boatman E Sayers for tenancy. His now retired father formerly rented them.

October 1945.

Fred Novis made an application for the tenancy of Capstan Stand No.54 and to surrender Boat Stand No.57. He also requested for tenancy of Capstan Stand No.27 at the Fishing Station. This was granted. As to Net Shop Nos.29 & 30 Parade Inspector Arnold reported on the dilapidated condition of the above, formerly tenanted by Thomas Sisk boat builder, who died February 1944. Notice to quit was to be served on his widow.

January 1946.

Lt Col. Stevens made an application to operate a Speedboat from the shore. This was granted and Boat Stand Nos.57 & 58 were allotted to him in addition to a Capstan Stand licence. The application made in January was later withdrawn in April 1946.

February 1946.

This month saw the retirement of an old Eastbourne Fisherman, Boatman and Lifeboat man Ernest 'Chinaman' Sayers, a member of the old Eastbourne seafaring family. He joined the Royal Navy as a 15-year-old lad in 1895 gaining a Long Service medal and serving 20 years in the Fleet Reserve. Re-enlisting in 1915 he saw active service on Minesweepers, and was involved in the Gallipoli Campaign. In 1918 he was back in Eastbourne operating Rowboats and his Motor Boat from his Stand opposite the Albion Hotel, Royal Parade. 1919 saw him start a long service with the Eastbourne Lifeboat. He recalled an occasion when out in bitterly cold seas, she started shipping mountainous waves. Ernie, who acted as steward aboard the Lifeboat 'James Stevens No.6', was ordered to issue tots of rum to the crew. As he stood pouring it out the 'James Stevens' lurched dangerously - *"but not one of the crew heeded the danger, they all had their eyes glued on the bottle to see I didn't drop it."* Ernest was a stalwart member of the Fishermen's Club and was Chairman for 12 years. Sadly he lost a son serving in the Navy in the 2nd World War.

May 1946.

The Chief Superintendents report for May.

New 2nd class Waterman licences were issued to Arthur Edward Allchorn and George Watkins.

George Grooms, licenced Boatman and Fisherman was granted the tenancy of Boat Stand Nos.66d & 66e formerly tenanted by the late Thomas Sisk.

Licence renewals were issued for Motor Boat Nos.6, 10, 11, 28 & 31.
1st class Waterman Nos.2, 19, 20, 36, 60 & 63.
2nd class Waterman Nos.91. 97.
Motor Boat Driver Nos.1, 22 & 32.

In view of petrol restrictions no Speedboats could operate for the 1946 season.

Nevertheless Speedboat operating applications were still made although there were no vacant stands and no petrol. However none were granted.

June 1946.

At the age of 82 years, Fisherman and Boatman Henry William Novis passed away in June 1946. He was the father of well-known and popular Fred 'Tinker' Novis. Henry along with other crew members of the Eastbourne Fishing lugger 'Thistle' survived a severe storm at sea in the English Channel in 1893. The French Fishing Boat 'Avenir' rescued them.

September 1946.

The first Regatta to be held since 1939.

December 1946.

A report showed that the 6 Speedboat Stands along Marine Parade were divided equally between 2 applicants, a Mr. Webb for Nos.57-59 and Holiday Amenities Ltd. for Nos.60-62 for the upcoming 1947 season.

The Eastbourne Boatmen were criticised in the national press for the high costs of their boat trips. This proved not to be the case. A pre-War trip to the Lightship cost 1/6d. This had risen to 2/-. All things considered this was hardly excessive.

April 1947.

The Deputy Chief Constable gave the April report on licences, amongst which after renewals a new licence was issued in respect of the Rowing Boat 'Eileen' to George Grooms.

A 2nd class Waterman licence to Alan Pitcher of 216, Seaside, was granted.

June 1947.

Still no Speedboats operating due to the petrol shortage but come August rationed supplies were available.

September 1947.

A complaint was made by the Boatmen of the E.F.B.P. Society about an amphibious

DUKW vehicle being used to ferry passengers to Speedboats being operated by Francis Hannington-Lee of 2, Ludlow Court, Silverdale Road. There were some problems over Hannington-Lee as his application for a 1st class Waterman and Motor Boat Driver licence, which had been denied. The Council listened to the Boatmen and stopped the use of the DUKW.

(DUKW - ex-military amphibious WW2 transport vehicle commonly known as a 'duck')

December 1947. The Sayers Family

An application by Edwin 'Ned' Sayers for the transfer of Net Shop No.51 and Capstan Stand Nos.32 & 40 at the Fishing Station, previously his deceased father's, was granted - Sayers being a bona fide Fisherman and Boatman.

Ernest Harold Sayers of 35, Latimer Road was secretary of the firm Messrs. Sayers Bros. Fishermen & Pleasure Boat owners. He requested the transfer to that firm as was at present constituted; the Net Shops, Capstan Stands and Boat Stands referred to below. The reason for the application was that Ernest Harold,

Sail Pleasure Boat 'Albatross' with fishing registration number. NN115, on Sayers Brothers Boat Stand 1911.

William Walter, Stanley George and Harry Sayers constituted the firm, but Harry Sayers had now left the business.

At the Fishing Station, Net Shop Nos.45 & 50, Capstan Stand Nos.35 & 39, Net Shop No.46 and Capstan Stand Nos.36 & 36a. Also Parade Boat Stand Nos.39-45 inclusive, Capstan Stand Nos.36, 36a, 37, 38 & 38a, Boat Stand No.51 and Capstan Stand No.52, were tenanted by Harry Sayers and transfer to the firm Sayers Bros. was sought. Boat Stand No. 53 was at present tenanted by William Sayers and transfer was also sought. All the above were granted.

The Sayers were a numerous Fishing, Pleasure Boating and Lifeboat Service family on par with the Allchorns

1930. 'Old' Ned Sayers varnishing oars ready for the start of the season. Note the cane Rowboat backboards.

Boatman Ernest 'Glaxo' Sayers and Pleasure Boat 'Southern Queen' 1959.

and other Eastbourne seafaring families. Some Sayers stories having already been mentioned previously in this record. Fishing and Boating off the beach at Eastbourne from the early days, Sayers, along with the Allchorns became the last surviving pair of families to ply for hire with their big motor launches through from the 2nd World War until the 1960s. Their last big boats being 'Eastbourne Queen' and 'Southern Queen', which they sold to the Allchorns when Sayers ceased Boating in 1965.

As previously mentioned, they traded on par with the Allchorns, Sayers having established their prime Boat Stand site in a groyne just west of the Pier. 'Pincher' Hide's family and other Eastbourne Boatmen once operated part of this site.

The Allchorn Boat Stand was just a few groynes further west, opposite Victoria Place now renamed Terminus Road. Competition for business was keen between the families as day-trippers spilled onto the Parade from Victoria Place, especially those years after the War and before foreign holidays became the norm. Eastbourne people of those years will remember the large Boatman 'Glaxo' Sayers standing on the lower parade booming out *"Nice day for a trip"* and likewise a less noisy Allchorn calling *"Boat just leaving for Beachy Head"*.

Sadly a sound not heard these days on the seafront. Strangely these two prominent seafaring families were known as Sayers 'Knucklows' and Allchorn 'Donkeys'. These titles well known among the beach fraternity, the origins of which are 'lost in time'.

The following is from an interview published in the Eastbourne Herald, with Henry Sayers back in October 1944.

"In the piping times of peace, Henry Sayers, 'Harry' to his host of friends, was known to thousands of visitors to Eastbourne beach. He has been a licensed Boatman for forty-three years since 1901 and in all that time, except of course for the War period, he has looked after people who wanted to hire a boat or indulge in a little rod or line Fishing. Indeed the seafront has been not only his livelihood, but also his very life. He belongs to one of the

Sayers Brothers 'Britannia' Boat trip ticket 1912.

oldest Fishing and Boating families in Eastbourne. Several generations of Sayers have followed these honourable callings and no doubt in years to come will still be found tending their boats and nets.

'Harry' is very proud of his record. He has grown up with Eastbourne as the saying goes, and he is as jealous of its good name as he is of his own. It is with pride that he will point out the house where he was born in 1876. Then it was 14, Warrior Square, now it is 39, Latimer Road. It is only a few yards from his present house, 76, Latimer Road.

The Sayers Family on Eastbourne Parade.

But what a change has come about in the passing years! 'When I was boy' he will tell you. 'I rowed a boat along what is now Rylstone Road.' In those days when the tide was up, you had to 'watch out'. In Redoubt Road for instance, arches were built to let the water run away and at some places 'pug boards' were put down to stop it seeping into the houses. 'Harry' continued and told that he and his brother 'Ted' Sayers (he died in 1937) were in partnership on the beach. They had 3 Motor Boats and about 12 Rowing Boats, which they plied for hire to visitors. In the winter they went fishing for herring and sprats.

Sayers Brothers Pleasure Boats C.1950. Foreground shows converted Brighton ex-Lifeboat 'Grace Darling'.

Sayers Brothers Motor Pleasure Boat 'Britannia' just leaving for a trip.

After 'Ted's' death his two sons Ernest and William (Harry's nephews) came into the business, which was interrupted by the War. 'Harry' tells of the part the firm's Motor Boats played in the Dunkirk evacuation, when everything that would float was wanted to bring our men off.

Sayers Brothers Motor Pleasure Boats. Left -'Eastbourne Queen' right -'Southern Queen' C.1960.

Boatman 'Young' Ned Sayers telling a story 1954.

Rowboats of Ned Sayers 1954.

The Sayers' boats were 'Eastbourne Queen', 'Grace Darling', and sadly the 'Britannia', which did not come back, she being lost off Dunkirk. When the War is over we shall go back to the boats. (Which is exactly what happened and they successfully traded up to 1965).

'Harry' went on to tell of his connection with the Eastbourne Rowing Club. Started to row back in 1895 and winning many Regatta races and trophies along the South Coast for many years."

In 1947 the long established boating firm of Messrs. Allchorn Bros. was also going through changes at the same time as the Sayers Brothers.

The following explains it from a report of an application submitted for Albert 'Sam' Allchorn, (of 56, St Philips Avenue, secretary of the firm Messrs. Allchorn Bros, Fishermen & Pleasure Boat owners), for the transfer of the under mentioned Net Shops etc. to himself, and brothers William and Frederick Allchorn. Albert, John and Thomas Allchorn previously held the agreements. Brothers John and Thomas Allchorn had now left the firm.

At the Fishing Station Net Shop Nos.36, 37, 38, 47 & 48, Capstan Stand Nos.29, 31, 37 & 38, the Parade Boat Stand Nos.21, 29, 30, 31 & 34 and Capstan Stand Nos.22, 28, 32, 32a, 33, 35 & 81: All transfers were granted.

January 1948.

A Lt. Browne applied for a licence to give trips in a DUKW, from the foreshore: Not granted.

February 1948.

John Allchorn of 3, Desmond Road, made a request for the tenancy of Net Shop No.48 to be transferred from Messrs. Allchorn Bros. to himself, a bona fide Fisherman: This was granted.

A stiff breeze and wet feet!

John also explained that he and brother Thomas Allchorn of 39, Ringwood Road had obtained permission from Henry Boniface of 63, Channel View Road, subject to the Committee's approval, to use his Capstan No.17 and Boat Stand No.20 at the Grand Parade. Boniface had no Pleasure Boats at that time and he was willing to the let the Allchorn brothers have use of the Stand.

They also asked permission to re-erect a concrete bed upon which to place a motor winch on the Capstan referred to. The previous concrete bed was destroyed during the War years.

They wanted permission to place a pay box on the Boat Stand as permission was given many years ago to Boniface subject to a weekly fee of 1/-. Both men had held 1st class Waterman licences for many years and both were Fishermen having a good knowledge of local conditions. They were reliable and capable Boatmen. All the applications were granted.

Aboard Sayers 'Eastbourne Queen' Boatman Alec Huggett at tiller. Eddie Knight standing aft. C.1950.

So we see that John and Tom Allchorn set up 'Pleasuring' with their Motor Boat 'Endeavour' in opposition to their brothers just along the beach.

That same month an application was made for 2 Ship's Lifeboats to operate off the beach as Pleasure Boats. The Council, not keen on any more operators, denied the request.

April 1948.

The Chief Constable again took over the reporting of licencing at the Watch Committee meeting.

New licences were issued for Motor Boat Drivers George Punyer, Stanley Sayers, and Geoffrey Carter.

2nd class Waterman licence to Thomas Wootten and a transfer of George Watkins 2nd to 1st class Waterman licence.

A Pleasure Boat/Rowing Boat licence for 'Dawn' owned by Mike Hardy was granted.

The Chief Constable also stated that an application had been received from A J Foley of the E.F.B.P. Society, on behalf of 6 boat owners for an increase in fares for Pleasure Boats as follows: -

Motor Boat hire - whole boat carrying up to 12 persons - proposed 15/- to 30/-.
For boats carrying more than 12 persons - £2.
And the following new suggestions not covered in 1920 Bye-Laws: -
For every person carried, at separate fares from 3/- to 4/- and pro rata under the hour.
Rowing Boats - for hire of the whole boat (with Boatman) from 3/- to 5/-.
Hire of whole boat - (without Boatman) from 2/- to 3/6 and pro rata under the hour.

The fares for Pleasure Boats were governed under the Bye-Laws made 2nd June 1920. The foregoing was submitted for consideration and discussion with the Entertainments & Pleasure Grounds Committee. In June, the Council adopted the above and incorporated them in the Bye-Laws.

Also at the above meeting the Town Clerk spoke on the subject of Pleasure Motor Boats. He stated that new regulations were to be brought in requiring that a person in charge of a Motor Boat was to be an experienced Boatman. Boats were to carry at least 2 lifebuoys, 2 smoke signals and at least 1 portable fire extinguisher. It was then resolved that a requirement for all future licences would be that 2 smoke signals were to be carried.

Albert 'Sam' Allchorn applied to use a DUKW amphibious vehicle for the purpose of hauling Motor Boats down to low water and across the sands at low tide. This was not granted. Regarding this application, a letter was submitted from the E.F.B.P. Society stating that it was made without the Society's approval. The Committee noted this.

An application by Boatmen Tom and John Allchorn to have a ringbolt fitted in the low wall at the foot of the bank opposite their Boat Stand on the Grand Parade was granted.

June 1948.

An application was made by Allchorn Bros. for the Motor Pleasure Boat 'Enchantress' to be equipped with a personal address system. There were no objections to it being used at sea, but not at anchor or near the beach and it was prohibited for touting. Another first for the Allchorns, which was soon to be followed by their main competitors Sayers Bros.

Licence renewals issued that month were: -
Motor Pleasure Boat 'Waverley' - Fred Novis.
Motor Pleasure Boat 'Britannia III' - Sayers Bros.
Motor Boat Driver licence renewals - George Watkins and Henry Cherry.

Tom and John Allchorn were granted tenancy of Net Shop No.44 at the Fishing Station, vacant since 1945. Also the use of a concrete shelter to be built by the applicants to repair boat engines etc. was granted subject to the approval of the Borough Surveyor.

September 1948.

The Home Office suggested to the Council that new Bye-Laws be raised governing Pleasure Boats. One suggestion being, no Pleasure Boat shall ply for hire more than 3 miles from the shore.

An application from Stanley Sayers of 13, Woodgate Road, for Net Shop No.43. The applicant was a member of the firm of Sayers Bros, engaged in Boating in the summer and Fishing in the winter: Granted. The renewal of the licence for Pleasure Boat 'Hibernia' owned by Mike Hardy was granted.

March 1949.

The Chief Constable's report for March.

A new licence for Rowing Boat 'Christine' owner George Grooms was granted.

A request by Alan Pitcher for an upgrade from 2nd class Waterman (since 1947) to 1st class was not granted.

R Dutton's request for a 2nd class Waterman licence to 1st class was granted.

Motor Boat Driver No.5 and 1st class Waterman Nos.3, 18, 26 & 27 Licence renewals were granted.

June 1949.

A 2nd class Waterman licence issued to Edward Charles Knight and a licence for the 'Eastbourne Queen' Motor Pleasure Boat owned by Sayers Bros. were both granted.

July 1949.

Another renewal of licence for 'Hibernia' owned by Mike Hardy was granted.

October 1949.

J H Grooms of 4, Cavalry Crescent, made an application in October, for Capstan Stand No.25 at the Fishing Station. Grooms held a 1st class Waterman licence and was employed by Messrs. Allchorn Bros. He owned a Fishing boat and intending to make his living with it during the winter. The application was granted.

November 1949.

Parade Inspector Humphrey spoke of proposals afoot to discontinue his job. His duties were to be taken over by a member of the Entertainments & Pleasure Ground Department. In due course at a meeting of the Entertainments & Pleasure Grounds Committee in November, it resolved the principal of the Parade Inspector's duties being undertaken by a member of the General Manager's staff, and the police to undertake some duties including the supervision of Pleasure Boats.

January 1950.

It was resolved that the Police would carry out the duties of licencing Boatmen and boats etc. The Chief Constable would be responsible and submit applications to the Watch Committee. The Town Clerk stated preparation, sealing and issuing of licences was a matter for him and would remain so. Mr. H Chester was made new Parade Inspector.

March 1950.

A 2nd class Waterman licence was issued to Roy Prodger.

2nd class Waterman & Motor Boat Driver licences were issued to A Cornelius, Edward Sayers and Neville Dean.

In that month the renewal of Motor Boat licences came up and the following were issued: -
Sayers Bros. - 'Eastbourne Queen', 'Grace Darling' and 'Britannia III'
Allchorn Bros. - 'Enchantress' and 'Endeavour'
F. Novis - 'Waverley'
M Hardy - 'Hibernia'

The above shows Eastbourne's Pleasure Motor Boat operators for the year 1950 - Allchorn and Sayers Bros. off the Grand Parade, Novis and Hardy off Marine and Royal Parade.

It would appear that John and Tom Allchorn were back in the family business, with the Pleasure Boat 'Endeavour' being licenced by Messrs. Allchorn Bros.

Sayers boat 'Grace Darling' was an ex Brighton Lifeboat.

May 1950.

To make business more difficult for the Boatmen, the Council introduced 'pedalos' on the beach granting a licence in May to Pedalo Craft Ltd. The Entertainments & Pleasure Grounds Committee gave permission for 20 'pedalos' in total, to operate off the Redoubt area.

September 1950.

What appears to be the first lady Waterman licence 2nd class was issued to Miss June Rosemary Matthews. The report by Parade Inspector Chester stated that he had tested her swimming and recommended the application be granted. (It is not known whom she worked for.)

It appears that the Police had ceased to deal with licencing applications as the Committee minutes show the Town Clerk submitting an application for licences in respect of the 'William Allchorn', 'Britannia III', 'Eastbourne Belle' and 'Southern Queen' all of which had been passed by the Council's Inspector of Motor Vehicles and Motor Boats. The Parade Inspector recommended all the above.

New regulations governing Licenced Pleasure Boats & Boatmen were in a report submitted by the Town Clerk.

"Regulations to be observed by owners of Pleasure Boats carrying more than 12 passengers upon the granting of a passenger certificate by the Ministry of Transport."
1. To take out insurance.
2. No use of loud hailer Public Address system to tout.
3. Every person employed in or about the boat shall hold the appropriate licence issued by Eastbourne Corporation.
4. The person in charge of the boat - Skipper, to hold 1st class Waterman & Motor Boat licences.

5. The Engineer to hold a Motor Boat Drivers licence.
6. All other persons to hold 2nd class Waterman licences.
7. To keep within 3-mile limit.
8. To carry at least one pair of oars.
9. Two smoke flares.
10. Two lifebuoys
11. A proper lifebelt for each passenger.
12. Buoyant apparatus capable of supporting not less than 60% of passengers for which the boat is licenced.

March 1951.

Following applications for new licences, the following were issued: -
1st class Waterman to P Cohen. Also to A Bolden and Albert 'Sam' Allchorn who already held 2nd class licences.
A 2nd class Waterman licence was issued to Brian E Allchorn son of 'Sam'.

April 1951.

New Speedboat regulations were introduced with an annual licence fee of 5/-.
Motor Boat licence renewals listed were shown as: -
Sayers Bros. - 'Southern Queen' and 'Britannia III'
Fred Novis - 'Waverley'
Motor Boat Driver licences were issued to A F Huggett and G Carter.

June1951.

Transfer from 2nd class to 1st class Waterman of A N Sayers, G Punyer, E J Sayers, E Knight, G Carter and H Cherry.

2nd class Waterman licences were issued to W Wood and L Pentecost.

February 1952.

The Parade Inspector submitted the following applications for transfer of 2nd class Waterman to 1st class to take effect from 1st April 1952.
Henry W Boniface - 2nd class to 1st class No.88.
Charles Seale - 2nd class to 1st class No.82.
Neville Dean - 2nd class to 1st class No.85.
Alan Pitcher - 2nd class to 1st class No.84.
All were granted.
Motor Boat licences were issued to: -
No.5 'Hibernia' - Mike Hardy.
No.10 'Britannia' - Sayers Bros.
No.22 'Waverly' - Fred Novis.

The above licences were granted subject to the Transport Manager passing the boats as being mechanically efficient.

April 1952.

The Parade Inspector submitted applications for new licences for William Allchorn Jnr. of 40, Desmond Road and Walter Powney both for 2nd class Waterman: Granted. Also licence No.25 for Speedboat 'Golden Arrow V'. (Off the Pier?)

1st class Waterman licence issued to F Morrow and the 'pedalos' still going strong with a renewal licence issued.

June 1952.

The following licences were issued: -
1st class Waterman to P Stevens.
2nd class to Fred Elstone, C Wright and D Callaghan.
A Motor Boat Driver licence was granted to Peter Stevens.
A Rowing Boat licence for 'Seaflower' owned by Edwin Sayers, 48, Latimer Road was granted.
New Pleasure Boat Bye-Laws were proposed and were referred back for discussions with the Eastbourne Fishermen's & Boatmen's Protection Society.

February 1953.

Pleasure Boat Bye-Laws - The Town Clerk reported that the Home Secretary had confirmed Bye-Laws made in respect of above by Eastbourne Council and they were to come into operation from 1st March 1953.

Licence renewals for the month reported by the Parade Inspector were: -
Motor Boats -
No.5. 'Hibernia'
No.10 'Britannia III'
No.22 'Waverley'
Speedboats -
No.25 'Golden Arrow V'
No.26 'Golden Arrow IX' (So two Speedboats operating in 1953.)

The transfer from 2nd class Waterman to 1st class for Brian Allchorn No.92 and William Wood No.96 were confirmed.

A new licence 2nd class Waterman to Robert Milton, of 151, Seaside, having passed the test.

June 1953.

Twenty 'pedalo' licences were renewed.

February 1954.

Licence renewals in February, saw the Entertainments Manager submit applications for the following: -
New applicant for 2nd class Waterman was John Bassett of 35, Sidley Road. He attended an interview and the licence was granted.
Motor Boat licence renewals -
No.5 'Hibernia'
No.10 'Britannia'
No.22 'Waverley'

Speedboat licence renewals -
No.25 'Golden Arrow V'
No.26 'Golden Arrow IX'

The above licences were renewed subject to Eastbourne Transport Manager being satisfied to the mechanical efficiency of the boats. (The above boats were not subject to a Board of Trade inspection. Messrs. Allchorn Bros. and Sayers Bros. big Pleasure Motorboats were for some years subject to Local and Board of Trade inspections. Eventually only the latter was necessary.)

April 1954.

The Entertainments Manager who submitted the following 2nd class to be transferred to 1st class issued Waterman licences: -
W J Allchorn, 2nd class No.83 to 1st class No.48.
R Prodger, 2nd class No.87 to 1st class No.49.
W Powney 2nd class No.89 to 1st class No.50.
D Callaghan 2nd class No.100 to 1st class No.51.
F Elstone 2nd class No.101 to 1st class No.47.
All were granted.

April 1955.

Licence renewals, submitted by the Entertainments Manager.
Motor Boat renewals -
No.5 'Hibernia'
No.22 'Waverley'
Speedboat renewals -
No.25 'Golden Arrow V'
No.26 'Golden Arrow IX'
All granted.

Pleasure Boat Bye-Laws - The Town Clerk reminded the Committee that in July 1954, all Boatmen had agreed to pay increased charges for their Boat Stands on the beach or foreshore and had signed new agreements relative thereof. The Council was to approve maximum fares for Pleasure Boat trips and to submit these to the Home Secretary for confirmation and amending of the Bye-Laws. All Boatmen had signed the new agreements. The Committee resolved to repeal Bye-Laws 4 & 5 regulating mooring places for Pleasure Boats & vessels, as they had long since had no practical use or meaning.

New charges to be introduced were as follows: -

Rowboats.
Hire of whole boat for 1-hour (with Boatman) 6/-
Additional 30 minutes (with Boatman) 3/-
30 minutes or less (with Boatman) 3/-
Hire for 1 hour (without Boatman) 4 persons 4/-
Ditto exceeding 4 persons 1/- for each additional person.

Motor Boats by mechanical power.
Whole boat carrying up to 12 persons 30/-
Every additional 30 minutes pro rata per hour 15/-
Every person carried by trip at separate fares
Between 45-60 minutes 4/- each
Between 30-45 minutes 3/- each
Less that 30 minutes 2/- each

Speedboats.
5 minutes 3/6d

The above came into operation on the 1st September 1955.

February 1956.

The Town Clerk recommended the following conditions be added to Pleasure Rowboat licences: -

"The boat when carrying passengers for hire shall (except when hired without a Boatman) have on board, and being in charge of, a person holding a Boatman's licence issued by the Council". This was approved.

Licence renewals - The Entertainments Manager submitted the following as shown in the 'Book of Licences'

Motor Boat renewals -
No.22 'Waverley'
Speedboat renewals -
No.25 'Golden Arrow V'
No.26 'Golden Arrow IX'
All granted subject to the Transport Manager's approval.

No renewal for the Pleasure Boat 'Hibernia' - the Hardy family having ceased 'Pleasuring'. So only 'Tinker' Novis was to be seen operating his Motor Boat 'Waverley' from his stand just east of the Queens Hotel, Marine Parade and George Grooms with his Rowing Boats. They were the last of the Boatmen east of the pier.

The Hardy family's Motor Pleasure Boat 'Estella' The big boat to the left of photo 1915.

The Hardy family were another of the Eastbourne seafarers who had served the town well as Fishermen, Pleasure Boatmen and in the Lifeboat Service - mostly having their boats on site along the Marine and Royal Parades.

Michael 'Jersey Mike' Hardy succeeded Henry Boniface as Coxswain of the Eastbourne Lifeboat in 1924, and with his brave crew effecting many gallant services through to 1950. 'Jersey Mike' a name not forgotten in the annals of the Lifeboat Institute.

The Hardys were among the first Boatmen to go motorised having the 'Estella' built by J S Gowland. The 'Estella' proved a fine vessel serving as a Fishing boat and for

Pleasuring during the summer season. Known as a friendly benevolent family, the Hardys regularly entertained large numbers of orphans from the Post Office Orphans Home for many years starting in the early 1920s. They charitably took the orphans and Post Office employees on sea trips on their visits to Eastbourne - a happy day out for the 1st World War orphans.

May 1956.

The Entertainments Manager submitted an application from G L Kirby of 87, Dudley Road for a Waterman licence 2nd class, which was granted.

July 1956.

The Town Clerk submitted an application from John B Durrant of 102, Manor Road, Hastings for a Waterman licence and Motor Boat Driver licence. He had passed the required tests and was granted the same. It appears that the Town Clerk had authority to submit the above as well as the Entertainments Department - autocratic it would appear.

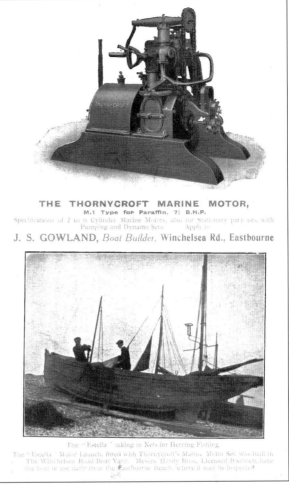

THE THORNYCROFT MARINE MOTOR,
M.1 Type for Paraffin, 7½ B.H.P.

Specification of 2 to 6 Cylinder Marine Motors, also for Stationary purposes, with Pumping and Dynamo Sets.   Apply to

J. S. GOWLAND, *Boat Builder*, Winchelsea Rd., Eastbourne

The "Estella" taking in Nets for Herring Fishing

The "Estella" Motor Launch, fitted with Thornycroft's Marine Motor Set, was built in The Winchelsea Road Boat Yard. Messrs. Hardy Bros., Licensed Boatmen, have the boat in use daily from the Eastbourne Beach, where it may be inspected.

Advert. J.S. Gowland, Boat builder of the 'Estella' 1912.

February 1957.

Referring to licence renewals, the Entertainments Manager submitted several applications and records show that the term 'Waterman' had ceased to be used. Now titled 'Boatman' only with no distinction shown between 1st & 2nd class.

All licences were to run annually from 1st April - 31st March instead of issuing and renewals at various times of the year.

Motor Boat renewal -
No.22. 'Waverley'
Speedboat renewals -
No.25. 'Golden Arrow V'
No.26. 'Golden Arrow IX'
All granted subject to Transport Manager's approval.

February 1958.

Licence renewals - the Entertainments Manager submitted following applications:-

Motor Boat renewal -
No.22 'Waverley'
Speedboat renewals -
No.25. 'Golden Arrow V'
No.26. 'Golden Arrow IX'
Granted.

March 1958.

The Entertainments Manager submitted an application from Denzil C Phillips, of 9, Command Road, who passed the required test. He was granted a Boatman licence.

February 1959.

The Entertainments Manager submitted the following licence renewal applications:

Motor Boat renewal -
No.22 'Waverley'
Speedboat renewals -
No.25. 'Golden Arrow V'
No.26. 'Golden Arrow IX'
Granted subject to Transport Manager's inspection at to mechanical efficiency.

April 1959.

The Entertainment Manager submitted Boatman and Motor Boat Driver licence applications from Colin Albert Allchorn of 63, Channel View Road and Michael Longley of 35, Latimer Road. Both passed tests and were granted licences.

July 1959.

H W Moon of 9, Command Road was granted a Boatman and Motor Boat Driver licence.

February 1960.

The Entertainments Manager submitted a licence report.

Motor Boat renewal -
No.22 'Waverley'
Speedboat renewals -
No.25. 'Golden Arrow V'
No.26. 'Golden Arrow IX'
Granted.

A Boatman and Motor Boat Driver licence was granted to R Brown of 87, Royal Sussex Crescent,

June 1960.

New Boatman licence applications from Frank Chapman of 67, Avondale Road, Albert Hutchinson of 19, Commercial Road and Frank Ronald Tyhurst of 48,

Commercial Road - All were all granted plus a Motor Boat Driver licence granted to Albert Hutchinson.

February 1961.

The Entertainments Manager submitted licence renewal applications for the following: -

38 Boatman licences
24 Motor Boat Driver licences
1 Motor Boat licence
46 Rowing Boat licences
All were granted.

March 1961.

In addition to the above, the Entertainments Manager made application for 4 Motor Boat licences and 4 Boatman licences, which were granted.

A request to operate small Motor Boats was made by Messrs. R Bradford and N Lambourne - Maximum speed 8-9 mph, no propellers, to carry 5 passengers, no windlass or huts required. A small ramp was to be used and the Committee required a demonstration. This was successful because permission was given for 2 boats to operate from groyne Nos.45 & 46.

A further request to operate two Sports cruisers, one 26 ft long, the other 19 ft long, from the beach during summer season was denied. The Committee voted 3-2 against.

May 1961.

The Entertainments Manager submitted new Boatman licence applications for M J Sheppard and R Wheeler. These were granted after the usual tests.

July 1961.

A new Boatman and Motor Boat Driver licence was issued to C Coburn.

February 1962.

The Entertainments Manager submitted applications under the following headings: -Boatman, Motor Boat Driver, Motor Boat and Pleasure Boat (Rowing) licence renewals. No further details are shown.

A fresh application was made by Bradford & Lambourne to operate 6 boats during the coming season as opposed to the 2 for the previous season. The Committee agreed and they were granted Boatman, Motor Boat Driver and Motor Boat licences for 6 boats, 6 out-board motors and a control Motor Boat to operate from April.

May 1962.

The Committee also granted to Bradford & Lambourne Boatman and Motor Boat Driver licences to operate 2 out-board Motor Boats and a control Boat from groyne Nos.45 & 46 at the Redoubt.

Bradford & Lambourne requested that their rent be reduced from £150 down to £75 per annum as the 1961 season had been bad - only 32 days had they been able to operate. The Committee agreed and reduced accordingly.

February 1963.

Boatman, Motor Boat Driver, Motor Boat, Speedboat and Rowing Boat licence renewals were submitted by the General Manager of the Entertainments & Catering Department and all renewed to 1964.

He also submitted applications for Motor Boat Driver licences from Brian Allchorn, Fred Elstone and Ron Wheeler: All granted.

Under the heading 'Hire of Small boats - Messrs. Bradford & Lambourne', the renewal of Motor Boat Driver and Motor Boat licences in respect of 6 out-board Motor Boats on groynes Nos. 45 & 46 were granted.

Speedboat licence - the Town Clerk submitted an application from Albert 'Sam' Allchorn for a Speedboat licence. He stated that at their meeting in December 1962, the Committee had granted Mr. Allchorn permission to operate a Speedboat from the section of the beach west of the Pier, from which he already operates motor Pleasure Boats: Granted for a year commencing 1st April 1963.

May 1963.

The General Manager of the Entertainments & Catering Department submitted an application for a Boatman licence from T Tonks. After interview by the Committee, Tonks was granted a licence.

Regarding Bye-Laws with respect to Pleasure Boats - the Home Secretary confirmed they should be in operation 1st July 1963.

October 1963.

Parade Inspector W R Edwards resigned as from December 1963 after 4½ years in the job.

December 1963.

Bradford & Lambourne were granted licences to operate 8 small Motor Boats for the next season.

Arthur Roland Ricketts was appointed Parade Inspector as from January 1964.

February 1964.

The General Manager of the Entertainments & Catering Department submitted renewal licence applications.

Bradford & Lambourne licences were renewed as in previous years.

October 1964.

New Boatman and Motor Boat Driver licences were submitted by the General Manager for W G Poolman and were granted.

The year 1964 appears to have been the end of the Watch Committee dealings with Pleasure Boating and Licencing as no further details emerged from the minutes up to April 1968. This coincides with the end of the Eastbourne Borough Police Force in 1968 when it was amalgamated into the Sussex Police Force.

Also there is no trace to date of the 'Book of Licences' and foreshore plans showing Boat and Capstan Stands numbered and identified to individual Boatmen and individual Boatman licencing details. Enquiries at the East Sussex Record Office and the Town Hall have proved fruitless.

The following is the last of any details regarding 'Pleasuring' that I have been able to find from the Entertainments & Catering Department Committee minutes.

April 1965.

An application by Messrs. Allchorn requesting permission for a 1000-gallon diesel tank alongside their Net Shop at the Fishing Station was granted. Reference was then made about new premises to be built. This refers to the demolition of the Fishing Station and the building of new Net Shops for the existing Fishermen and Boatmen. The rebuilding and redevelopment was finally completed around 1974.

The Town Clerk read a letter from the E.F.B.P. Society on behalf of Fred 'Tinker' Novis. It requested permission for their member to place his Pleasure Boats on a section of the beach approximately opposite the York House Hotel, Royal Parade, instead of on a site immediately east of the Pier, from which he had operated for a number of years.

The Society pointed out that due to the loss of beach east of the Pier, the sea at high tides now reached the promenade wall. Consequently on occasions, Mr. Novis was unable to leave his boats upon the beach but had to lift them up onto the promenade.

The General Manager stated that he had no objections to Mr. Novis using the section of beach requested. The Town Clerk referred to the licence granted to Mr. Novis for a term of 14 years from 1st April 1955. (N.B. a 14-year licence)

The Committee resolved that Mr. Novis be granted permission to transfer his boats to the eastern part of the section of beach lying between groyne Nos.48 & 49.

Sadly 'Tinker' Novis was to die in 1966 and with his passing it appears no more Pleasure Boats were to be seen plying for hire east of the Pier - George Grooms having retired in October 1965.

The Town Clerk read the Committee a letter from Mr. G F Grooms stating that on medical grounds, he had been unable to operate his Rowing Boats from the foreshore and had also been unable to find anybody to operate them for him. In accordance with his agreement with the Council, Mr. Grooms had paid half the sum due in respect of the 1965 season, namely £3. 5s. 0d. Mr. Grooms asked that in the circumstances the second payment should be waived: Granted.

So by 1965 it was only the Allchorn family operating off the Grand Parade with the motor Pleasure Boats 'William Allchorn' and Sayers boat 'Southern Queen' (acquired when Sayers Brothers ceased trading that year). The last Rowing boats plying for hire on the beach were those owned by Edwin 'Ned' Sayers, for hire off the beach between the Pier and Bandstand. They finally disappeared in 1967.

Over the years among those old members of the 'Sailing/Pleasuring' days to pass away was Albert 'Sam' Allchorn, a stalwart of the Eastbourne Fishermen's & Boatmen's Protection Society Club.

Sadly the 1990s saw the deaths of three of Eastbourne's old Fishermen and Boatmen all passing away in their 90s namely: Fred 'Mucky' Erridge, John 'Jack' Prodger and John 'Jack' Hurd - surnames that go back hundreds of years in the Eastbourne seafaring community.

After the 2nd World War there were less Boatmen along the Parades. Some that operated on Marine and Royal Parades were George Grooms, Fred 'Tinker' Novis, Mike 'Jersey' Hardy and family - the Prodger and Hurd families having ceased operating by the outbreak of the War.

Those operating on the Grand Parade were Allchorn, Sayers and Boniface. Not many when one compares the pre-War years and further back to when the seafront was alive with cries of "nice day for a trip" and "the boat's just leaving". The visitor at one time catered for by numerous Rowboats, trips to Beachy Head and the Lightship by the bigger sailing boats, followed in later years by the motor powered boats, fine lined vessels built by local boat builders, such as Simpson, Gausden, Sisk, Gowland, Pragnell and Lower and Cantell of Newhaven.

Sadly all gone but for the Allchorn boats 'William Allchorn' and 'Southern Queen' still plying off the beach at Grand Parade under the ownership and operated by Jason Foster, proprietor of Eastbourne Marine Ltd.

Eastbourne Pleasure Boatman Brian Allchorn with his pleasure boats 'Southern Queen' and 'William Allchorn'.

Chapter Six

Beach Launching and Recovery of Boats at Eastbourne.
By Brian Allchorn. Pleasure Boatman.

Boats have been launched from time immemorial using greased wooden slides known locally as 'trows' down the shelving shingle beach into the sea. This can be a labourious process for, as can be appreciated the shingle beach is seldom flat and level but is usually in a series of banks and ridges caused by the weight and direction of the wind and water. Getting boats over these undulations was either done by the use of blocking in the hollows - blockings being thick pieces of wood, wooden hatch covers, old railway sleepers etc, on top of which the trows were placed until the boat was over the last ridge at high water mark. From there on the beach is level down to the sea.

The men would push the boat to cries of 'ahoop, ahoop' and when they got the boat moving it would change to 'kip 'er going, kip 'er going'.

Also employed was a form of Beach Anchor to which a pulley block was attached and a wire rove through from a winch, through the block and onto the stern of the boat thus: -

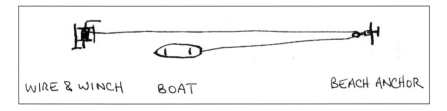

WIRE & WINCH   BOAT   BEACH ANCHOR

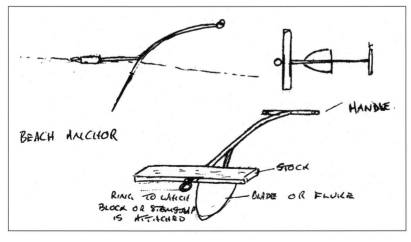

The Beach Anchor was also more often used to check boats down the beach when they were on an even slope and thus likely to run away. The boat's stern strap (the wire strap passed through the round hole in the keel at the bow, used to haul boats back up the beach) being attached to the ring on the wooden stock and the boat stopped by the person on the handle pressing down, thus digging the blade/fluke into the shingle beach or released by lifting it out or part way out controlling the descent down the beach.

Beach Anchors were not used after motor winches became the general means of retrieval. Motor winches were usually equipped with an efficient brake and the speed of descent could also be controlled by this method. In the old days when boats were recovered by capstan or hand winch there were no such sophisticated devices.

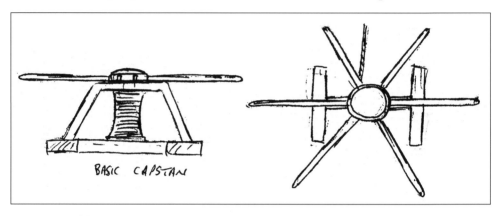

BASIC CAPSTAN

Recovery of boats was initially by hand capstan - an upright drum of wood with provision at the top for a number, usually six, of horizontal bars fitted into slots. A man was put onto each one of these to push and walk round in a circle thus turning the capstan and winding in the wire. The number of men needed of course varied with the size of the boat being hauled up. There was always an element of danger in this method. Lives were indeed lost when a bar broke under the strain and the preceding bar flew back under the weight of the boat striking the unfortunate man in the head.

The wooden hand capstans were succeeded by cast iron hand winches (or land crabs as they were known locally), which consisted of two 'A' frames, a wire drum to which a large geared driven wheel was attached and a set of driving gears with

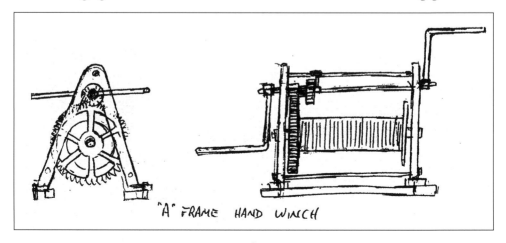

"A" FRAME HAND WINCH

provision for a single or double purchase. A metal pawl would engage into the teeth of the large geared driven wheel to prevent running back when hauling had ceased and in some cases a rudimentary brake was used.

These could be dangerous if used with the pawl disengaged, especially when hand operated by just one person. Under heavy load and with a loss of grip on the handle, it would fly back rapidly and could cause serious injury. Two men were the usual number to operate the 'A' winch.

There were also larger 'A' frame winches with longer handles to which four men could lend their weight to the task.

Present day motor winches take most of the hard work out of it and also give the ability to use a 'beach plough' (usually a heavy wooden board about 6ft x 6ft x 2ft thick with attached handles and chain) by which boatmen could 'plough' the tops of the ridges into the hollows and leave a nice even flat stretch of shingle beach which made life much easier. It was essential for large Pleasure Boats such as the 'William Allchorn', which at around 30 tons weight could in no way be pushed up and over banks of shingle. Ploughing was a hard task but well worth it for the ease of work afterwards.

Launching and Recovery of Row Boats (Skiffs).

Rowing boats or 'Skiffs' as the Boatmen always know them had toggles on short strops fore and aft. Two each side by which four men or even two could manhandle them up and down the shingle beach using 'trows' for the heavier Skiffs. To work them out across the sands at 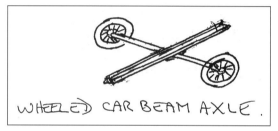 low tide, a board about 6ft-8ft long attached at right angles to an old wheeled car beam axle was used, the Skiff being pulled up onto it and then wheeled across the sands.

Loading and Unloading Pleasure boats.

In the early days of Pleasure Boating, boats were nosed into the sea during fair weather and passengers put ashore with a form of portable stollage. This method was still used on occasions during the 1950's, but then only to offload passengers if the boat was put ashore and hove up complete with passengers. Often on the last trip of the day or if the weather had turned inclement, small landing stages were constructed using old wagon wheels.

This was very much the case with the William Allchorn Family Pleasure Boat Business until, in 1936 they purchased the old Eastbourne pulling and sailing Lifeboat 'James Stevens No.6'. Then a proper landing stage was constructed using the wheels and axles of the Lifeboat carriage. This served well until the late 1970's when, whilst working in choppy conditions the boat 'William Allchorn' surged against the landing stage. There was a 'crack' and it was discovered the spokes on one of the large 6ft diameter wheels had broken. Temporary repairs were made but new wheels and axles would be needed.

A problem in the modern age? Not for the 'Allchorns'. Plans were drawn up and steel was rolled to their specifications, which they prefabricated. The work took a couple of winters, as all the other maintenance work on the boats had to be done working as always to a tight schedule, but it was finally completed in 1981. New wheels, new axles, a new frame and top were towed up to the Boat Stand along the sand on the last available suitable tide.

To enable passengers to access the landing stage and thence board the big Pleasure Boats, a series of 'nenplanks' (plank walkways) forming small stages on wheels, twelve in number, each around 16ft long which were put on or off as the tide ebbed and flowed. All twelve were needed at low water, two being sufficient at high tide. The whole nenplanks assembly was pulled out by winch via a block attached to a large baulk of timber buried deep, just inside low water mark and pulled back in as the tide flowed, by another winch.

On spring (long) tides it was not possible for the boats to get to the landing stage. It was then during the early years that large Row Boats, known as ferry boats were used to take people out to the Pleasure Boats lying at anchor. This was a protracted process as the ferryboats only carried twelve passengers. The passengers then had to climb up a stepladder hooked over the gunwale to board the Pleasure Boat. This was a somewhat excitingly precarious experience for the boat tripper especially when the sea was a bit choppy. To save rowing and if conditions were right, some boatmen would push the ferryboats alongside the Pleasure Boat - a much quicker process.

All this changed when 'Allchorns' purchased an ex army D.U.K.W. amphibian vehicle. At low water this enabled some 35 people to be ferried from the landing stage, across the sands and into the water until the front wheels began to lift indicating there was sufficient depth of water for the Boat to come alongside and take the people aboard.

The D.U.K.W. made the Boatmen's life easier in other ways. In the early days before vandalism became such a problem; the boats were pulled up onto the beach at the Boating Stand on Grand Parade. In order to get the boats afloat for work at low water in the mornings, they would be launched at 4.30 am and anchored off, getting 30 minutes later each day until it got back to a normal 8.00 am start. This of course was repeated every fortnight throughout the season until September when the dark mornings made it too dangerous. With the D.U.K.W. however it was found that with care and keeping the Boats on greased trows, the Boats could be pushed out. This method of launching was almost always successful but on odd occasions a boat would get stuck and had to miss a trip waiting for the tide to float her.

In later years and in fine weather, at the end of the day the Boats 'William Allchorn' and 'Southern Queen' would be anchored in the bay to the east of the pier where there was good holding ground. They would pick up the crews with the D.U.K.W. and take them out again next morning - easy. The Boats used to sit out in the bay with the evening sun on them, advertising themselves. Hotel owners on the front would assure their guests of fine weather next day as 'the boats are anchored off', but in reality all it meant was a fine wind forecast.

There were occasions when on an ebbing tide, the Boat stayed alongside the landing stage a little too long, took the ground and was unable to get off. This meant giving the passengers their money back - Not good for business.

Another hazard was a pile of granite, which had been the cargo of the sailing vessel 'Sea flower' that sank just west of the Pier in the 1800's. I was skippering a boat in the 1970's, when she ran aground there luckily without damage and re-floated after 5 minutes on a flowing tide.

Times were hard in my father's (Albert Allchorn's) younger days and I've heard him tell how, when there was no money, they had at times to resort to 'limpet pudding' (limpets collected off the rocks and cooked to eke out what food they had). It should be appreciated that the Allchorns were a big family of 11 children - usually all hungry. Despite this, grandfather (William) had his priorities right. If the home needed something and the Boat needed something and there wasn't enough money for both the Boat won - for as he said, *"without the Boat we can't earn"*.

Grandmother would complain when the spratting season arrived in November; *"I suppose the house will soon be covered in sprat scales"* to which he retorted, *"the time to moan my girl, is when there are no sprat scales"*.

Hooker running.

Some of the Boatmen, when it was too rough to work in the summer would dress themselves up in sorts of garish garb and go 'hooker running'. This involved launching one of the big skiffs (Row Boats) out through the surf then turning and running ashore on a big wave, not unlike modern day surf boarding except they used a boat. A crowd would gather to watch and they would go round with a bucket collecting for the Leaf Homeopathic Hospital situated then in Marine Road, their favourite cause. These Boatmen, known as 'Redskins', would put up a board stating when and where they would be performing, sea conditions permitting.

The Winter Months & Fishing.

Come the end of the season in October, the boats and gear would all be taken away from the seafront. Winter maintenance began. Engines and shafts were removed for overhaul and work done on the boats when weather permitted, bearing in mind it was not possible to put boats undercover in the days before the big Net Shop was built. So a lot of work was done outside.

With five brothers to do the work there was often time to spare, so they went fishing during the winter. Fishing followed a set pattern as the year progressed in those days. Some spratting was done in January/February and 'hooking' or 'long lining' (its correct term) out back of the Sovereign Lightship (now Light Tower), the sprats providing the bait. The boats in those days often returning laded with cod 14-20 lbs in weight, conger, tope and dogfish. The fish were off loaded into a hand barrow without wheels, something like a wide robust wooden stretcher, with a handle at each corner carried by two or four men dependent on the load.

The tubs of line were taken to the net shop (shed) where they were cleaned and re-baited ready for next day. This was often done by candlelight during the evening, after the men had been home to have a meal and a warm. Most fishermen hated 'hooking' for as they said *"you were never done and always seemed to have a line in your hand"*. The late Tom Allchorn's definition of misery was *"coming in from back of the lightship with toothache, a hook in your finger and a smart breeze off the land"*.

Some trawling also took place, but in the main January, February and March were the lean months when they overhauled boats and gear and fitted up and mended nets. Potting for crab and lobster usually began in earnest in March and went through to October with trawling and some trammel netting going on as well. Spring 'dogging' took place mainly through April and May, hooking again but using whelk for bait and of course working in warmer lighter and pleasant conditions catching dogfish or rock salmon (huss to the general public). Then in October, the herring season began and went through into December. The herring also providing bait for those starting 'hooking'. Herring drifting, being a night time occupation, is hazardous these days due to the amount of set nets in the sea all with 'danns' (floats with flagged poles attached) which cannot be seen in the dark and against which drift nets can wrap themselves.

In the old days no fisherman would dream of having any sort of fixed gear in the sea when the spratting or herring drifting season arrived, but times have changed - not for the better. (Depletion of the sprat and herring has brought about this bad fishing practice)

Meanwhile work went on the Pleasure Boats and engines ready for the inspections, which were carried out each year. Engines were stripped out and laid out along with propeller shafts all ready for the Board of Trade Examiner to check them over. Given the 'OK' they were rebuilt and put back into the Boats that had undergone their hull surveys at the same time as the engines were inspected. And when all was ready for

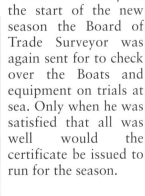

the start of the new season the Board of Trade Surveyor was again sent for to check over the Boats and equipment on trials at sea. Only when he was satisfied that all was well would the certificate be issued to run for the season.

Marine and Royal Parades C.1890 'Boats for hire'.

Royal Marine Parade C.1890.

Grand Parade C.1900.

Grand Parade. C.1900.

Grand Parade. C.1900.

Good day for a sail. Allchorn Pleasure Sail Boats 1905.

Nice day for sail 1908.

A busy day for Rowboats 1921.

Competition for the Boatmen - Seaplane flights off Eastbourne beach. Post card originally sent September 1919. The writer states 'cost per trip one guinea' (£1.1s.0d in old (real) money).

A Royal Parade Boat Stand 1938.

All part of the service 1910.

Paddling and sailing on the sands, Eastbourne 1905.

'Steady as she goes' 1930.

Eastbourne Regatta C.1930. 'Walk the pole'.

East of the Pier. Note the gap in the railings for the passage of Rowboats.

1937. Boatmen on Grand Parade to west of the Bandstand. Left - 'Ted' Hide. Right - Harry 'Early Doors' Allchorn. Harry used to call 'Early Doors' at his part time job at the Royal Hippodrome.

Eastbourne Regatta C.1930. A Boatman 'Up the pole'.

Eastbourne Boatmen C.1900.

1937. Boatmen Harry 'Early Doors' Allchorn and 'Ted' Hide.

Boatman 'No.74', Eastbourne beach C.1930.

Eastbourne Boatmen C.1930.

A happy band of Eastbourne Boatmen C.1930. Left - right, Ernest 'Glaxo' Sayers, Jim Boniface, unknown, unknown, extreme right Jesse Chester.

Grand Parade c1915. Jack Hurd recalled some of the boatstand owners as: Right to left -
Boniface, Ned Sayers, George Penfold, Allchorn and Hide.

Grand Parade c1915. A calm morning for the pleasure boats.

C1900 loading the 'Britannia'.

C1905 dandy rigged sailing yacht 'Brittania' under full sail.

Eastbourne Regatta c1908.

C1910 Eastbourne Aviation Co. competition for the pleasure boatmen.

Eastbourne lugger rigged pleasure boat 'Mallard'.

Boatmen crew of pleasure boat 'Mallard'.

Royal Parade boatmen c1920 with Prodger Pleasure Boat 'Ocean's Gift'.

August 1939. Flag Day for veteran boatman Alleyn Sayers.

Boatman Jack Elms and his telescope 1935.

Royal Parade boatmen make friends 1934.

Boatman: William Henry 'Sausage' Grooms. Father of Boatman George 'Young Sausage' Grooms.

Albert 'Tuppy' Sayers - Old Eastbourne Pleasure Boatman.

William 'Laddie' Simpson, boatman, fisherman and lifeboatman. Portrait painted by Charles Charles, artist on the pier 1912.

Nicknames

Nicknames were common throughout the Fishing and Boating Fraternity from way back to the present day. It is said nicknames were first used by the Fishermen to identify themselves when involved in smuggling activities, against detection by the Excise and Coastguard men.

Nicknames of Fishermen - Boatmen - Lifeboat men.

Compiled by Ted Hide from family and other sources.

Nickname	Name
Chalky	Charles Ernest Hide
Dot	George Hide
Navarino	James Hide - Uncle of Dot
Pincher	George Merrick Hide - Son of Dot
Bones	Charles Hide - Son of Dot
Gruff	George Hide - Son of Pincher
Lulu	Luke Hide - Son of Pincher
Admiral	Osman Hide - Son of Pincher
Old Bollard	William Hide - Cousin to Dot & Navarino
Crutch	William Bollard Hide - Son of Old Bollard
Young Bollard	William Bollard Hide - Son of Old Bollard
Codgy & Red Fred	Frederick Hide - Son of Old Bollard
Keen Eyed Dicky	Richard Hide - Son of Old Richard Hide
Garibaldi	Weller Sayers
Pork	Samuel Huggett Snr.
Pork	Samuel Huggett Son of Pork Snr.
Bungay on the Rocks	John French
Storey	James Adams
Old Screw	Reuben Wood
Slippery	F Weakford
Cuckoo	George Hookham
Gospel	? Hall
Elmo	Jack Elms
Gish	? Huggett
Knuckle	Harry Sayers
Workhouse Bill	William Sayers
Old Jack Muck	Walter Sayers
Bird	Richard Francis
Skinny	Fred Hurd
Curly	? Gibbs
Old Tom, The Peoples Friend	Thomas Bennett
Spanish Jack	John Garcia
Tommy Ruin	Thomas Swain
Old Lad	Jesse Huggett Snr. Lifeboat Cox'n
Joker	Joseph Huggett. Father of the above Lifeboat Cox'n
Lord	Edwin Matthews
Dusty	Henry Matthews

Sailor	? Mitchell		Merry Legs	William Allchorn
Ratchet	Albert Addington		Early Doors	Harry Allchorn
Garbutts	Henry Thomas - Lifeboat crew mechanic		Margarine	Tom Allchorn
			Old Bogey	William Allchorn
Grunt	Fred Hurd		Misere	Jack Allchorn
Old Father	Ben Erridge		Gammy	Henry Allchorn
Chum	Walter Hide - Grandson of Bones Hide		Sam	Albert Allchorn
Bluenose	George Prodger (Meads)		Billy Bags	William Boniface
Camboy	W Sayers - Rowing Club Cox 1880		Salvation	Tom Boniface
			Old Harry	Harry Boniface
Stagger	Harry Hendy - Lifeboat crew		Clapper	Jim Boniface
			Jumpy Joe	Joe Boniface
Tuppenny	Tom Wood		Effit	Henry Boniface
Itchy Boo	? French...died 1916. He married daughter of Joe Carter, Eastbourne's first Policeman		Smuggler	George Erridge
			Killcraft	William Erridge Snr.
			Alligator	William Erridge Jnr.
Chinko	Fred Benjamin Erridge		Quack	George Erridge
			Dandy Boots	Fred Erridge

From the 1860s, nicknames only: -

Soldier.

Crab.

Old Nick.

Young Nick.

Free.

Scuttle.

The following are nicknames compiled by the late Tom Reed, Frank Smith and Fred (Mucky) Erridge

Nickname	Name
Donkey	William Allchorn
Old Grannio	Harry Allchorn
Chissel	William Allchorn
Two Thumbs	Ted Allchorn

Paddy Jack	Richard John 'Jack' Erridge
Skins	Harry Erridge
Cocky	Alfred Erridge
Muckey	Fred Erridge
Catseyes	Fred Huggett
Squarty	Philip Huggett
Cesspool	Jack Huggett
Hollands	Tom Huggett
Jimbo	Jim Huggett
Old Mug	Philip Huggett
Golden	Jesse Huggett
Tishy	Fred Huggett
Cesh	Fred Huggett
Magic	Fred Hurd

Ackapay	Fred Hurd	Dummy	Will Matthews
Tuppy	Albert Sayers	Nick	Will Jackson
Old Rig	Alleyn Sayers	Cassy	Reuben Reed
Sharky	Harry Sayers	Sharp Eyes	Fred Reed
Chinaman	Ernest Sayers	Tinker	Fred Novis
Mutt	Arthur Sayers	Lala	Jack Mockett
Glaxo	Ernest Sayers	Elmo	Jack Elms
Nucklow	Harry Sayers	Gulliver	Oliver Wood
Jazzy	Nelson Sayers	Goosey	Bill Wood
Laddie	William Simpson	Bruiser	Brian Wood
Flummy	Tom Prodger	Tarwood	Will Wood
Kruger	John Prodger	Bungay	Jack French
Juicy	Will Prodger	Rocky	Doug French
Manhole	Jack Prodger	Puff	Philip Grant
Norley	Charlie Prodger	Diddly	Bert Grant
Katty	Charlie Prodger	Gorbil	Jack Tuxford
Crickets	Joe Prodger	Coco	Harry Hewett
Young Will	William Prodger	Quack	Sam Oliver
Trunky	John Colstick	Reuben	Jack Knight
Snob	Jim Merritt	Diddler	William Godden
Dust	Henry Matthews	Bewlin	Frank Smith
Goat	Ebb Matthews		

Licence Reports

The following record of 'Pleasuring' Licence totals issued over the years 1891 to 1965 were obtained from minutes of the Eastbourne Watch Committee, under references DE /A/6/ 1-11 and are held at East Sussex Records Office, Lewes.

Parade Inspectors Annual Licences reports.

March 1891.

1st class Waterman	72
2nd class Waterman	21
Sailing boats	27
Rowing boats	155
Capstan Stands	26
Ladies Bathing Machines	131
Gents Bathing Machines	114

Conduct of Boatmen - generally good.

March 1892.

1st class Waterman	75
2nd class Waterman	19
Sailing boats	27
Rowing boats	170
Capstan Stands	20
Bathing Machines and Offices	249

Conduct of Boatmen - generally good.

March 1893.

1st class Waterman	80
2nd class Waterman	24
Sailing boats	30
Rowing boats	175
Capstan Stands	20
Bathing Machines and Offices	249

Conduct of Boatmen - generally good.

February 1894.

1st class Waterman	79
2nd class Waterman	33
Sailing boats	29
Rowing boats	196
Capstan Stands	35
Bathing Machines	251

Conduct of Boatmen - generally good.

February 1895.

1st class Waterman	68
2nd class Waterman	27
Sailing boats	25
Rowing boats	188
Capstan Stands	29
Bathing Machines	251

Conduct of Boatmen - generally good.

March 1896.

1st class Waterman	68
2nd class Waterman	30
Sailing boats	25
Rowing boats	189
Bathing Machines	237
1 fatal drowning	

Conduct of Boatmen - satisfactory.

March 1897.

1st class Waterman	66
2nd class Waterman	27
Sailing boats	22
Rowing boats	172
Bathing Machines	232
Offices	7

Conduct of Boatmen - satisfactory.

April 1898.

Printed Reports

Boats	167
Waterman	79

No Further Details

April 1899.

Waterman Licences	75
Pleasure Boats	170

No Further Details

1900-1913 - No records found of Boat & Boatman Licences issued.

Chief Constable's reports of Annual Licences.

April 1914.
1st class Waterman	64
2nd class Waterman	42
Motor Boat Drivers	17
Sailing Boats	11
Rowing Boats	187
Motor Boats	9

April 1915.
1st class Waterman	72
2nd class Waterman	35
Motor Boat Drivers	23
Sailing Boats	9
Rowing Boats	171
Motor Boats	9

Watermen now engaged on active service, not charged for licence.
Entertainment licences for beach still being issued.

April 1916.
1st class Waterman	69
2nd class Waterman	36
Motor Boat Drivers	25
Sailing Boats	2
Rowing Boats	109
Motor Boats	7

March 1917
1st class Waterman	72
2nd class Waterman	40
Motor Boat Drivers	28
Sailing Boats	2
Rowing Boats	107
Motor Boats	5

March 1918.
1st class Waterman	68
2nd class Waterman	40
Motor Boat Drivers	26
Rowing Boats	89

No Sailing or Motor Boats Shown

April 1919.
1st class Waterman	55
2nd class Waterman	29
Motor Boat Drivers	20
Sailing Boats	1
Rowing Boats	123
Motor Boats	4

April 1920.
1st class Waterman	65
2nd class Waterman	33
Motor Boat Drivers	27
Sailing Boats	3
Rowing Boats	169
Motor Boats	6

March 1921.
1st class Waterman	73
2nd class Waterman	38
Motor Boat Drivers	30
Sailing Boats	4
Rowing Boats	173
Motor Boats	14

March 1922.
1st class Waterman	81
2nd class Waterman	43
Motor Boat Drivers	39
Sailing Boats	1
Rowing Boats	172
Motor Boats	16

March 1923.
1st class Waterman	107
2nd class Waterman	35
Motor Boat Drivers	42
Sailing Boats	3
Rowing Boats	179
Motor Boats	7

1924. No records found.

1925. No records found.

March 1926.
1st class Waterman	96
2nd class Waterman	37
Motor Boat Drivers	53
Pleasure Boats	210

March 1931.
No totals given. Report states 'Refer to Book of Licences'.

March 1932.
No totals given. Report states 'Refer to Book of Licences'.

March 1933.
1st class Waterman	78
2nd class Waterman	30
Motor Boat Drivers	49
Rowing Boats	149
Motor Boats - None Recorded	

March 1934.
1st class Waterman	77
2nd class Waterman	27
Motor Boat Drivers	52
Rowing Boats	141
Motor Boats	11

March 1935.
1st class Waterman	72
2nd class Waterman	26
Motor Boat Drivers	49
Rowing Boats	147
Motor Boats	11

March 1936.
1st class Waterman	72
2nd class Waterman	34
Motor Boat Drivers	49
Rowing Boats	124
Motor Boats	11

March 1937.
1st class Waterman	70
2nd class Waterman	23
Motor Boat Drivers	45
Rowing Boats	124
Motor Boats	8

March 1938.
1st class Waterman	67
2nd class Waterman	19
Motor Boat Drivers	44
Motor Boats	3

March 1939.
1st class Waterman	65
2nd class Waterman	17
Motor Boat Drivers	44
Rowing Boats	116
Motor Boats	10

May 1940.
1st class Waterman	42
2nd class Waterman	6
Motor Boat Drivers	27
Rowing Boats	110
Motor Boats - None Recorded	

April 1945.
1st class Waterman	34
2nd class Waterman - None Recorded	
Motor Boat Drivers	22
Motor Boats	7
Rowing Boats	58

April 1946.
1st class Waterman	39
2nd class Waterman	7
Motor Boat Drivers	30
Motor Boats	6
Rowing Boats	61

April 1947.
1st class Waterman	41
2nd class Waterman	9
Motor Boat Drivers	30
Motor Boats	8
Rowing Boats	62

April 1948.
1st class Waterman	43
2nd class Waterman	1
Motor Boat Drivers	33
Motor Boats	6
Rowing Boats	54

March 1949.
1st class Waterman	40
2nd class Waterman	12
Motor Boat Drivers	34
Motor Boats - None Recorded	
Rowing Boats	53

March 1950.

1st class Waterman	32
2nd class Waterman	12
Motor Boat Drivers	33
Motor Boats	6
Rowing Boats	54

March 1951.

1st class Waterman	33
2nd class Waterman	14
Motor Boat Drivers	36
Motor Boats	6
Rowing Boats	54

February 1952.

1st class Waterman	49
2nd class Waterman	7
Motor Boat Drivers	35
Motor Boats	3
Rowing Boats	54

February 1953.

1st class Waterman	45
2nd class Waterman	5
Motor Boat Drivers	36
Motor Boats	3
Speed Boats	2
Rowing Boats	56

February 1954.

1st class Waterman	57
2nd class Waterman	6
Motor Boat Drivers	36
Motor Boats	3
Speed Boats	2
Rowing Boats	55

February 1955.

1st class Waterman	46
2nd class Waterman - None Recorded	
Motor Boat Drivers	30
Motor Boats	2
Speed Boats	2
Rowing Boats	54

February 1956.

Boatman	44
(1st/2nd class - no distinction)	
Motor Boat Drivers	29
Motor Boats	1
Speed Boats	2
Rowing Boats	50

February 1957.

Boatman	42
Motor Boat Drivers	28
Motor Boats	1
Speed Boats	2
Rowing Boats	47

February 1958.

Boatman	42
Motor Boat Drivers	29
Motor Boats	1
Speed Boats	2
Rowing Boats	46

February 1959.

Boatman	42
Motor Boat Drivers	31
Motor Boats	1
Speed Boats	2
Rowing Boats	48

February 1960.

Boatman	46
Motor Boat Drivers	33
Motor Boats	1
Speed Boats	2
Rowing Boats	46

February 1961.

Boatman	43
Motor Boat Drivers	29
Motor Boats	1
Speed Boats	2
Rowing Boats	46

February 1962.

Boatman	46
Motor Boat Drivers	31
Motor Boats	1
Speed Boats	2
Rowing Boats	45

February 1963.

Boatman	40
Motor Boat Drivers	29
Motor Boats	1
Speed Boats	2
Rowing Boats	40

February 1964.

Boatman	40
Motor Boat Drivers	31
Motor Boats	1
Speed Boats	2
Rowing Boats	38

February 1965.

Boatman	44
Motor Boat Drivers	35
Motor Boats	1
Speed Boats	2
Rowing Boats	37

The last records found shown above indicate Boatmen still renewing their licenses although there is no sign of activity on the beach other than perhaps 'Ned' Sayers and his Rowboats.

The Allchorn's 'William Allchorn' and 'Southern Queen' were the only pleasure boats operating and regulated by the Board of Trade.

Index

Index Of Names

A

Adams - 13, 14, 42, 43, 86, 176
Addington - 93, 131, 133, 136, 138, 177
Allchorn - 7, 17, 20, 28, 29, 31, 35, 36, 40-42, 45, 46, 60-62, 68, 69, 72, 78-80, 82, 84-89, 91, 93, 97, 102, 104, 106-111, 113, 115, 117-138, 140, 142, 144-151, 154, 156-159, 162-164, 167-170, 177, 183
Allen - 41
Andrews - 122, 131, 135, 136
Anson St.Clair-Ford - 28, 29
Argles - 94, 102, 107
Arnold - 109, 138, 139
Ashcroft - 129
Ashdown - 80, 93, 109
Austen - 53, 135

B

Bailey - 122
Barber - 23
Barfield - 62
Barnard - 56
Bassett - 131, 150
Bates - 45, 53, 54, 56-58, 60, 62, 63, 68, 73, 79-81, 88, 116
Beckett - 17
Bell - 41, 42
Bellamy - 67
Belsham - 128
Bennett - 20, 29, 36, 47, 51, 60, 62, 66, 92, 106, 176
Berry - 50, 51
Blackman - 130
Bolden - 149
Bomford-Emmerson - 72
Boniface - 7, 41, 61-63, 68-72, 80, 81, 84-86, 88, 89, 92, 94, 95, 102, 103, 106-113, 115, 118-122, 128, 129, 131-136, 145, 149, 152, 158, 169, 170, 177

Botting - 8
Bourne - 29
Bowler - 122
Bradford - 155, 156
Breach - 7, 14, 30, 31, 35, 36, 44-46, 55, 60, 62, 68, 72, 85, 98-100
Briggs - 68
Brown - 15, 36, 47, 68, 108, 128, 154
Browne - 107, 144
Bruce - 114
Butterworth - 129
Burr - 49, 52, 55-59, 73

C

Callaghan - 150, 151
Cain - 53
Campbell - 82
Cantell - 126, 127, 158
Carter - 145, 149, 177
Cavendish - 6
Chambers - 14, 21, 23, 45, 61
Chandler - 41, 77
Chapman - 154
Charlwood - 61
Cherry - 146, 149
Chester - 7, 85, 90, 110, 111, 114, 119, 122, 133, 135, 147, 169
Clark - 55, 131
Clarke - 68
Climpson - 23
Coburn - 155
Cohen - 149
Coleman - 41
Collins - 13-16, 19, 50, 51, 73
Colstick - 32, 68, 119, 178
Comber - 109
Compton - 52
Cook - 44
Cooper - 9, 15, 41, 42
Coppard - 100
Cornelius - 148
Couchman - 41
Cox - 123

Index of Pleasure Boats